On Being a Smart CIO

Lessons I've Learned as a
Chief Information Officer (CIO)
and Trusted C-Suite Adviser

Dr. Lance B. Eliot, MBA, PhD

DEDICATION

To my wonderful daughter, Lauren, and my wonderful son, Michael.
Faithful, Scholarly, Skillful, Courageous, Ambitious, and Forever Loving.

CONTENTS

Lance B. Eliot

ACKNOWLEDGMENTS

If I mentioned everyone that has been involved in my career and business development the list would seemingly be endless; I am grateful to all for their tremendous support. That being said, I would like to mention a few in particular.

To Warren Bennis, one of the greats on leadership and my doctoral advisor and mentor, for his calm and insightful wisdom and support. To Grace Hopper, the icon of computer history, whom I met on a lark at a conference while in high school and showed me the power of the nanosecond (my children have grown up hearing that story over and over).

To Ed Trainor, CIO extraordinaire, from whom I learned first-hand at an early stage of my career what it takes to be a CIO and appreciate his ongoing efforts as a colleague and friend. To Wendell Jones, a lifelong colleague and friend that will be forever missed. To Max Hopper, one of the greats of in the history of CIO's, whom I first met when I was asked to give him a lift from the airport to where he was speaking for a major IT conference and remained in contact as a colleague over many years.

To Bob Rouse, Cliff Higbee, Steven John, Phil Zweig, Madeline Weiss, June Drewry, Bart Bolton, Mike Rochelle, Ed Trainor, and all the other RFL Facilitators that continue to keep the SIM RLF program going (it's a great educational program, which I am honored to have helped contribute to, from the beginning, and still today).

To Kevin Anderson and James Hickey at Tatum, for their unwavering support (and thanks to Stu Werner too!). To Hunter Muller, for his perseverance in the quest to create a network of CIO's for the betterment of the CIO brand. Thanks to Ken Harris, DuWayne Peterson, Mike Brown, Jim Thornton, Abhi Beniwal, Jim Ellis, Al Biland, John Nomura, Jon Kraft, William Wang, Aaron Levie, Peter Kim, Jim Sinegal, and others.

And most of all thanks to Lauren and Michael, for their ongoing support and for having heard much of this material during the many weeks and months involved in writing it.

Lance B. Eliot

INTRODUCTION

Business needs Information Technology (IT). In today's world, IT has become the rocket fuel that drives business innovation and is transforming entire industries and how we conduct commerce. Take a close look at any modern enterprise and you will see IT being used throughout the firm, including in all major functions such as Finance, Operations, Human Resources (HR), Marketing, and so on. It is inescapable and pervasive.

Annual spending on IT has been pegged at approximately $3.4 trillion dollars globally, covering IT systems, IT services, enterprise software, etc. (based on research by notable research think tanks such as IDC, Gartner Group, Forrester, Computer Economics), and there are estimates of about 30 million IT professionals worldwide (about one-third in the USA). Who manages and leads all of these IT professionals? Who determines how the IT budget is spent? Who oversees the creation of IT systems in the enterprise? Who maintains the IT systems and keeps them running?

The "who" in this case of having overall responsibility for IT in an enterprise is the head of IT, often labeled as the Chief Information Officer (CIO). Being a CIO is a tough job. You are supposed to be aware of the continually changing technology landscape and be a top techie in the company. Meanwhile, you are supposed to be aware of the continually changing aspects of your business and have impeccable business acumen. You must be able to put out "fires" such as a cyber-attack breech that hits your core systems, while at the same time be mindfully scanning the horizon for disruptions headed toward your industry that could radically impact your business.

The CIO has the challenge and the opportunity to infuse IT within the enterprise and be a valued member of the C-suite that is helping the business to survive and even thrive. The CIO also has the potential for undermining the business and being the goat that failed to keep IT in the game and integral to the business. It's a two-edged sword and a high stakes role that not everyone is suited to undertake.

CONTEXT OF THIS BOOK

What makes for a good CIO? What makes for a so-so CIO? What makes for a rotten CIO? What do CIO's do and how do they operate? What are the latest trends in IT and how should they be approached? In what ways can IT be more effective in organizations? These are crucial questions that need to be examined, given the importance of the CIO role to the firm and to the leading and managing of IT in the enterprise.

Drawing upon my twenty plus years of experience in IT and also as a CIO, I carefully address these questions in this book. My background provides a wide range of perspectives on the nature of the IT function and business. I have been writing a popular blog (www.lance-blog.com) on IT and was urged by CIO's and various IT researchers and pundits to pull together some of my key pieces into a collective book. I write from the viewpoint of having been a CIO, an insider as to what CIO's really do and how they tick. I also served on the International Board of Directors for the largest CIO professional society, the Society for Information Management (SIM), and routinely interact with and hobnob with fellow CIO's and Chief Technology Officers (CTO's) at various IT industry events and conferences. This provides a larger context for my views as based on the perspectives of my peers and colleagues.

My experience includes having been a Partner at the nation's largest executive C-suite services firm (which is also part of the world's second largest professional services company), and I also founded and ran my own IT boutique systems integration firm. Thus, I have engaged with the C-suite and CIO's during the delivery of IT services as a consultant and seen as an "outsider" what makes IT work within firms. The role of management consultant offers a decidedly added understanding about businesses and I highly recommend for most CIO's that they try to have a stint in their CIO-career that includes doing consulting work.

Seat-of-the-pants practitioner experiences are crucial to knowing what really goes on in enterprises, but that alone is not enough to gain a broader sense of what IT is all about and how it should be managed. Having an academic perspective helps to provide balance and a macroscopic look at how IT fits into business. In my case, earlier in my career I was a professor at the University of Southern California (USC) and the University of California Los Angeles (UCLA) and taught both undergraduate and graduate level courses in business and computer science. I also conducted research in these fields, and besides publishing various books and journal articles, I frequently spoke at both academic and industry conferences.

I offer the above overview of my background so that you'll be aware of my perspective on the topics at hand. This book is intended to be an interesting and decidedly useful compilation of thoughtful pieces that cover the gamut of IT in business and especially with the harsh and trained eye of the CIO, illuminating the trauma and delight of leading and managing IT.

WHAT THIS BOOK PROVIDES

Many CIO's are so consumed by their day-to-day job that they do not have much chance of poking their head up and self-examining what they are doing and how their IT group is coming along. There is a treadmill upon which CIO's are placed and with their legs and arms strenuously pumping hard, looking outward beyond the treadmill can be problematic, whereas they know for sure that they need to keep all of their systems going in their enterprise and so should keep their nose to that grind. In fact, the percentage of CIO's that go to conferences or outside events is relatively small, partially because they just don't have the time to go, even if they have the desire to go.

For existing CIO's, I hope that you will find the material in this book to be stimulating. Some of it will be repetitive of things you already know. But I am pretty sure that you'll also find various "Aha!" moments whereby you'll discover a new technique or approach that you had not earlier thought of. I am also betting that there will be material that forces you to rethink some of your current practices. I am not saying you will suddenly have an epiphany and change what you are doing. I do think though that you will reconsider or perhaps retune what you are doing.

For aspiring CIO's, if you are toiling in IT and seeking to someday reach the top spot, I believe you will find this book quite helpful in your career pursuits. In my daily interaction with IT professionals such as programmers, business analysts, network specialists, and the like, they often are curious what are CIO's thinking about and what does it take to become a CIO. I believe this book can provide that understanding. If you are an existing IT manager or director, and bucking to become a CIO, I believe this book will help you to gauge what you need to know and do to reach that position.

For executive recruiters that try to find and match CIO's to C-suite openings, I believe you would find of value the perspective of how to dig deeply into the capabilities of CIO's and their way of thinking. It could quicken the time you take to evaluate candidates (time is money!). It could also lead to better matches and longer lasting tenure of the placements that you make.

For C-suite executives that are non-IT business leaders, this material offers a glimpse into what is happening in the world of IT and business. It might give you insights as to how to best make use of IT in your organization. It certainly should help you to work more closely and collaboratively with your CIO. And, provide an indication of what your

CIO is doing, why they are doing it, and how to measure the success of your CIO.

Finally, for researchers and students at the undergraduate and graduate levels, you might find this material an intriguing cross between the purely academic and the purely practitioner. Much of the academic writing on IT can be rather abstract and conceptual, leaving a gap between what is described in a prescriptive sense and what actually happens in the real world. In sharp contrast, much of the daily "purely practitioner" writing that one sees in the IT industry is not very thoughtful per se and is more akin to reporting on the latest new doodad.

For anyone choosing to use this book for teaching purposes, please take a look at my suggestions for doing so, as described in the Appendix. I have found the material handy in courses that I have taught, and likewise other faculty have told me that they have found the material handy, in some cases as extended readings and in other instances as a core part of their course (depending on the nature of the class).

In my writing for this book, I have tried carefully to blend both the practitioner and the academic styles of writing. It is not as dense as is typical academic journal writing, but at the same time offers depth by going into the nuances and trade-offs of various practices. The word "deep" is in vogue today, meaning getting deeply into a subject or topic, and so is the word "unpack" which means to tease out the underlying aspects of a subject or topic. I have sought to offer material that addresses an issue or topic by going relatively deeply into it and make sure that it is well unpacked.

STRUCTURE OF THIS BOOK

I have divided the material into three parts.

The first part consists of aspects that I believe are core to the book. They include defining and differentiating the CIO, CTO, and CDO roles, and offering my suggestions for what is a Smart CIO. We then dig into the aspects of SMAC, an acronym that encompasses the advent and impact to IT in an enterprise due to Social media, Mobile apps, Analytics, and the Cloud. Next, I cover Top 10 lists that reveal what IT is doing today. This is a perfect segue then into articulating various technology trends and how to find business value in them, including machine learning, neural networks, Internet of Things (IoT), and other high-tech topics. I top off the first part of the book by discussing the CIO 100, which are the annual best-of-the-best IT accomplishments of the year and include some of the most notable CIO's.

The second part of the book is about the "hot" topics in IT, including

DevOps, HCI, Ransomware, Hybrid IT, Consumerization of IT, Bimodal IT, and Shadow IT. Seasoned CIO's will be familiar with some of these topics, but not likely to the depth covered in these chapters. Within the IT industry, most CIO's are being bombarded via email and telemarketing to find ways to deal with or solve business and tech problems embodied by these topics. I offer a more reasoned and deeper look at the topics than is found in typical industry coverage.

The third and final part of the book has additional topics that I have grouped together for convenience but can really be read as distinct on their own right. I discuss the reporting relationship of the CIO, the rise of interim CIO's, the question about the level and importance of social intelligence for CIO's, the interaction of the CIO with the Board of Directors of a firm, the importance of involving IT in mergers and acquisitions, the use of Maslow's Hierarchy of Needs as a management tool, a discussion of what keeps CIO's awake at night, and end with a brief look at what CEO's tend to think of CIO's.

In November of 1958, the Harvard Business Review, an exalted business publication, published an article by Harold Leavitt and Thomas Whisler that stated there was a new technology taking hold in business and that for want of a single established name for it that they coined it Information Technology. Over 50 years later, it is evident that indeed IT is taking hold in business. Many of the topics covered in this book were completely unknown then. Probably 50 years from now, there will be a new set of topics that we didn't even think about today.

For those of you willing and interested enough to read this material and give it due consideration, I offer to you the Latin motto "Palmam qui meruit ferat," which means let him who deserves it bear away the palm. If you take into account what you read here and embody it into your efforts as a manager and leader, I confer upon you the badge or certificate of learned and mindful leader. Enough said.

Lance B. Eliot

.

CHAPTER 1

ROLES OF THE CIO, CTO, CDO

PREFACE

There are an abundance of C-suite titles being tossed around by companies today. We all know and accept a few of the commonly used titles such as the Chief Executive Officer (CEO) and Chief Operating Officer (COO) vaunted monikers. The role and responsibilities of the CEO are relatively easy to imagine and comprehend. The COO role is sometimes a little murky and many firms do not consistently embrace the role, but nonetheless we intuitively have a sense of what the COO does if there is one in a firm.

What title should be used for the head of Information Technology (IT) at your firm? If using the title of Chief Information Officer (CIO), how does that differ from having the title of Chief Technology Officer (CTO)? There is also an even newer title, Chief Digital Officer (CDO), which briefly had a moment of mania and now seems to have become less a darling than when it was first introduced. You might also be surprised to know that there was an earlier IT-era title of Chief Data Officer (CDO), and though it had not gained traction it miraculously seems to have gotten a second lease on life by the rise of today's Big Data and the emergence of Business Analytics.

In this chapter, I explore the myriad titles of the head of Information Technology. You might wonder whether it is important to consider the various titles and think instead that a rose is a rose, no matter what you call it. This though overlooks the notion that what we call someone and the nature of the title says a lot about what we expect of the role and the person. We could give someone the title of dogcatcher if titles don't really matter, and yet I think we'd all agree that upon hearing the word dogcatcher you have an immediate reaction and belief about what that role does and their value to the organization. Having an in-depth understanding about the various titles for the head of Information Technology and choosing the right one(s) is vitally important to whether a business will end-up gaining the ROI from their IT that they hoped and assumed they will be able to get.

CHAPTER 1: ROLES OF THE CIO, CTO, CDO

Who is leading the enterprise technology aspects at your firm? It could be a Chief Information Officer (CIO), which is a role that often involves overseeing and guiding the Information Technology (IT) of a firm. Or, it could be a Chief Technology Officer (CTO), a somewhat newer role than CIO and often seen as the head proponent for technology throughout a firm and especially for technology aimed at customers and the world outside the company. Or, it could be a Chief Digital Officer (CDO), an even newer role than CTO and that is seen as the savior for helping companies embrace digital throughout their firm and transform the company toward a digital future. Or, it could be a Chief Data Officer (CDO), a less commonly known role and that has a focus on company data, especially nowadays due to the rise in Big Data and predictive analytics.

If you are somewhat bewildered at so many CXO titles for the enterprise tech aspects, please be aware that you are not alone in your qualms. Not only are there a lot of titles, they even are confusing by repeating the CDO as both used for the Chief Digital Officer and for the Chief Data Officer. When someone tells you that they are the company CDO, you'd be safest to politely ask what the letter D stands for in their case.

I can make things even more confusing by sharing with you a few more of the alphabet soup meanings. For example, CIO is being tweaked by some to mean Chief Innovation Officer, suggesting that the traditional CIO role should be transitioned to being focused on ensuring innovation occurs throughout a firm, and that the Chief Information Officer role should be adjusted accordingly. Another one making the rounds is Chief Integration Officer, suggesting that the role of the former Chief Information Officer now should be one of integrating together the various parts of a firm, and tying together disparate systems and processes, along with the technology.

Dizzying. There are tongue-in-cheek versions of some of these titles too. For the CIO, there was a period of time when business was rushing to outsource their IT function, and so at the time some said that CIO should be Career Is Outsourcing. When the CTO title began to rise, some thought that firms would do away with their CIO's, and so the word was that CIO stood for Career Is Over. This has happened again with the rise of Chief Digital Officers, and yet the CIO's still seem to be maintaining their grasp. In fact, some see the pendulum as swinging back toward the Chief Information Officers, so much that some now like to say that CIO now stands for Career Is Outstanding.

Let's take a close look at each of the CXO leadership titles that are involved in the enterprise tech realm, and provide insights about the why and how of what they are.

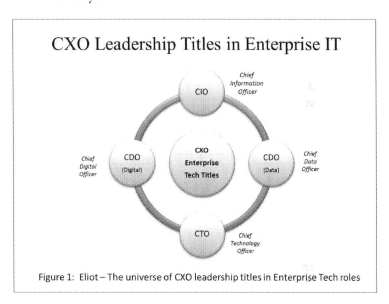

CXO Leadership Titles in Enterprise IT

Figure 1: Eliot – The universe of CXO leadership titles in Enterprise Tech roles

TECH LEADERSHIP ROLES

Many firms do not have any kind of C-suite title for their head of technology, and instead refer to the head of their IT and/or Tech by the title of say Vice President (VP), or Senior Vice President (SVP), or Executive Vice President (EVP). These firms do not believe that a C-suite title is warranted for their company. They view that it is OK to have a CFO, COO, CEO, and other C-suite titles, but that the head of IT or Tech is considered not equal in stature. Inch by inch, many of those firms are finding that by not having a C-suite title for the head of IT or Tech, they are considered falling behind of their competition in the notion of embracing the importance of being at the forefront of IT and Tech.

So some are now adding the C-suite title, but they might also be relegating the role to something less than a true top executive position. This can be both good and bad, in the sense that without being at the top of the food chain it can be very hard for the role to succeed. Being buried under some other functional area can be limiting to what the role can accomplish, simply due to the hierarchical nature of how firms work. Some think that well they are a matrix organization and everyone is kind of equal, but of course this is rarely the case in that in the end most firms still ultimately are guided by the hierarchy whether explicit or implicit.

The titles of CIO, CTO, CDO are the commonly used CXO leadership titles that are representative of these roles. Even if your firm does not have any of these actual titles, the odds are that you might have someone essentially performing the role, though using a different title. Factors used to compare these roles include whether the role is expected to have Business acumen, Tech proficiency, Data deftness, or Digital prowess.

For the CIO, the perception is that such a role is supposed to be very business oriented. This suggests that they are also not especially tech savvy or focused, nor data savvy or focused, nor digital savvy or focused. Furthermore, the perception is that the CIO is usually tasked with internal IT, such as for the ERP systems and other internal systems, but not particularly focused on the external systems for customers such as embedding systems into the products and services of your company.

For the CTO, the perception is that the role is supposed to be heavily techie in orientation and experience. They are up on the latest hot technology and stay at the forefront of hot technology. The perception is that they might not be as business savvy as the CIO, and nor especially savvy in data and nor digital.

For the Chief Data Officer (CDO), they are considered a heavyweight in data. They are keenly interested in and care about how data flows within your firm, outside your firm, and leveraging data to the maximum ways possible. So they are considered strong in the data aspects, but not so strong in other aspects such as business, tech, or digital.

For the Chief Digital Officer (CDO), they are considered a digital wizard. They are keenly focused on making sure that a firm transforms to embrace digital throughout all aspects of the firm. They are on the look for ways in which your industry will be disrupted by digital. Meanwhile, they are considered as less business savvy, less tech, less data, than the other CXO tech leadership titles.

Now that I've laid out that elaboration, allow me to say that most actual CIO, CTO, CDO's are now angry at those above elaborations. Why would they be angry? Because most would say that those are false stereotypes about each role. The CTO might be broiling to suggest that they are somehow not business savvy, or not data savvy, or not digital savvy. They might even insist that the reason they were hired as CTO was because the firm wanted someone that was a wizard in each of those realms. The CIO might bristle that they are not somehow digital savvy, nor tech savvy, and nor data savvy. And also be miffed that they are considered as somehow only being focused on internal systems. The CDO's, whether Chief Data Officer or Chief Digital Officer, would likely also be fuming about how they are being characterized.

And they might indeed be right. They could each have a high rating within their own presumed area of expertise, and have a medium in all of the other facets. Of course, they might argue it should be high in those other facets rather than medium, but anyway I am just making the point that the stereotype described earlier should be taken with a grain of salt. Generally, there is not an across-the-board accepted and standardized definition for each of the CIO, CTO, CDO roles, and each firm tends to define the role as befits their particular firm.

This can be confusing when trying to compare one firm against another, as you cannot necessarily assume that just because someone at Firm X has the title of CTO that they are the same in their role as the role performed at Firm Y with the title of CTO.

In theory, each of the CIO/CTO/CDO's titles has an intersecting element, and they each have a non-intersecting element that makes them each distinct. How much of an intersection there is, and how much of a non-intersection there is, are all up to debate. I wish that I could say that a CIO is always this and that, a CTO is always this and that, and the CDO's are always this and that. Alas, it is been an evolving effort of having these vaunted roles emerges and along the way it has been a meandering path rather than a nicely laid out path.

FACTORS INVOLVED

You might be wondering why these roles have emerged and evolved? Good question. Here are some of the key factors involved:

- Often driven by the individual
- Strengths of the individual are a determiner
- Weaknesses of the individual are a determiner
- Executive peers viewpoints count
- Politics within the firm make a difference
- Needs of the firm
- Pressures from outside the firm
- Can include glamour aspects
- Can be fad based
- Overall a mixed bag

Let's next explore these factors. Sometimes, the roles have been driven by individuals. In some firms, they had a person in let's say the CIO role. Maybe that person was stuck in their ways and was not interested in or willing to take on the kinds of technology aspects that the firm thinks needs to be managed. Rather than fighting against the CIO, such firms would adopt a new position, the CTO. Some firms embraced the CTO role, not necessarily due to the CIO's individual limitations, but sometimes due to the placement of where the CIO was in the organization. Maybe organizationally the CIO was placed in a circumstance where the aspects of what they wanted a CTO to do would not be amenable, and even though the CIO could do the role, they weren't in the right place and the organization did not want to shake-up the tree accordingly.

Another reason for adopting a CTO when there is already a CIO was that (it was argued) the CIO would be overwhelmed if they tried to take on both the CIO duties and the perceived CTO duties. Rather than swamping the CIO, and also endangering other facets of the business that needed a CTO capability, such firms opened up the new role of CTO. You can go ahead and repeat the last several paragraphs and substitute the Chief Data Officer (CDO) in each place that I mentioned the CTO, and you can likewise repeat it and substitute the Chief Digital Officer (CDO). In other words, in many cases there were firms that for various organizational, political, or individualistic reasons opted to adopt a CTO, or CDO's roles.

There is also the potential of pressure from outside a firm. A Board member of Company Z sees that a Chief Digital Officer at another firm has completely transformed that company into a digital age firm. The Board member then puts pressure onto the CEO of Company Z that shouldn't they also have a Chief Digital Officer? Lo and behold, then the firm adopts a CDO accordingly. Notice that this might have nothing particularly to do or say about the existing other CXO tech leaders in Company Z, other than that the perception is that the Company Z needs to have the adopted role. This could then be duplicative of what the firm already has in place, or could genuinely be an important addition and refocus for the firm.

I mention this above aspect that the added role might be quite worthy, since I don't want to leave you with the impression that having these various roles is necessarily duplicative or bad.

In fact, there have been fads involved in these roles. Whereby the business world gets excited about one of these roles, and firms clamor to put someone in place. Riding a fad can be good, and the firm can be enriched by doing so. On the other hand, sometimes firms become a bit bulky with too many of these tech leadership roles. The result is that there is confusion within and even outside the firm as to what each of the CIO/CTO/CDO's in that firm are responsible for.

HIERARCHY OF THE CIO/CTO ROLES

Let's consider for the moment the CIO and CTO roles. In some companies, they have a CIO and do not have a CTO. Let's label that as Scenario #1. This is the most frequent aspect of today's companies overall, namely that they tend to have a CIO (or equivalent though with a VP/SVP/EVP title), and no CTO as yet.

The next scenario is the circumstance of having a CIO and a CTO, in which the CTO reports to the CIO. That's considered Scenario #2. Here, the firm has opted to create a CTO role, and placed the CTO under the CIO. Some would say this is good, allowing the CIO to then take on the duties of a CTO by having a new head that will then help to keep the CIO from being overburdened. A contrarian might argue that the CTO is buried underneath the CIO and will not be able to do widespread kinds of CTO things.

This takes us to the Scenario #3. In this scenario the CIO and CTO are considered peers. They might either both report to the CEO, or maybe both report to the COO, or maybe one reports to the CFO and the other to the COO, etc. Either way, they are considered roughly equal in the hierarchy and neither is strictly above the other. Some would say this is a good way to structure things because you then get both working toward their each respective strength. The downside is that sometimes they are working at odds with each other, not clear on who has what turf. This can lead to head banging and ultimately undermine both.

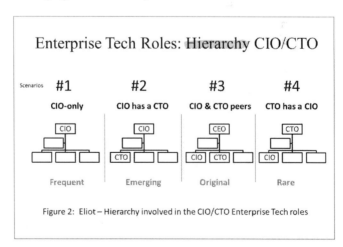

Figure 2: Eliot – Hierarchy involved in the CIO/CTO Enterprise Tech roles

For many firms that were the first to adopt a CTO role, they set about making the CIO and the CTO equal in the hierarchy. Their thinking was that they needed both to be able to stand tall. In some firms there has been a move toward a different organization setup which we'll call Scenario #4, wherein the CTO has a CIO reporting to them. This is a rarer circumstance. Usually, this might be seen in a high-tech company that especially reveres technology so the CIO is less crucial than the CTO.

HIERARCHY OF THE CIO/CDO ROLES

We have covered the hierarchy aspects of the CIO/CTO. There are other variations, of course, and the matter can become more complex when you toss into the mix at company that has multiple divisions or business units, each of which might have some combination of CIO's and CTO's. In any case, let's next look at the CIO/CDO roles.

We will have a similar set of potential arrangement as described in the CIO/CTO configurations. Scenario #1 is the CIO-only role and there is not yet a CDO. Scenario #2 is the CIO and CDO as peers, which is what companies are tending to do when they first adopt a Chief Digital Officer. Fewer firms are adopting Chief Data Officers and so for the moment I'll lump together the CDO's and usually be implying the Chief Digital Officer rather than the Chief Data Officer.

The same trade-offs as before are in existence when having the CIO and CDO as peers. On the one hand, they both might work together well and cover their each role tremendously, or they at the other extreme might be butting heads and there is internal confusion over what each does.

Scenario #3 has the CDO reporting to the CIO. Some firms like this approach because they believe it augments the CIO, while other firms eschew doing this because they believe that in their organization the CDO would not see the proper light of day.

Scenario #4 has the CIO reporting to the CDO. This might happen in firms that believe they need to radically transform their firm and so have opted to put the Chief Digital Officer above their CIO. Their thinking is that this will help drive the CIO toward reconstituting the existing systems as part of the digital transformation.

I am purposely not declaring that any one particular way of these is right and the others are wrong. That's what I sometimes get asked by CEO's and I politely say that it is an overly simplistic way to see things to assume that out-of-the-blue one could declare a particular configuration as good or bad. Each organization has its own flavor and needs, and so the nature of the roles needed and reporting will be best ascertained by examining that specific firm.

I might also add that it is equally important to look at an existing firm and root out whether their CIO/CTO/CDO's roles are in proper places and alignment. For a specific firm, it is relatively easy to see what makes a good fit. To say generically that all firms should be fit a certain way in terms of their CIO/CTO/CDO's is nonsensical and I assure you that there is not one shoe that fits all.

HIERARCHY OF THE CIO/CTO/CDO ROLES

Suppose we consider that a firm could have a CIO, CTO, and a CDO (one or more). There are a lot of potential organization structure combinations and permutations, but I have narrowed it to just three that seems most popular.

Scenario #1 involves the CIO overseeing the CTO and CDO. This tends to occur when there is a CIO that is considered in a firm as a great leader and able to undertake the technology aspects and the digital aspects of the firm. The CTO and CDO are able to undertake their efforts under the auspices and glow of the CIO. That same scenario can breakdown if the CIO is not well regarded at the top of the firm. Furthermore, even if they are well regarded, it can breakdown if either the CTO or the CDO believe themselves to be poorly placed in the organization.

These facets need to be worked out.

Scenario #2 has the CIO/CTO/CDO as peers. This sometimes happens in firms that have a CIO that they thought was best augmented by another CXO tech role, perhaps first doing so with a CTO. They maybe then found that the CTO was overly techie, and when they wanted to go the digital route they then brought in a CDO. This might work out Okay, assuming that all three are able to work collaboratively. Obviously, this can breakdown if each perceives themselves as competitive to each other. Turf wars can then dominate their time and attention.

Scenario #3 depicts the CIO at the top, having a CDO that reports to them, and then a CTO reporting to the CDO. There are lots of variations like this, in which we could place any one of the roles above or below the other. As earlier suggested, the chemistry between them and the nature of their role definition will determine whether this kind of structure will work out well or not.

WRAP-UP ABOUT THE CIO/CTO/CDO ROLES

Here is a recap of key points that we've covered:

- CIO/CTO/CDO roles are not a strictly distinctive standardized accepted set of roles,
- Each role has presumably a particular capability and purpose,
- The reality is that for most companies the roles are blurred,
- Factors impacting the roles include the firm history, culture, etc.
- Titles do mean something and are indeed important,
- Reporting relationships mean something and are important,
- A particular configuration might be good and well aligned,
- A configuration can be poorly aligned and adversely impact a firm.

There is not a national or international agreement as to what the CIO/CTO/CDO's roles must be per se. There are certainly various definitions, but firms are able to decide for themselves what they think each role is. For most companies, they have evolved over time an understanding of what the CIO/CTO/CDO roles are. There is at times a shake-up when a new CEO comes on-board, or when some other exigency forces the firm to reconsider what name plates to use and what the roles will be for.

I am sometimes told or overhear others that say the title doesn't mean anything, and that there is too much preoccupation with whether someone has the title of CIO or CTO or CDO. I respectfully disagree with them in that I assert that titles do matter. The employees in the firm are quite aware of titles, as are those outside a firm. You can make-up some crazy titles within a firm, but it will have a confusing meaning to the outside stakeholders. In spite of the confusion about exactly what a CIO or CTO or CDO does and how they differ, people inside a firm and outside a firm have an intuitive and immediate sense of what those titles confer.

If titles don't matter, then presumably we could give the CEO some other title (or maybe no title at all, which imagine that confusion), likewise for the CFO, etc. I am also sometimes told or overhear others saying that where you report in an organization is also of little or no importance. Sorry, but reporting relationships do have meaning. Someone once said to be me that we are all humans and all equal. Well, yes, we are all humans, and so you could say we are all equal in that sense. But, when it comes to companies, the hierarchical structure is still king, and regardless of how you matrix things or try to flatten things out, people will still perceive that there is a structure implying hierarchy, even if not explicitly so stated. It's human nature and how humans work collectively.

You might meanwhile be wondering should your firm have a CIO, should it have a CTO, should it have a CDO's? Those are the kinds of questions that should indeed be asked. Of the various combinations and permutations of the CIO/CTO/CDO's, none is the supreme right way to do things in your firm. For your firm, the right number of such roles and how they are aligned is something that needs to be tuned to your specific firm. If the CIO/CTO/CDO roles are poorly aligned, it will be a mess and the tech within and used for outside your firm will likely be a Frankenstein. If the CIO/CTO/CDO roles are well aligned, it will produce a resulting success of tech within and outside your firm, and a thing of great beauty.

Lance B. Eliot

CHAPTER 2

ON BEING A SMART CIO

PREFACE

The name of this book has a purposely provocative title by the seemingly simple use of the word "smart" in it (this is equivalent to click-bait). The title has a sense of action to it, encouraging the reader to seek to be a Smart CIO. There is an implicit challenge in the title, forcing existing or potential CIO's to wonder whether they are a Smart CIO or not. Non-IT executives might be curious too as to what a Smart CIO is, and whether they have one in their midst. Executive search partners might chuckle at the title of the book since they find themselves often dealing with less-than-smart CIO's and likely have their own definition of what a Smart CIO consists of (and colorful derogatory phrases for the ones that are less-than-smart).

This mind teasing title was not by accident. Having worked with and for many CIO's and having been a CIO, I am convinced that those CIO's that ultimately survive and indeed thrive do so because of their smarts. But what does this mean to say or assert that someone is a Smart CIO? I think it is reasonable and expected that anyone that claims to be a Smart CIO should have some kind of definition or barometer that helps gauge the appropriateness of making such a claim.

Even more importantly, I firmly believe that at least we should be having a dialogue about what makes for a good CIO versus a not-so-good CIO. The problem with the not-so-good ones is that it continues to poison the barrel. Most C-suite executives already have a muddled if not at times lowly opinion of their CIO, and tend to carry this onto the backs of all

CIO's. A number of years ago, while I was serving on the board of a prestigious association of CIO's, we launched an educational program to try and uplift CIO's toward what I am now calling a Smart CIO stature. Part of my drive to write this book has been to continue that now sputtered goal, and in this chapter there is an outline of what I believe a Smart CIO is all about. You are welcome to disagree or argue with my definition, and at least I'll know that it got us to think more explicitly and overtly about this vital topic.

_____

CHAPTER 2: ON BEING A SMART CIO

Not all CIO's are equal. There are topnotch CIO's that really know their stuff. There are struggling CIO's that are not quite yet up to par. And of course there are all different flavors and variations of CIO's in-between. The type of CIO that seems especially adept at being a CIO is one that is a treasure to the profession and is highly successful in the CIO role.

What makes the difference between a so-so CIO and the "right stuff" CIO? I assert that the key is being a Smart CIO. A Smart CIO is the best kind of CIO and achieves success both within their firm and in the larger community of the CIO profession. I have purposely chosen to use the word "smart" and I realize that it might rankle some that find the word "smart" to be abrasive, elitist, or otherwise objectionable. There are those that might prefer to use a word like the Shrewd CIO, the Savvy CIO, the Alert CIO, or maybe even the Bright CIO (do they light up a room?). Those are certainly feasible alternatives, but I still prefer the word "smart" as will be explained next. Admittedly the word "smart" is loaded with potential baggage and could be interpreted in a negative way. I'd like to carefully and thoughtfully unpack the word "smart" and offer a detailed explanation for why I think it is a suitable means of denoting the key to being a topnotch CIO.

Put aside for the moment any preconceived notion of what the word "smart" means to you. Let's have an open dialogue about what the word could mean and how it applies to CIO's. If at the end of this discussion you are still frothing about the use of the word "smart" then at least you'll know what I intended by its use and you are welcome to come up with some other phrasing as you might so wish to do.

DEFINING THE SMART CIO

The word "smart" usually denotes someone with high intelligence. I am avoiding using the phrase "Intelligent CIO" because the word "intelligence" tends to have an even more complicated and confounding image than does the word "smart." There is an ongoing debate for example about the use of Intelligence Quotient (IQ) tests and whether an IQ test actually measures intelligence or not. For many, the notion of being intelligent refers to a strictly cognitive kind of notion, having an ability to do hard math or have deep thoughts.

There have been many backlashes against the use of IQ tests and the pigeon holing people based on seemingly questionable and artificial ways of gauging intelligence. There are also arguments that being intelligent does not necessarily translate into intelligent behavior. In other words, you might be very intelligent, but only within your own head, and when trying to convert that intelligence into something useful or practical in the real-world that one does not have to directly correlate to the other.

Some also argue that there is a book learning kind of intelligence, the learned type that you use in school, versus a contrasting seat-of-the-pants intelligence. The seat-of-the-pants intelligence is intelligence gleaned from everyday interaction with the world around us. Those that try to portray extremes would say that the book learning intelligence is often a kilter of the real-world and generally pie-in-the-sky kind of intelligence.

Meanwhile, those that have the seat-of-the-pants intelligence are seen as real-world oriented and practical, but then criticized as not being able to see a bigger picture and perceive the world beyond their own experience base. The presumed advantage of the book learned intelligent is that the person is infused with knowledge far beyond what they themselves could garner in just their own limited day-to-day interactions of the world.

This brings us around to an important underlying tenant of being a Smart CIO, namely, smartness here means that you have a strong ability to acquire knowledge and skills, and then be able to act upon those acquisitions. The fields or domains underlying the aspects of being a CIO are continually changing, whether it is the technology that CIO's deal with, or the business practices and approaches that they need to know and utilize. A Smart CIO is one that is able to acquire the knowledge and skills and keep the acquisition ongoing for both the technical realm and the business realm. It is not enough though to merely or only just obtain the knowledge and skills, since you need to also be able make use of that knowledge and apply those skills in a demonstrative way. A Smart CIO is more than a cornucopia collection of mental capabilities; they also act upon those capabilities and leverage their mental capabilities to the hilt.

This notion of smartness also encompasses having sound judgment. We probably all know seemingly highly intelligent people that at times appear to exercise very poor judgement. This is again another reason I am avoiding saying the Intelligent CIO and instead saying the Smart CIO. A Smart CIO exercises good judgment. Does this mean that the Smart CIO is perfect and always exhibits sound judgment? No, I am not creating a false god-like image, and openly acknowledge that a Smart CIO is a human being, meaning that from time-to-time they might not display sound judgment, and their smartness might wane at times. It will happen. On the other hand, by-and-large, for most of the time, and especially when it counts, they do indeed exhibit sound judgment.

A Smart CIO has passion for what they do. They are not just robotically performing the job of CIO. They believe in their role as a CIO and have passion for it. This passion is also shown as they do their work. It is not just hidden within them, but is instead an aura that is presented while they are performing as a CIO. They are also engaged, acting in a manner that shows they care and are involved.

A recent movement in the debate over IQ has led to the emergence of the assertion that people presumably also have an Emotional Quotient (EQ). Some would argue that IQ omits the emotional aspects of life and being human. As such, there has been created the EQ, capturing another dimension of a form of intelligence and intelligent behavior. In the CIO realm, this had sparked debate and discussions about whether CIO's should or do exhibit a sufficient level of EQ. There is even a name given to this as known by the Social CIO or Socially Intelligent CIO.

I am including into the Smart CIO that they do have some kind of sufficient and capable EQ or social interaction capabilities. So far, it seems like a tall order to be considered a Smart CIO. But there's even more. As a "chief" and "officer" of a business, the CIO also needs the leadership capabilities to properly and appropriate lead the IT function and work with their fellow executives such as the CEO, COO, CFO, CMO, etc. The Smart CIO needs leadership capabilities and also management acumen. They need to have an astute business sense.

As the "information" word is also a part of the CIO acronym, the Smart CIO also needs to be technology literate, and be aware of and using when appropriate the latest in technology and systems trends. They need to know not just about the technology, but also the underlying informational aspects and digital aspects too.

USING AN ACRONYM FOR SMART

You might already be aware that the computer field is filled with lots of acronyms. We seem to relish making up acronyms for all sorts of techie bells and whistles. You might also already know that the word "SMART" has been turned into an acronym for other uses. For example, when trying to set goals, some would say that you should make "SMART" goals, meaning that they are Specific, Measurable, Attainable, Relevant, and Time-Based. It's a somewhat clever and memorable way to keep in mind what you need to do when setting goals and you can use the "SMART" acronym to remind you of what you need to know.

Let's see if we can conjure up an acronym to fit with the Smart CIO. I would assert that a Smart CIO is **Systematic, Mindful, Adaptive, Respected,** and **True.**

Systematic means that the Smart CIO plans out what they do, they are think in a systems way, and they realize and take into account that systems have many components and those components interact with each other. I am not referring simply to the technology side of being systematic, but also including the business aspects of being systematic, the organizational and company politics of being systematic, and so on.

Mindful means that the Smart CIO does things not by random chance or by being haphazard. Instead, they think about what they are doing and going to do. They are mindful of the consequences of the choices and decisions they make. They are mindful of how to enact those decisions and choices.

Adaptive means that the Smart CIO is able to adapt as conditions change. The business might change. The technology might change. The industry might change. To these changes, the Smart CIO is able to readily adapt. They adapt on a timely basis. They adapt willingly. They adapt as befits the circumstance.

Respected means that the Smart CIO is respected for what they do and who they are. Having such respect is crucial to performing their role. Without having respect, even though they might be able to command others to act, the added aspect of having respect will carry them further along. They have goodwill that acts as a reservoir of support, and the respect that they have is earned respect and not just respect by title alone.

True means that the Smart CIO is authentic. They are who they present themselves to be. Trying to act as a Smart CIO is not likely to fool anyone for very long. The trials and tribulations of being a CIO are a tremendous wear and tear. There is a truth about them and they are known for honoring their word and being real.

We can now refer to the Smart CIO as the SMART CIO with this added acronym. I am not particularly a fan of such acronyms and so have opted to continue here with referring to the Smart CIO without the acronym. The acronym might be handy if you think it an easier way to remember what the picture I am painting of what a Smart CIO is.

DIGGING DEEPER INTO THE SMART CIO

Whenever I refer to the Smart CIO, I usually get someone that wants to right away heckle and tosses out the idea that there must be the Dumb CIO's if there are Smart CIO's. Well, Okay, you could certainly say that there are Dumb CIO's and I can see how one would think of it as the opposite side of the coin of the Smart CIO's, but I think the word "dumb" is an overly saturated word with all sorts of confounding meanings. If you want to go that route of using the word "dumb" then I suppose you could also say there are Dull CIO's, Light CIO's, Unaware CIO's, and so on.

I'll even help out and offer an acronym using the word "smart" but tries to suggest the opposite of what was intended with the SMART acronym. Rather than Systematic, Mindful, Adaptive, Respected, True, the negative polarity of the Smart CIO might be said to be Sloppy, Mindless, Anchored, Reclusive, and Two-faced. Anyway, I don't find it especially productive to play the game of trying to identify what is the opposite of the Smart CIO. Instead, I would claim that the Smart CIO is like a temperature gauge. There are those that are at a less level of yet being a Smart CIO, and those that are at a higher measure of being a Smart CIO. If you fall below a minimum threshold, then I would suggest that calling someone a Smart CIO is no longer valid and actually misleading.

To further explore the Smart CIO definition, let's use a handy quadrant.

Quadrants of Smart CIO™

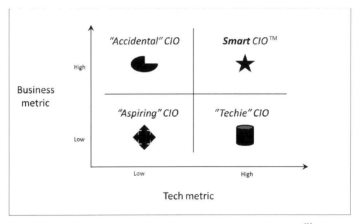

Figure 1: Eliot – The range of levels and being a Smart CIO™

We'll keep things simple and offer that there are two main dimensions of gauging a Smart CIO.

First, there is the business metric, along the vertical axis. The business metric is loosely stated as ranging from low to high. Imagine that within this business metric we are bundling all of the earlier stated aspects about being business savvy. Next, along the horizontal axis, let's put the technology metric. The technology metric is also loosely stated as ranging from low to high. This technology metric is considered bundled with all of the earlier indicated technology aspects about a Smart CIO.

Generally, the Smart CIO is in the upper right corner. They exhibit a High score on the business metric and a High score on the Tech metric. We'll use a star to indicate this is the rock star and aim for being a Smart CIO. What about the other three quadrants?

There is the Low-Low quadrant, meaning a CIO that is lacking in business and in technology. As mentioned earlier, there are some that would try to maybe label these as being "Dumb CIO's" but I'll instead politely call them "Aspiring CIO's." I do this because I would assert that assuming they are actually acting as a CIO, I would hope that they might realize they are well below what is expected and hoped for becoming a Smart CIO, and that they would seek to embellish their business and technology acumen accordingly.

One potential concern about these Low-Low CIO's is that they can at times inadvertently poison the barrel and make a black-eye for all CIO's. We've probably all seen this happen, wherein a CEO with a CIO that is not up-to-the-task is not seen as an individual that is poorly performing, but instead perceived as a blanket representation of all CIO's. In such cases, the CEO will often ban the role of CIO, mistakenly commingling an individual that was not up to the CIO role with the general notion of the CIO role. We know that if they had filled the role with a Smart CIO they would realize the value of a CIO.

There is quadrant of a High on the business metric and Low on the tech metric. Typically, this indication of someone with top business acumen but low on the tech side is commonly seen when a firm decides to put a non-IT person into the CIO role. Perhaps someone from the Operations side of the company is well trusted by the firm and knows the business really well. The company thinks that they can drop the person into the CIO role, and whatever tech stuff is needed won't be much of a concern. These CIO's are sometimes called the Accidental CIO.

I would argue that this is a dangerous kind of CIO. There is danger because if they are insufficient in their technology smartness, they can make decisions involving technology that lead the firm down a bad path. I realize that some would say that the business-only CIO can be augmented by surrounding them with techies, but this usually doesn't work out very well. The business-only CIO gets multiple tech opinions from those around them and cannot judge which is best or worst. They also cannot provide much guidance or mentoring to their techies and will often be perceived poorly by the techies that feel like the person just doesn't get what they are telling them. I am not saying that the Accidental CIO is always doomed to failure. I would say that an Accidental CIO should be striving toward the Smart CIO quadrant, augmenting their business prowess with sufficient tech capabilities and awareness.

The last quadrant to discuss is the High on tech and the Low on business, the classic "Techie CIO." This has been the mainstay for many years. CIO's that came out of the technical ranks and ultimately rose to the CIO title. Unfortunately, this tended to make a bad name for CIO's and the ongoing accusation that CIO's are not business savvy. Similar to the Accidental CIO, I would hope that a Techie CIO would realize the limitations of not having the appropriate business acumen and would be seeking to add that prowess to become a truly Smart CIO.

I am saying that ultimately the CIO's in the other three quadrants should all be striving toward the top right corner and become a Smart CIO. This is not so that they can somehow walk around with a badge that says they are a Smart CIO, but because if they embody the ingredients of a Smart CIO they will be running IT more effectively and efficiently and strategically for the company. I would also emphasize that being in the top right corner is not a birthright and nor a spot that once achieved is everlasting. It is actually somewhat common to see a Smart CIO that falls behind and drifts downward, bordering onto the other quadrants. They need to be continually fighting to stay in the upper right corner. As mentioned earlier, if they are mindful they will realize that they are falling behind, and if they are adaptive they will update and change to keep themselves properly fit.

NATURE VERSUS NURTURE

In the debate about being intelligent, there are some that argue that a person is born with a set amount of intelligence. You can then either use it or not. But, if you are born with perhaps a lower level of intelligence, you are stuck. Nothing you can do will rise you up. In many ways, this depiction of intelligence is misleading and generally debunked. It does bring up an interesting issue, namely, the classic debate over nature versus nurture. Is a person born with certain characteristics and as such they are deemed for or best suited for certain things in life?

This is an ongoing debate in the leadership realm. Some say that leaders are born as leaders. They claim that you cannot make someone into being a leader. They then point to certain charismatic leaders as proof of this claim. It is a bit of spurious proof and I am not going to get mired into that debate here. Instead, let's contemplate whether the Smart CIO is born that way or can they be nurtured into it?

One viewpoint is that for some elements, such as the leadership component, they must be born with it, while the other parts can be learned. In fact, it is frequently stated that you would be best to hire someone with business savvy and teach them the techie stuff, rather than get a techie and try to turn them into a business savvy person. That being said, I assure you that I have seen business savvy people that could not gain the techie side, and I've seen techies that took just fine to the business side.

A brush stroke kind of assertion on this is probably weak in terms of trying to claim that all techies are not suitable to being migrated into the business side, and equally questionable to say that al business savvy types are readily migrated into the tech. My position is that the nurture wins out over the nature argument for the Smart CIO, assuming that the individual that we are considering is really meeting the earlier stated characteristics. A person of a smart mind and embodying the willingness and desire, I believe, can be mentored, coached, educated, and trained into the Smart CIO role.

TRENDS AND ACTION STEPS

We earlier touched upon the aspect that a Smart CIO keeps up with trends. There are numerous evolving trends in the IT field, such as DevOps, Hybrid IT, Bimodal IT, and so on. It is expected and incumbent upon a Smart CIO to be up-to-speed on these trends. That being said, it is worthwhile to clarify what it means to say that the Smart CIO needs to be up-to-speed on the trends.

One might leap to the conclusion that the Smart CIO must embrace the trend and accept it and adopt it. That's not what I am saying and nor implying. Awareness of a trend means that the Smart CIO is aware of the emerging trend. They know what it consists of. They learn about how it is valued or not valued. They contemplate seriously how they should embrace it, or not embrace it. This means that they do not ignore trends. I point this out because some CIO's will by the waving of their hands just shrug off a trend that they know little about. That's not a Smart CIO.

Some CIO's will blindly fight a trend, and try to ridicule the trend by making belittling comments. The frequent such exhortation is that "seen that, done that," even though they might not have actually ever really have done it. That's not a Smart CIO. A Smart CIO would dig deeply enough into the trend to have a proper understanding for it, and if they believe it is not worthy they would have a handful of solid reasons to back their findings. Some CIO's brush aside a trend as a fad. A Smart CIO realizes that even if a trend is a fad, the fad aspect can be leveraged and used for other means that otherwise might not get attention or resources. Each of these above points take us around to the notion of the mindfulness of the Smart CIO and the adaptive capabilities of the Smart CIO.

If you are an existing CIO, I hope that this elaboration will be of use to you. It might open your eyes to facets of the CIO role that you knew about but maybe has fallen by the wayside in the harsh hectic day-to-day role as a CIO. For any researchers or observers of CIO's, perhaps this elaboration will spark ideas on how to further assess and probe on the CIO role.

.

CHAPTER 3

SMAC: SOCIAL, MOBILE, ANALYTIC, CLOUD

PREFACE

There has been a grand convergence of several technology trends in the last several years that has taken the IT field by storm. In particular, four of those technology trends have been bundled together into a catchy acronym known as S-M-A-C. Anyone tuned into the latest buzzwords in the IT field have been talking about SMAC, even though there admittedly are many in IT that have not necessarily heard the acronym per se and are not specifically familiar with it. If you haven't heard it, you are about to become part of the brotherhood or sisterhood of those that know it.

The letter S is for Social, meaning the advent and adoption of Social Media. Social Media became popularized via consumers and in society at large, and then in catch-up mode many IT groups within companies began to realize that they needed to jump onto the same bandwagon and help their company become social media savvy. In this case, the idea is to use social media as a platform within the company for internal communications, and then also work with the marketing and corporation communications side of the company in aiding the social media efforts to the outside world.

The letter M in SMAC is for Mobile devices and mobile apps, the letter A is for Analytics such as Big Data and Business Analytics, while the letter C is for Cloud as in the use of the cloud for storing of data and the housing and running of applications. Each of the four technologies are now considered part of the "table stakes" for any CIO in terms of making sure that their company is active in SMAC. Furthermore, the CIO needs to make sure that the IT group is versed in SMAC and able to collaborate with the rest of the firm in adopting it.

––––––––

CHAPTER 3: SMAC: SOCIAL, MOBILE, ANALYTIC, CLOUD

Have you heard about SMAC? If you don't know what I am talking about, you'd better keep on reading, since otherwise you'll be uncool and not in touch with one of the latest Information Technology (IT) related trends. SMAC is the hot acronym that is being spoken at all of the trendy IT conferences. SMAC is whispered by executive recruiters trying to assess whether a CIO candidate is up to par. SMAC is the new hip way to quickly convey to someone else in the know that you are in-the-know. It stands for Social, Mobile, Analytics, and Cloud, or "SMAC" for short.

Before you say, hey, what's the big deal, let me tell you why those four simple letters are a big deal. A really big deal. Right now, business leaders are looking at their IT function and saying, what have you done for me lately? It does not matter that the CIO has kept the systems humming, the PC's calculating, and the network plumbing flowing. It does not matter that the CIO has averted hackers from cracking into the corporate systems. Well, that last one does matter, since otherwise the CIO would probably be summarily canned (yes, think of some recent major newsworthy incidents, and you'll see what I mean).

Anyway, businesses want to be competitive, and SMAC is the simplest way to express that notion, at least in a techno lingo. In a kind of Morse code, the utterance of SMAC is saying this: *Tell me what you know — and what you have done — in Social Media, in Mobile Apps, in Analytics, and in the Cloud. Seems pretty simple. It actually is not.*

Any CIO worth their salt will need to recount what they IT function has contributed toward the business making use of Social Media, doing so in a manner that has substantively aided the business. Likewise, recount what the IT function has done in the development and deployment of Mobile Apps that substantively aided the business. Likewise (again), recount what the IT function has done in providing Analytics capabilities, such as the now famous Big Data, and how that has substantively aided the business. And, likewise (again!), recount what the IT function has done in the adoption of Cloud computing, doing so in a manner that substantively aids the business.

LIGHTWEIGHT SMAC

I purposely included the "substantively aids the business" in each of the four arenas. I say that because there are some that try to get bye by saying, oh yes, they know about Social Media, they dabbled with Mobile Apps, they reviewed Analytics, and they tried out the Cloud. Sorry, that won't cut it. That's, at best, lightweight SMAC.

Lightweight SMAC is defined as a kind of SMAC that means you have been at the fringe of these latest IT trends, but you have not truly jumped into the midst of it. Some even try the gambit of hey, they personally use Social Media like Facebook, and they keep their personal vacation pictures and selfies in the Cloud. Notice that I had said "substantially for the business" which means that you do SMAC for the business, for the company, across and within and throughout the company. Personal SMAC is just more lightweight SMAC.

Another attempt at some SMAC tomfoolery is the attempt to get away with the three-out-of-four, or two-out-of-four, or even one-out-of-four gambit. In other words, suppose that the CIO has implemented various Cloud related systems, perhaps putting a bunch of core apps into the cloud, and doing so such that it substantially helped the business. OK, that's good. But, it's not good enough. The one-out-of-four is not enough. Certainly, having done two-out-of-four, such as both Social and Mobile are better. Still, though, not enough. Three-out-of-four, let's say Social, Mobile, Analytics, you are getting closer to completeness, but still not there.

I know that it seems like an unfair hurdle, but, yes, you need to be versed in and have accomplished grand things in all four. Otherwise, you are a lightweight. Fighting words, I realize.

INSUFFICIENT SMAC

Recent surveys show that most companies are quite dissatisfied with IT at their firm in the following specific respect: The IT function is not introducing new technologies as fast, nor faster than and not as effectively as their competition. That usually translates into insufficient SMAC. For example, the firm sees competitors actively using Social Media, pushing out tweets, leveraging their Facebook presence, and so on; meanwhile, at your firm, the Social Media is more like anti-Social Media with hardly anything to show, and certainly not something to crow about.

The firm sees competitors with really cool Mobile Apps that their customers appear to be downloading in droves. Meanwhile, you don't even have a Mobile App. The firm hears through the grapevine that their competition has tons of data that they are mining, and they are finding ways to boost revenue, get closer to the customer, and cut costs. Meanwhile, you have a ton of data, but it just that, a ton, a big lardy ton, and no one in your firm has any means to try and slice or dice it. Finally, the firm sees competitors that have dumped their old legacy applications and moved into graceful new applications available on the web, via the Cloud.

All in all, they see their competitors as leaps and bounds ahead, doing "heavyweight" SMAC. You, unfortunately, are insufficient SMAC, the lightweight SMAC plodder. Now, I realize that some CIOs will say, wait a second, my business leaders might be fooled into thinking the competition is doing all those things, but it is really smoke and mirrors, a lot of puffery. Yes, there are quite a number of tall tales that are being told these days. I call it the pie-in-the-sky SMAC. But, you trying to claim that the King has no clothes, won't really endear you to the business leaders in your firm. Indeed, it will probably make you seem just doggedly outdated and overly defensive. In short, you need to give in. Give yourself over to SMAC.

THE SMAC PATH

How can you become SMAC worthy? First, you should be at least doing research on how SMAC is being used in your industry. How far along is Social Media adoption in your industry? How about Mobile Apps? How about Analytics? How about the Cloud?

For the Cloud, keep in mind there essentially three levels of Cloud use, namely, SaaS, PaaS, and IaaS. SaaS is "Software as a Service" and basically means apps that are offered over the web. PaaS is "Platform as a Service" and basically means tools and services for building and deploying apps .IaaS is "Infrastructure as a Service" and basically means the infrastructure such as servers, networks, operating system, storage capacity, etc. These three elements are usually referred to as the "Cloud Computing Stack" which means, when thinking of these levels as stacked on top of each other, how you are using those three stacks. As an aside, you are encouraged to look at the National Standards and Technology (NIST) standard definition for cloud computing: http://csrc.nist.gov/groups/SNS/cloud-computing/. Take a look (if you like), and then come back here and continue reading.

Second, those of course are just technologies, so also make sure to think "business" too. IT has been forever accused of wanting new toys, i.e., new technologies, just for the sake of it. Avoid that likely accusation by getting your key end-users and business leaders involved in the assessment of where SMAC is in your industry. Put together a strategic level IT plan that encompasses SMAC. Third, don't rush, but also don't delay. There is a temptation to get onto the SMAC bandwagon and wantonly start a bunch of initiatives in Social Media, in Mobile Apps, in Analytics, and in the Cloud. Resist that temptation. Resistance though does not mean taken no action. It means to be thoughtful, mindful, and systematic.

I know that many CIOs eschew the trendy buzzwords that seem to continuously emerge in the IT realm. Whether you like it or not, the SMAC buzzword is catching hold. Putting your head into the sand is, well, dangerous and probably job threatening. Take a realistic look at your company, and gauge your SMAC portfolio. If you rated your company on say a scale of 1 to 10 (with 10 being best), on each of the elements of SMAC, how would you rate? What can you do to start moving up toward a 10 on each of the four elements? Your company depends on it. Your job depends on it.

CHAPTER 4

CIO'S TOP 10 LISTS

PREFACE

In everyday society we seem to delight in seeing Top 10 lists. Some of you might recall the popularity of comedian David Letterman's nightly Top 10 lists that were gags about the latest items in the news. We pay attention to the Top 10 lists of songs and movies. Sports teams are ranked into the Top 10. In essence, reducing a complex world down into a short list of ten important items is helpful and simplifies things for us.

There are several Top 10 lists in IT that are about CIO's and frequently used by CIO's. Similar to everyday Top 10 lists, such lists in the IT field are handy to provide a focus and a convenient means to see what's up and what's down, and an indicator of what's in and what's out.

Being aware of the CIO-related Top 10 lists is crucial to understanding what CIO's are interested in and where their attention is going. In one sense, what is on the list is nearly as revealing as what is not on the list. If you look at a particular Top 10 list and don't seen an aspect on it that you think deserves to be there, it could mean that CIO's don't agree that it belongs in the top rankings. This can either be because you are over-inflating something that you believe strongly in, or it could be that the CIO community has not yet come around to knowing about or accepting whatever it is. In any case, these Top 10 lists are like X-ray machines into the minds of CIO's and you ought to be examining the X-ray results to know what is happening.

———

CHAPTER 4: CIO'S TOP 10 LISTS

There are a plethora of "Top 10" lists in IT that purport to provide insights about what is hot in IT and what is not hot. Generally, such lists can be very useful as a barometer of what CIOs are thinking about and what the needs of IT in business are all about. I have chosen to examine the latest set of Top 10 lists that appeared in a recent study done by the Society for Information (SIM), a prestigious association of some 3,000 CIO's and CTO's worldwide. As full disclosure, I tend to believe in the survey by SIM due to my having been involved with SIM for many years, including having served on the Board of Directors for SIM. I am quite familiar with the rigorous nature of their studies and the thoughtful manner in which their research is conducted.

The Top 10 lists that I am going to discuss are reflected in a published SIM study entitled "Issues, Investments, Concerns, and Practices of Organizations and their IT Executives: Results and Observations." I provide herein an excerpted version of some of those lists for purposes of discussion and evaluation.

Rather than trying to talk to individual CIO's one-by-one about what they care about, it is handy to have a survey of hundreds or perhaps thousands of CIOs, offering then an across-the-board perspective on what is trending. A particular CIO can then compare what they consider their most important considerations to the Top 10 lists, and ascertain whether their own personal lists and the survey produced lists are akin to each other, and gauge what other CIO's as their peers are interested in or not. It can be a wake-up call for some CIO's that get mired in topics perhaps due to familiarity or tradition.

Non-CIO executives are often also interested in these lists, since they might wonder whether the IT of their organization is tracking with what other firms are doing. Is their CIO seemingly concerned about the same topics? Are there topics that other firms care about but that their firm seems to not be caring about?

Vendors often find these Top 10 lists equally helpful, providing insight into the mindset of CIO's, the purchasers and approvers of the wares sold by the vendors. Some vendors will discover that the wares they are selling are perhaps toward the bottom of a Top 10 list (or not even appearing in the Top 10 at all), thus explaining why they find themselves constantly going against the grain when trying to sell their product or service. Some vendors will recast their wares into the top items of the Top 10 list, in hopes that their product or service will get greater attention and better sales.

CIO's will at times find it useful to cite a Top 10 list when trying to justify a new technology in their organization. By showcasing that the aspect has been ranked as a high priority by many other CIO's and organizations, the CIO seeking to embrace that new technology can perhaps get their own company to embrace it too. Most companies do not want to get caught off-guard and discover that some technology has emerged and that other firms think it is important and yet their firm does not equally rank it. Given the intense attention to disruptive innovations that are changing industries radically, firms no longer are as willing to fall behind in terms of the latest systems and technologies.

The Top 10 lists are also helpful to aspiring CIO's that are curious as to what existing CIO's are thinking about. When working further down inside an IT hierarch, the perspective of what is important can often be very narrow, shaped by the functional part of IT that the staffer is in. If you are a specialist in networks, the odds are that you view only networks and infrastructure as the most paramount focus for the IT function. By seeing a CIO's Top 10 list, the IT staff can gain a broader perspective about the nature of the IT function and also be more supportive of their CIO by realizing what is overall of most importance.

WHAT THE RANKINGS MEAN

One question that often comes up about these Top 10 lists is whether or not it is important or significant that an aspect is ranked in a particular order. In other words, some say that anything on the Top 10 list is important, otherwise it would not have even made the upper ten at all and be somewhere further down on the list. Though it is true that making the Top 10 list does indicate that an aspect is overall noteworthy, I would also argue that where the aspect lands within the top ten is also significant. I say this because in IT there is only so much available in the IT budget and such limited resources and time and attention; you ultimately do need to make tough decisions about which piece of the pie gets the smaller versus the larger slice.

An item ranked at the top of the Top 10 list is invariably likely going to get more dollars of the IT budget, more attention by the CIO, more scrutiny and consideration than say the bottom of the Top 10 list. This does not mean that you can therefore ignore or disregard the bottom of the Top 10 list. It just means that the higher ranked items are indeed of greater value and attention, and so accordingly should get and deserve to receive more of the pie.

I like having these Top 10 lists because it does force CIO's into making the difficult conscious choice of what is more important. In the day-to-day efforts of running IT, it can become easy to shift one's attention from crisis to crisis, and lose sight of the big picture. By referring to the Top 10 list, it can shake you out of the daily crisis mode and remind you of the overall and overarching direction that you need to go.

The Top 10 list is also handy to spark discussions about anything that you think is not in the Top 10 but that should be in the Top 10. If there is an aspect that a CIO believes warrants being in the Top 10, that's fine, and the question then becomes where it does fit into the Top 10, and what else needs to come off the list? It is easy to just want to have something added to the list, but much harder when you then need to figure out where it ranks and thus what else must come off the list to keep the list still at just a Top 10.

Finally, this brings us to another point, namely, you don't need to be wedded to the list as being only ten items in size. You could expand the list to say 15 items or even 20 items. Many studies will have the list at those larger sizes, and then only report to the media the Top 10 for brevity and ease of comprehension. If you are curious about why a particular item appears to be missing from a Top 10 list, take a look and see if a fuller list exists and then see where the missing item fits on that longer list.

TOP 10: IT MANAGEMENT ISSUES

Let's consider first the list of the "Top10: IT Management Issues, " which includes these elements in ranked order from most important (ranked #1) to less important (ranked #10):

1. Alignment of IT and the Business

2. Security and Privacy

3. IT Time-to-Market

4. Innovation

5. Business Productivity

6. IT Value Proposition

7. IT Agility and Flexibility

8. IT Cost Reduction

9. Business Agility and Flexibility

10. Business Cost Reduction

#1. Number 1 on this particular list is Alignment of IT and the Business. This aspect about alignment is nearly always in the top few positions of the list for key IT management issues. Why is it consistently ranked so highly? The reason for being so highly ranked is pretty straightforward. If the IT function and the business are well aligned then it means that what IT is providing as products and services to the business should be a good fit, and the business will be pleased with what IT is doing. If there is misalignment between IT and the business then almost nothing else on the list is probably going to work out well anyway. The odds are that anything else on the list will not be what the business wants.

Aligning IT and the business is hard work. It is something that is continually in flux. That's also why it remains so highly ranked, it is not like something that you can just do once and be settled with it. Instead, day after day, week after week, month after month, the CIO must constantly be striving to gain alignment of IT and the business. That being said, I do not intend to suggest that IT and the CIO are to merely go hat in hand to the business and say, hey, tell me what you want. Doing so is fraught with difficulty. Many businesses are unsure of what they want. They need sufficient coaching and guidance from the CIO to be able to grasp what makes sense for the business and what does not make sense.

Notice that I am not saying that the CIO dictates this to the business. Sadly, some CIO's have done so, acting in a dictatorial way, and the end result is usually that the business is greatly dissatisfied with the CIO, and with IT. The CIO needs to work with the business in a collaborative fashion to figure out how IT and the business can be best aligned.

#2. Number 2 on the list is Security and Privacy. This item fluctuates on these Top 10 lists, sometimes floating further down on the list. Right now, given the various cyber-attacks and ransomware viral issues, the topic of security has risen up toward the top of the list. Privacy is also tacked onto the security topic since the ability of cyber attackers to grab private data and expose it has made the privacy of data increasingly important to companies. As Big Data continues to increase in popularity with businesses, the privacy aspects gets larger and larger. Furthermore, regulation by governmental entities about keeping data private by a business adds more teeth to the privacy needs. A breech of privacy can impact customers, and can also bring potential criminal persecution against companies that allowed the privacy violations to occur.

#3. Number 3 on the list is IT Time-to-Market. Companies are finding that the marketplace is moving very rapidly and so their firm needs to respond quickly too. If a new mobile app is needed by a business, it usually needs it right away. If a new web site is needed by a business, it is usually needed right away. Getting IT systems rapidly up and going has become even more crucial than it has in the past.

If the IT function cannot respond quickly enough, the rest of the business is going to suffer. If the rest of the business begins to suffer because of the speed of response by IT, the odds are that the business will decide that it will find someone else to handle IT that can do so more quickly. This is the basis for much of the outsourcing of IT activity today, being done in hopes of gaining a speedier time-to-market for IT.

#4. Number 4 on the list is Innovation. Businesses do not want to be disrupted by innovation that someone else comes up with before they do. The expectation is that IT will help the business be innovative. By identifying new technologies and how to deploy those technologies, the business will be aided by IT in achieving overall innovation. This is a tough aspect to sometimes help achieve in a business. The IT function often has its hands full with keeping the legacy systems going. Being able to innovate requires the resources to do so. It also requires the mindset for it. Often, an IT function will not have within it the IT staff that is ready for and willing to be innovative. Even if the IT is so staffed, often the business itself will be resistant to innovations, in spite of what overall battle cry might be heralded.

#5. Number 5 on the list is Business Productivity. This is a classic item on the list, namely that IT should help the business be more productive. Labor when armed with technology should be more productive. Less labor can often do more by being armed with the right kind of technology.

#6. Number 6 is the IT Value Proposition. This is a classic item too, and a vexing one. What are we getting for our IT investment? That's what CEO's and CFO's are fond of saying. Where is the value in our IT? Are we over-investing in IT? Are we under-investing in IT? CIO's are faced with justifying the cost and the benefits of IT. This usually happens in a big way during the annual budget cycle. It can also occur throughout the year, especially if the business and IT are misaligned. Misalignment almost always leads to accusations that the IT Value proposition is just not there.

#7. Number 7 on the list is Agility and Flexibility. Agility refers to the being able to nimbly get things done. Flexibility refers to being readily able to adjust to accommodate business needs, and do as the needs fluctuate. In the past, IT often collected requirements and then a year or two later rolled-out a system meeting those requirements. Today's world moves so fast that the odds are that those requirements six months down-the-road would be outdated and need to be changed. Being able to accommodate that kind of change is met when an IT function is agile and flexible.

#8. Number 8 on the list is IT Cost Reduction. Businesses want to know that they are spending the least amount necessary on IT. Did we get a good price on those software licenses? Are we paying a competitive price for our use of those cloud services? Is there fat in IT that can be cut out? Other executives of the firm want to be reassured that every penny going into IT is crucial, well spent, and not wasted spending.

#9. Number 9 on the list is Business Agility and Flexibility. Similar in some ways to item #7, this aspect is about having IT aid the business overall in being agile and flexible. Are there ways to design systems that encourage the business to be agile? Can you deploy systems that aid the business in becoming more flexible and able to adjust to changing customer needs and tastes?

#10. Number 10 on the list is Business Cost Reduction. Similar in some ways to item #8, this aspect is about having IT aid the business overall in reducing costs. Can the new systems help reduce the cost of manufacturing? Reduce the costs of providing services to our customers? What ways can the deployment of IT enable the costs of the business to be reduced?

That's then the Top 10 list of IT Management Issues. For most CIO's, there is nothing earth shattering on the list. The list contains the items that they contend with each and every day of the week. CIO's though might find of some special interest the ranking of the Top 10. Would you agree or disagree that for example security and privacy should be #2 on the list? If you are a CIO that thinks it should be in say tenth position, is that because you don't think that security and privacy is particularly important for your business? Or because you think you have it solved and so it is not worthy of being so highly ranked? Those kinds of questions are useful to ask. By doing so, it reveals your own assumptions about what is important to you, and what is possibly or presumably important to the business.

TOP 10: CIO WORRIES

Next, let's consider the list of "Top 10: CIO Worries," consisting of:

1. Security and Privacy
2. Alignment of IT and the Business
3. IT Talent Shortage
4. IT Time-to-Market
5. IT Agility and Flexibility
6. IT Credibility
7. Business Continuity
8. IT Value Proposition
9. CIO Leadership Role
10. IT Disaster Recovery

Much of this list is similar to the IT Management Issues list. Like two horses jockeying for position, the top two are "Security and Privacy" and "Alignment of IT and the Business" (which were the top contenders in the IT Management Issues list, though flipped in sequence).

It makes abundant sense that the Security and Privacy item sits at the very top of the CIO worries. Most CIO's are kept awake at night fearing that a sneaky cyber-attack on their corporate systems will not only wreak havoc on the company data, but also damage the reputation of the company and otherwise make IT also seem incompetent or worse. Each morning that the CIO wakes-up and during the night there has not been such an incursion, they breathe a sigh of relief, at least for moment, they at least made it through one more night safely.

There are some items on the CIO Worries list that do not appear on the IT Management Issues list. For example, ranked third in the CIO Worries list is the IT Talent Shortage. CIO's know that finding high quality IT talent is a huge challenge these days. Without having the proper talent in place, the IT function won't be able to meet the needs of the business. Finding and attracting IT talent has become an important part of being the CIO of a modern business.

Ranked number six is IT Credibility. Many businesses have a rather dim view of their IT function. At times, IT has not delivered on what was promised. Projects run late. Systems go over budget. These are all aspects that reduce the credibility of IT. Without credibility, the rest of the business will not believe what IT has to say, and will often subvert IT. The rise of so-called shadow IT is often due to the business deciding that it will do IT on its own, rather than using a centralized IT for the business.

CIO's need to work tirelessly to regain credibility. Plus, even assuming that credibility can be gained, it is only kept when the IT products and services are consistently meeting expectations. It takes a lot of hard work to gain credibility. It takes only one bad apple of an IT system that goes awry to then wipe out the credibility that had been so earnestly earned.

Ranked number 7 is Business Continuity, and in a somewhat similar fashion at number ten is IT Disaster Recovery. Businesses today are confronted and bombarded with natural disasters and manmade disasters. The IT function should aid the business in ensuring business continuity. Likewise, IT itself should be prepared for disasters and have appropriate IT disaster recovery preparations in place and ready to be invoked.

The other CIO worry that appears on the CIO Worries list and does not appear in the IT Management Issues list is item #9, namely the CIO Leadership Role. Why is the CIO worried about the CIO leadership role? It is a "keep my job" worrying concern.

The CIO is wondering if he or she has the leadership chops needed to properly lead the IT function and work with the business to achieve alignment. And, does the business think that the CIO has that leadership acumen? If the CIO does not have the leadership capabilities, or if the business believes that the CIO does not, it could mean that the CIO might be facing a pink slip soon.

TOP 10: IT INVESTMENTS

Another interesting list consists of the "Top 10 IT Investments," consisting of:

1. Business Intelligence
2. ERP
3. Security
4. App Development
5. CRM
6. Data Center/Infrastructure
7. Cloud
8. Network/Telecomm
9. Legacy Applications
10. Virtualization

This is where the IT budget is being spent in terms of capital and other systems related spending. Business Intelligence systems are at the top. This has been the case in the last several years and will continue for a while. Besides the rise of Big Data, the newer rise of the Internet of Things (IoT) will further increase the hunger by the business for Business Intelligence systems.

Next is ERP, Enterprise Resource Planning systems. These are the core systems of the business, usually consisting of the financial and accounting systems, along with the operations systems. Though maybe not the darling of attention like it once was, nonetheless to keep the business running takes a sizable and ongoing investment in ERP.

Third on the list are systems for security. This could almost be higher on this list, given that it is ranked as the number two item on the IT Management Issues list, and the number one item on the CIO Worries list. Most CIO's are already relatively well invested in security, so they probably opted to list its third on this list. Plus it tends not to be as costly as the Business Intelligence and ERP investments. Of course, it is also something that many businesses under-invest in, either due to the CIO or due to the business not having a willingness to make sizable investments in security. Regrettably, many firms won't make sizable security investments until after they get hit by a major security attack.

Ranked at number 4 is applications development, which is a sizable investment as firms increasingly want new apps and want them rapidly built. At position number 5 is CRM, Customer Relationship Management systems. These systems for sales and marketing are still coming along strongly, though not as much as during their heyday a few years ago.

Investments in Data Centers and Infrastructure are at position number 6. And at position number 7 is the Cloud. Then at position number 8 is the Network and Telecommunications. These three are all grouped about the same place on the list. They are items focused on the plumbing of IT and ensure that the systems of IT have a place to be run and be accessed.

Ranking at 9th on the list is Legacy Applications. These are the applications that are continuing to keep the business running. Ongoing investments in those applications are necessary to ensure that they meet ongoing and changing business needs.

In many IT groups, the staffs that maintain the legacy applications are unfortunately treated as second-class IT citizens, while the IT staffs developing new applications get all the glory. This can create friction within IT that needs to be overcome. The CIO needs to acknowledge the importance and value of the legacy applications and that team too.

At item #10 on the list is virtualization. A relatively techie topic, and once higher on the list, the adoption of virtualization by IT has become relatively common and accepted. The ongoing investment is not as much as was the initial cost to get virtualization up and going.

TOP 10: IT TECH SKILLS

Let's now consider the "Top 10: IT Tech Skills," consisting of:

1. Business Intelligence
2. Security
3. Information Architecture
4. Functional Area Knowledge
5. Enterprise Architecture
6. App Architecture
7. Agile Software Development
8. ERP
9. User Interface/UX
10. IT Project Management

These are the topmost tech skills that CIO's are looking for in their technical staff. By-and-large, you will notice that the tech skills being sought are well matching to the IT Investments list. For example, ranked number one as a tech skill is Business Intelligence, while indeed the top IT investment is Business Intelligence.

Let's take a look at some of the tech skills that maybe are not so obvious and self-explanatory. Ranked at position four is "Functional Area Knowledge." This refers to having an understanding of a functional area, whether it be say accounting knowledge to be able to help work on accounting systems, or maybe insurance industry knowledge if working on insurance industry systems.

Ranked at number nine is User Interface and User Experience (UX) skills. This refers to being able to design applications that have good and working interfaces to the end-users of the application. In some cases, the application is being developed for use by end-users within the business. In other cases, the application is being built for use by the customer or client of the business. Providing a good user interface or UX is essential to gaining adoption of an application.

Ranked at number 10 is IT Project Management. Some would argue that this is more of a business skill (which we'll see again, in a moment, when looking at the next column). For IT project managers involved in highly technical systems, they need to have a mix of both technical skills and business skills, and so the reason for it being listed on both the tech skills and the business skills lists.

TOP 10: BUSINESS SKILLS FOR IT

An IT function won't get very far if it only consists of technical skills. There is also a need for business skills. Here's the list of the "Top 10: Business Skills," for IT, consisting of:

1. Strategic Thinking
2. Leadership
3. Systems Thinking
4. Business Analysis
5. Change Management
6. Innovative
7. Problem Solving
8. Emotional Intelligence
9. Decision Making
10. Project Management

Ranked at position number 1 is the ability to think strategically. This is a vitally important business skill since it involves being able to work closely with the business to make sure the right kinds of systems are being built and deployed. Many businesses and IT groups waste a lot of resources by building and deploying systems that have little or no strategic value to the business. By having the strategic thinking skills in IT, this can hopefully be averted.

Next are leadership skills, needed to guide the IT function appropriately. Having systems thinking skills (ranked #3) and business analysis skills (ranked #4) are all about being able to analyze what the business needs are, and then designing systems that can properly meet those needs.

Change management (ranked #5) is about ensuring that as new systems rollout that the business is able to change to make use of those new systems. Often, a business is mired in old processes and outdated ways of doing things. When a new system rolls out, the business clings to the old ways and won't properly make use of the new system. This then often causes the new system to be considered a flop. The business suffers because it isn't exploiting the presumed beneficial aspects of the new system. Thus, an important business skill in IT is being able to help and manage the changes that need to be made by the business.

The other business skills in the list are relatively self-explanatory, except perhaps for position eight, Emotional Intelligence. Emotional Intelligence is about having an ability to empathize with others. Traditionally, IT has not been very empathic with the emotions of the business. Taking a stale and somewhat robotic tone, those in IT often ignored the emotional reaction of the end-users. For example, replacing an existing system can be difficult for some end-users that are familiar with and comfortable with an older system. By having the ability to sense these emotional concerns, those in IT with keen emotional intelligence can better ensure that systems are aligned.

IT BUDGET CATEGORIES

An item from the SIM survey that I thought might be of interest to discuss is the latest in terms of IT Budget Categories as a percentage of the total IT budget:

- Hardware: 16%
- Software: 18%
- Facilities: 6%
- Employees: 38%
- Consultants: 6%
- Contractors: 6%
- Cloud Services: 10%

Though this is not a Top 10 list per se, it is a list that I thought would be valuable to mention. For many CIO's, they are continually struggling with how to slice up their IT budget. What portion should go toward hardware? What portion toward software? Etc. Vendors are often keenly interested in this facet too, since it reveals how much the CIO can potentially spend on these categories.

The hardware spending on the average of the CIO's surveyed was about 16% of their budget. Software is about one-fifth of the IT budget, coming in at 18% of the IT budget. Facilities are 6%. The biggest chunk of most IT budgets is the spending on the IT employees. As shown, it is on the average about 38% or say nearing half of the IT budget. Spending on consultants is 6%, and on contractors is 6%.

For IT groups that have outsourced much of IT, the spending on the IT employees is quite a bit less than the 38%, and those costs shift over to the consultants and contractors categories.

Cloud services are now around one-tenth of the IT budget. This is a shift from the hardware and software part of the budget, moving into a somewhat new category involving the cloud. These expenditures are for using cloud services such as AWS and the costs too for storage via those cloud services.

WRAP-UP ON THE TOP 10 LISTS

Every year, various IT industry research groups release the latest Top 10 lists for IT. Be on the look for these lists, and keep up-to-date as the composition of the lists change and shift. From year-to-year, the rankings will tend to bounce up or down a little bit within each list, but not much. In fact, items coming off a list or new ones getting added onto a list are usually a gradual process. Thus, you can anticipate that when you look at next year's list it will be relatively similar to the lists you've seen herein.

You might be rooting for something to get onto the vaunted Top 10 list, or clamoring for something to rise up higher on the list. I wish you good luck. In any case, knowing what is on the Top 10 list can be important as an informed participant in the IT industry and for anyone in business that cares about IT.

CHAPTER 5

TECH TRENDS AND BUSINESS VALUE

PREFACE

Leading and managing an IT function is a continual balance of being versed in technology and also being astute in business. We have seen over and again that often an IT function becomes enamored with a technology that becomes so-called shelfware. This means that it is some kind of technology that IT heralded and spent money on, and yet it is not being used by the business. It sits on the shelf, collecting dust. This wouldn't be so bad except for the fact that precious resources were expended to get or make it. Furthermore, there were lost opportunities that could have used those resources and had a true payoff for the business.

I don't want to only point the finger at IT. There are nowadays many end-users and non-IT managers in businesses that do the same thing that IT had been doing for years. Vendors have at times opted to go around IT and sell their wares to end-users and non-IT managers directly. They do so under the claim that IT will just get in the way or otherwise befuddle or mangle a technology that could really help the business. Sure, this is certainly a valid concern and criticism in some cases, but it also opens the door to circumstances where end-users and non-IT managers get themselves into the shelfware predicament. What they thought was going to be the greatest new toaster turned out to not be usable, or they did not know how to properly adopt it (which perhaps IT could have helped to make sure it did get adopted).

It is important to take a look at what technologies and technology trends there are, and then overlay that with trying to ascertain the value that the technology might have to the business. Saying this is a mouthful, for sure, and needs to be "unpacked" (a terms that seems to have crept into our cultural vocabulary). The unpacking of what are the latest technologies and how they can impact the business is best done in a collaborative manner with the business and IT, working hand-in-hand.

CHAPTER 5: TECH TRENDS AND BUSINESS VALUE

Everyday there seems to be a new technology that pops out of the woodwork and becomes the darling of IT fashion. Often, these "hot" technologies are accompanied by exhortations that it is the next best thing since sliced bread. Furthermore, you are cautioned and even threatened that if you don't jump on-board that you will suffer dire consequences, including presumably a career dead-end, possible job loss, and probably even incurable bad breath.

One of the perhaps most important activities for any IT executive consists of helping to curate these emerging technologies and ferret out which ones are ready for investment and which ones are not. This is what many non-IT executives expect that their IT executive will help do for them. Given that the IT executive is supposed to be tech savvy, it seems fitting and directly relevant that the IT executive should be on top of this.

That being said, some IT executives get themselves into a bind by being the only one at their firm that is involved in keeping up-to-date on the latest technologies and assessing them. This solo approach is usually a bad sign, namely it suggests that the IT executive is acting separately from the business. Plus, there is at times a tendency to have a kind of so-called "technology lust" toward exciting new technologies, which is not necessarily the right business reason to want a new technology.

It is crucial that the CIO or CTO involve the business directly in the ongoing assessment of new technologies and collaboratively ascertain the value that such technologies might or might not provide to the business. One increasingly popular organizational mechanism includes establishing an IT-related Center of Excellence (CoE), or an equivalent kind of R&D element to bring together the techies with the business members of the firm. The CIO or CTO goes out of their way to ensure that there is appropriate representation from other units and functions of the firm, and does so in more than a perfunctory way. A perfunctory way is usually just asking for anyone from other departments and then in a hollow manner assigning them to be part of the CoE. That's not going to do much good, and in fact is likely to harm the CoE and the whole notion of having the CoE.

In past years, progressive CIO's and CTO's tried to get these kinds of new technology organizational assessment entities going and were often rebuked. Why should other parts of the business "waste" their limited resources towards such an internal effort? Won't it just involve sitting around and getting to play with new toys? We have "real" work to do, those other business heads would say, and come back to me when you've vetted something that I should truly care about. This head-in-the-sand response has lessened in many respects. Today, the cry for all businesses to become digital businesses has spurred companies to reconsider how they do business. They are bombarded with examples of companies and competitors that are making facets of their business into digital winners, positively impacting not only the internal running of the firm but also the products and services being delivered to customers.

Let's take a look at the aspects of new technologies and how businesses are transforming in the fast paced digital age.

BUSINESS TRANSFORMATION

There is a lot of talk these days about transforming the business. What does that mean? It indicates that businesses are changing how they do business, undoing and altering prior practices and transforming into something that will presumably be stronger, more resilient, more efficient, more effective, and intending to be more profitable and maximize shareholder wealth.

Businesses are doing so for purposes of being better at what they do, but also to avoid being squashed by competition or being otherwise put out of business or battered. The word "disruption" is a key part of why companies are seeking to transform. The popular example of Uber is an indicator of what it means to disrupt an industry. Conventional taxi and limo services were dramatically disrupted by the introduction of Uber and other Uber-like car transportation services. It had been hard to hail a taxi, the quality of the taxi car was often dismal, the taxi driver was frequently sour and unpleasant, the paying for the taxi ride was difficult and cumbersome, etc. The Uber and Uber-like services found a means to either eliminate those pain points or at least reduce them.

Some would say that the "friction" between the consumer and the act of getting a ride was reduced and instead the whole experience has now become one of a pleasant nature rather than a dread. Firms want to avoid getting disrupted and they know that the Uber and Uber-like firms all used technology as a cornerstone for bringing about the disruption in the ride hailing industry. So, by prospering and appropriately embracing new technology, a firm can avoid becoming disrupted or at least mitigate the disruption impact.

Embracing the new technology involves transforming the business from where it is today and into something different that integrates the technology into crucial aspects of the business. Besides avoiding being disrupted, firms would like to take things a further step forward and be the disrupter. In other words, it's one thing to be ready for and make sure that your firm can withstand a disruption, that's a defensive type of posture, while it is another way of thinking to go ahead of the pack and be the actual disrupter, that's a proactive posture.

That sounds reasonable, you might say, and then wonder what new technologies might have that potential for being disruptive and therefore should be cooked into the transformation of the business. Glad you asked. Let's take a look at this next.

TECH TRENDS AND HYPE

I realize that at this juncture you might be eagerly awaiting a list of which technologies to be considering for your firm. Before we jump there, let's again keep in mind that the technologies will only be of genuine value if they can have an impact on the business. If a new technology is exciting as a technology but it cannot be ascertained as to how a business can leverage it, we would be back into the realm of looking at something that though interesting does not have an actual payoff.

It can be hard to figure out whether a new technology will or will not make an impact to a business. This requires that both the technologists and the business collaborate on making such a determination, as earlier emphasized herein. In fact, some businesses prefer to be "fast followers" that wait until someone else has figured out how to make a connection between a new technology and positively impacting the business. They cleverly wait until others have tried and sometimes failed, and then cherry pick from those that successfully integrated a new technology. They quickly grasp the brass ring and don't let it go around a couple of times, doing so in hopes of being early enough to be at the lead of the pack, but not have been one of the pack that struck out by being too early.

A fast follower strategy has tradeoffs. You might not time it well and end-up actually being a late follower when you were actually aiming to be a fast follower. Or, you might go too fast, falsely thinking that a technology is ripe and wanting so much to be a fast follower that you end-up at the so-called "bleeding edge stage" of a new technology.

The laggards are firms that wait until the technology is so proven that most of the rest of the market has already embraced it. For them, they view that the cost of being a fast follower or even worse being a bleeding edger is generally foolhardy. Once something is tried-and-true, then and only then will the laggard adopt it. This does have some merits in that by then the way in which the adoption should occur is usually more well established, as is the predictability of how much of an investment is needed and what the payback will be.

The laggard though faces potential business disruption like a large tidal wave that might wash over them and collapse them. By the time that the laggard acts, the wave of adoption by speedier firms can be so significant that the laggard has already lost the game. Today, we see conventional taxi and limo services that are struggling to adopt the same technologies and approaches of Uber and Uber-like companies, but their outdated business models and their laggard-like adoption might ultimately doom them.

A well-known tech research company called the Gartner Group has popularized a technology adoption graph known as the Hype Cycle. Take a look at Figure 1.

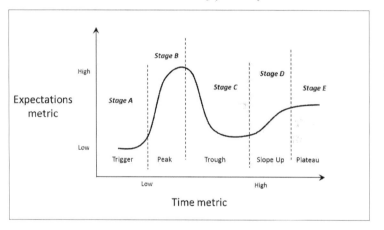

Figure 1: Eliot – Crucial to be aware of the innovation and tech hype cycles

Along the X-axis is time and along the Y-axis is expectation. There is an undulating curve that starts on the left side of the chart as being low in terms of expectations and at the low of time. This is what I will refer to as Stage A of a new technology. During Stage A, a new technology gets introduced into the world. There is some kind of trigger that makes it seems attractive and interesting. Gradually, there is momentum built-up that this new technology has great promise. The curve then proceeds upward, getting higher and higher on the expectations metric. This brings that technology into Stage B. At some point, the expectation peaks, reaching a super high point, and then once the excitement start to wear off, it begins to turn downward.

As shown in Stage C, a new technology can lose steam and drop down into a trough. This frequently happens when few can figure out how to profit from the technology in terms of turning it into something useful and usable for business. Eventually, for some technologies, once the kinks are worked out, it begins to come back and starts to rise again. This is shown in Stage D, whereby the technology has finally gotten successful adoptions and is clawing its way back upward in terms of expectations of merit.

Usually, the technology then flattens out at some level of expectation that is more than where it started but less than where it peaked. This is Stage E, when the technology has reached a plateau and has found its balance in the marketplace in terms of adoption. For the latest version of Gartner's Hype Cycle, take a look at this *Forbes* URL on the topic: http://www.forbes.com/sites/louiscolumbus/2016/08/21/gartner-hype-cycle-for-emerging-technologies-2016-adds-blockchain-machine-learning-for-first-time/#120dc2b01ef2. It gets updated annually by Gartner.

Currently, Stage A has technologies such as Virtual Personal Assistants, Internet of Things (IoT) Platforms, Smart Robots, Neuromorphic Hardware, and so on. Stage B, the peak reaching stage, currently has Machine Learning, Autonomous Vehicles, etc. Stage C, the trough, currently has Natural Language Question Answering, Augmented Reality, etc. Stage D, which they call the slope of enlightenment, contains Virtual Reality, and they don't list any specific technologies in the Stage E.

I am bringing to your attention the Hype Cycle to ensure that when you think about new technologies that you are also thinking about where they fit in the cycle of usefulness and utility to business. Whether you agree or not with Gartner's latest placement of current technologies into the various particular stages, it is more important to be considering that you should be indeed contemplating and considering where any new technology fits in the curve.

If you believe that a particular technology is currently in say Stage A, it likely means that if you are going to adopt it, you are going to be a bleeding edger. Your risks are higher. You are betting on something not yet proven. It might not be clear yet as to how the technology will help the business. And so on. If you believe that a particular technology is currently in say Stage D or Stage E, it likely means that the technology has stabilized, it is better understood from a business ROI perspective. You are likely not a fast follower per se and more likely a laggard.

Seeing how a research firm like Gartner has classified new technologies is useful as a gauge to compare to your own firm and its assessment of the technologies. Keep in mind that your firm might see a particular technology in a different light than what an overarching graph depicts. For example, if your firm already has been using AI technologies and needs to be at the forefront to remain competitive, you might perceive that say Machine Learning is actually toward Stage D now rather than its position of Stage B.

Also, realize that the undulating curve is just one such curve of potential technology adoption. Not all technologies necessarily go through this shape of a curve and through each of the stages. It is possible that a technology might for example arise in Stage A and skip directly to Stage E.

BUSINESS VALUE CHAIN AND TECH

We have now taken a look at how new technologies tend to arise over time and undergo adoption. But, you might naturally ask, adoption for what aspects of the business? One of the useful ways to consider how a new technology might impact a business involves looking at the Value Chain of the business and considering how technology plays a role in each piece of the business. Take a look at Figure 2.

Tech Trends and Value Chain Impacts

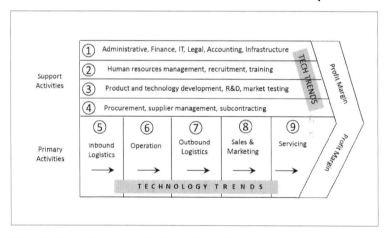

Figure 2: Eliot – Leveraging the Porter Value Chain to gauge tech trends impacts

The Value Chain was initially popularized by Michael Porter and the diagram provides a handy depiction of the elements and activities of business which lead to creating value. I have labeled each portion with a number, ranging from 1 to 9. The first four numbers (1 through 4) are considered support-related activities of a business. The last five numbers (5 through 9) are considered the primary activities of a business.

Under the support activities, we have: (1) Administrative, finance, IT, legal, accounting, infrastructure, (2) Human resources management, recruitment, training, (3) Product and technology development, R&D, market testing, and (4) Procurement, supplier management, subcontracting. There are of course other support related activities that aren't overtly named on the diagram due to brevity, but you can assume are included. For your particular firm, fit any such unnamed support activities into whichever of the aforementioned four buckets seems most sensible for your business.

The primary activities of the business are considered (continuing the count): (5) Inbound logistics, (6) Operations, (7) Outbound logistics, (8) Sales & Marketing, and (9) Servicing These primary activities are the advent of your products and services and at some point in these activities involves likely some kind of direct interaction with your customers. I have found quite useful the overlaying of new technologies onto the Value Chain, trying to ascertain which new technologies can be useful for a particular piece of the Value Chain.

A new technology might be useful for more than just one piece. Also, sometimes a new technology might be initially best oriented towards an internal use among the support activities, and then once so proven it moves outward into the primary activities. This can happen in the other direction too, namely that a new technology is adopted in a primary activity and then once proven it gets adopted into a support activity.

Part of the reason that I urge you to consider using a framework such as the Value Chain is that often when a new technology is being considered by a firm it is done so in a narrow manner. For example, suppose the HR group is interested in using Machine Learning as an approach to cull through thousands of applicants and help determine which are the most promising for hiring purposes. The IT group perhaps helps in this assessment and focuses on this particular use case. What might be missed is that Machine Learning might be applicable in other parts of the business too. Why would that matter?

Sometimes trying to justify the cost and effort toward adopting a new technology can be hard on the basis of a single use case. If the same technology can be applied to other parts of the company, it can sometimes be more readily cost justified. There are economies of scale gained by leveraging across the company. Multiple portions of the company might be able to pony up the needed resources by each contributing toward the larger overall cost.

Often, a pinpoint use is what instigates a spark of interest in a company toward a particular new technology, and it is then incumbent upon the CIO or CTO to have an overarching perspective and help consider how the technology can be applied across the company. This is in fact one of the greatest joys and challenges often for a CIO or CTO, trying to aid the firm in seeing technology on a more macroscopic scale and across the breadth of the company. The flip side of this coin is that when trying to take a single use case and enlarge to more of the company, it can inadvertently lead to delays in adoption as more hands get involved and a larger dialogue takes place.

TECH TRENDS THAT ARE HOT

We are now finally at a point where it makes sense to start discussing specific new technologies and emerging tech trends. Rather than just describing what the new technology consists of, we can now also consider what stage of marketplace adoption is it in, where might it be going, and also why would it be potentially useful to business as seen through the framework of the Value Chain.

Algorithms

One of the most touted "new technologies" is the rise of the power of algorithms. What does this mean? Generally, it means that the underlying series of steps or formulas that are used in a company's computer systems is becoming increasingly valued and crucial to the business. You might say that we've had algorithms since the start of the computer field, and so why is this something new or worthy of any special attention.

The argument made for the advent of today's algorithms is that we are able to take more of what humans might be doing algorithmically and infuse that into software and systems. This can be done more readily now since the ability to develop such software and systems is markedly easier today and can be more economically readily made available than before. Let's take an example to showcase this. The Consumer Financial Protection Bureau (CFPB) is using an algorithm developed by the research think tank Rand that determines the likelihood of someone being racially discriminated by an automobile lending company. For example, the CFPB is seeking $80 million from General Motors based on alleged discriminatory lending practices as "revealed" by the use of the algorithm.

The Rand algorithm makes use of large data sets such as census data and geographic data and tries to estimate the likelihood that someone is of a particular racial base. It does this based only on the address of where the person lives and their last name. They call it the Bayesian Improved Surname Geocoding (BIGS) system. There is heated debate about whether this algorithm is right or wrong, good or bad, but nonetheless the point is that it is an algorithm and it is being used for a business related purpose.

There are dangers inherently in using algorithms. There is an implicit assumption that an algorithm is correct. There is an implicit assumption that the base algorithm has been correctly implemented in software or a system. There is an implicit assumption that the algorithm works correctly for the aspects that it is intended, and that it is not being used for aspects for which it is not intended.

One illustrative example of these kinds of dangers is the introduction of Tay by Microsoft. This was an AI chat bot that ultimately went haywire due to how it was taking input from users and then altering its approaches. It began to emit insulting messages that were widely offensive. In this case, it did not do any substantive harm per se, but imagine if such an approach was used by a system that had more life-and-death types of consequences, such as running factory machinery, monitoring hospital equipment, or used in military systems.

A savvy CIO or CTO looks for ways in which aspects of the business can be turned into algorithms, exploring each area of the Value Chain, and ultimately identifying systems that could embody those algorithms, but also with the right protections and validation to help ensure that the algorithms are working appropriately. It is also important to ensure that the business is able to safeguard those algorithms including the Intellectual Property (IP) rights associated with them.

Machine Learning

Related to the topic of algorithms is the role of machine learning. Most would agree that machine learning is a subset of the field of AI. AI is an umbrella term that includes natural language processing, vision and image processing, machine learning, and other facets.

Machine learning refers to having a computer-based system that is able to "learn" as it runs and thus presumably improve its efforts over time. It is therefore a kind of intelligence or intelligent like behavior. I put the word "learn" into quotes because the notion that a computer is learning like a human learns is not quite what is meant by the use of the word "learning" in machine learning. Essentially, the details of how humans learn are still a mystery of science and it is not reasonable to claim that any computer system learns in the same manner per se as a human does. Therefore, the word "learn" is overloaded with all sorts of impressions and meanings, and should be used cautiously when referring to computer systems.

In any case, machine learning is usually based on either supervised learning or unsupervised learning. In the case of supervised learning, the system is guided by a human in a supervisory manner as to what is intended. For example, suppose we want a system that can identify houses and trees in a photograph or image. We could have humans label what are the houses and what are the trees, and the system then tries to generalize from the labeling to then identify in new images any houses or trees.

In contrast to supervised learning, in unsupervised learning the system would not use explicit labeling but instead use a form of reinforcement, whereby there is a reward function that provides guidance. The underlying reward function is part of a field of study known as the credit assignment problem, namely what kind of reward or credit should be used during learning and how should it be best be utilized. In the game Go, the moves will ultimately lead to winning the game or losing the game.

An unsupervised learning approach tries to utilize the win or loss to ascertain which moves were "good" and led to a win versus which moves were "bad" and led to a loss. For the image identification of houses and trees, we might have an unsupervised learning wherein the system guesses at which is a house or a tree, there is some kind of credit or reward for making a right or wrong guess, and the system tries to ascertain what to classify as a house or tree accordingly.

Artificial Neural Networks

Typically, a machine learning approach uses Artificial Neural Networks (ANN) to implement the system, often using ANN's for both the supervised or unsupervised learning approaches. ANN refers to a system that uses simulated neurons, crudely and simply modeled after biological neurons, and interconnects the simulated neurons in the same kind of notion as having biological neurons interconnected via synapses. This is done as a simulated approach of what we generally believe biological neurons are accomplishing. I emphasize that this is not to be misinterpreted or misunderstood as actually replicating in any ideal sense what the biological neurons are doing. It is an artificial and simulated approach.

Artificial neural networks have been around for several decades, but are having resurgence due to being able to now ramp-up the magnitude of how many neurons and interconnections that can be simulated and the speed at which they can be run. Some refer to ANN as "neural networks" and omit the word "artificial." This can be misleading in that the term "neural network" could refer to biological neural networks instead of computer simulated neural networks. In the context here of discussing artificial neural networks, I will at times just refer to ANN as neural networks to be more economical in discussing the topic.

The phrase "deep learning" tends to refer to machine learning that is using relatively large sets of simulated neurons and interconnections, being "deep" in the quantity of how many are involved. This has become increase in the number of simulated neurons has become feasible due to the advances in the underlying hardware and the dropping of prices for the underlying hardware. For example, the use of commonly available

Graphical Processing Units (GPU's) and Field-Programmable Gate Arrays (FPGA's) for simulating these artificial neurons has become economical given the rapid reduction in price, the improvements in miniaturization, and the increase in their capabilities.

Neuromorphic computers or architecture refers to whole computer systems that are shaped around the artificial neural network approach. One of the breakthroughs in having this kind of hardware was IBM's system launched in 2014 that contained the SyNAPSE chip with 5.4 billion transistors and an on-chip network of 4,096 artificial neural cores, allowing for a computer that could simulate 1 million artificial neurons and 256 million interconnections or synapses.

Per the earlier discussion about the Hype Cycle, the technologies of Machine Learning and the Artificial Neural Networks are still in the early stages, likely Stage A and Stage B. Businesses are still grappling with how to best use this technology. For purposes of undertaking natural language processing, there have been impressive improvements in being able to interact in a human-like natural language way via incorporating machine learning and ANN into the natural language processing capabilities. For your firm, consider what areas of the Value Chain could potentially be aided or disrupted by utilizing these technologies.

Internet of Things

The Internet of Things (IoT) refers to the connecting of "things" into the Internet that have previously not been readily considered electronic devices that can be somehow added onto the Internet. Clorox for example recently came out with a water pitcher that has a computer embedded into it for purposes of connecting the water pitcher onto the Internet. The user of the water pitcher can setup an automatic reorder for water filters, doing so via the Internet (using the Amazon Dash technology).

Gradually, we will see more and more of these kinds of additions onto the Internet. For example, clothing makers are anticipating having a computer chip embedded into the label of your shirt, pants, dress, etc. This will allow the clothing item to be connected to the Internet. You would be able to track where the clothing item is and other facets about the clothing item.

Some say that instead of calling this the Internet of Things that we should call it the Internet of Everything (IoE), implying that the word "things" is just not wide enough in terms of encompassing "everything" that will ultimately be connected onto the Internet. Another phrase is that the IoT or IoE will be a Digital Mesh. This suggests that we should think of not just things but also think of how they are interconnected via the Internet, along with the information and services associated with them.

Either way that you opt to name it, the point is that for businesses the advent of having all sorts of products being able to connect on the Internet will be a boon for some businesses and a bust for other businesses. Similarly, there will be old services that will no longer be needed or might need to be changed, and there are new services that might arise that are not needed or known today but that are feasible and needed once we have IoT or IoE. IT executives need to be working collaboratively with the business to ascertain how IoT et al will impact their business and their industry.

User Experience (UX) and the Ambient Experience

In earlier times of IT, we focused on the User Interface (UI) of how a system was designed and built to interact with the user of the system. This was broadened to focus on the entire sense of a User Experience (UX) when using a system. As an example of the power of UI and UX, Uber's interface has been recognized as one of the most well designed UI and UX's, and is considered one of the key factors in the rapid adoption and growth of the use of Uber.

An expression "Zero UI" has arisen to suggest that a user interface should be so easy to use that it is almost like the user doesn't even realize it is there at all. Another new buzzword is the "Ambient Experience" which refers to a UI or UX that remains continuous over time and adaptable across devices. For example, you might be using a system first on your mobile phone, then switch to using a laptop, then switch to using Augmented Reality via glasses, then switch to using Virtual Reality using a headset.

For CIO's and CTO's, consider what kinds of UI and UX you currently have on your existing systems. If the existing systems are hard to use and the user interface is clunky or obtrusive, you might then consider some of the newer technologies and techniques for user interfaces. The nature of the UI or UX can be a substantial determiner of whether or not a system is actively used or not. Sometimes firms put a lot of effort into the guts of a system but little effort into the interface, and then find to their chagrin a low adoption rate, due to the lousy interface in spite of whatever beauty might lie underneath it.

Chat Bots and Virtual Personal Assistants (VPA's)

Chat bots have become popularized in messenger applications. When using Facebook messenger, for example, you can have a software add-on invoked that tries to "chat" with you using natural language processing. The pizza chain Domino's has a chat bot that allows you to order a Domino's pizza. While immersed in a chat with your friend, you can invoke the

Domino's chat bot and order your favorite pizza delivered to your door. These chat bots will gradually become more pervasive and we'll see them occurring in all sorts of systems.

Virtual Personal Assistants (VPA's) are similar to chat bots. They usually though are about so-called personal assistant activities. For example, you are in Facebook messenger and suddenly realize that you wanted to have a meeting put onto your schedule for next Thursday. You bring up your VPA and in a natural language processing mode indicate to it that you want to meet with George on next Thursday, and the VPA then tries to figure out how to put this onto your schedule, akin to what a human personal assistant would do.

As indicated by the example above about the pizza chain Domino's, businesses need to be considering what chat bots and VPAs they should be involved in. If chat bots and VPAs are going to be "conferring" with customers and consumers, you don't want to be left out of that kind of conversation. Consider in what ways that chat bots and VPA's might impact your Value Chain at the primary activities, your company products and services, and in what way might it impact your internal support activities.

OTHER TOP TECHNOLOGIES

We have touched upon some of the top technologies such as machine learning, neural networks, IoT, chat bots, VPA's, and so on, but there are many others that continue to emerge. You need to establish an organizational mechanism to help remain aware and familiar with what is emerging.

As discussed earlier, it is useful for an IT function to establish a Center of Excellence or the equivalent, and use that CoE to keep up with the latest in technology, and how it fits or does not fit to your business. The CoE should be continually scanning the horizon for new technologies, even ones in their most nascent form. The CoE needs to be assessing the new technologies and be ready to communicate its findings. Sometimes this is done proactively by various communiques throughout the firm, and sometimes it happens reactively, as mentioned next.

There is an often told story of the CEO that while flying on an airplane informally talks with someone seated next to them, gets told about some new whiz bang technology, and the CEO immediately after getting off the flight contacts the entire C-suite executive team and orders that by gosh the company needs to adopt that technology. This happens more frequently than you might think.

Staying ahead of that kind of occurrence is important, and doing so by proactively having a CoE would allow the CIO or CTO to be able to quickly respond by saying that the company has looked at that technology and based on collaboration with the business has determined that it is this or that in terms of readiness for adoption by the business. This is better than madly reactively scrambling to figure out what the technology is and whether or not it might be applicable to the business.

If the CIO or CTO does not take on these kinds of trends tracking and assessing efforts, it then leaves a vacuum as to whom in the company should be doing this. Some CIO's or CTO's will think that perhaps the head of R&D for the company should be doing this. That might be appropriate, but at least the IT executive should have a hand in it.

Some companies don't trust or believe that their IT function is up to the task of running a CoE on technology. Thus, it can be difficult for those CIO's or CTO's to try and break into it within their firm. For them, it is often a long, slow, painful process of gradually gaining trust that the IT function can have a role and be a significant player in this.

Some CIO's or CTO's will say that they don't have the budget monies available for something like a CoE. This can at times be overcome by starting small, providing proof of the value of the CoE, and then going to set aside larger amounts for expanding the CoE. It also can be wise to seek out other fellow non-IT executives that could help shoulder the cost of the CoE, involving the business units or other functional areas, which collaboratively is desired anyway. There are many ways to skin a cat, as they say, and it is vital to find a means to keep up with the latest technologies and technology trends, and do so in business case manner.

CHAPTER 6

THE CIO 100 NOTABLES

PREFACE

The Academy Awards provides an opportunity for the entertainment industry to acknowledge its best directors, producers, actors, cinematographers, movies, and other notables. Each year, the entertainment industry examines what was produced that year and assesses itself. The grand ceremony of revealing the winners and celebrating their success is a highlight of the industry and adored by movie fans and entertainment industry stakeholders.

Likewise, in the IT field, there are annual events that acknowledge the accomplishments of companies and what they did with IT that year and how they achieved particularly extraordinary business results. The CIO is given the overall credit, though it is assumed and usually stated that the outstanding IT projects and systems were representative of their respective IT function and the commitment of their business executives and end-users.

It is exceedingly useful to be aware of this "Academy Awards" for IT, and I will examine one that is known as the CIO 100. The CIO 100 is an annual judging of some of the top IT efforts and culminates in an awards event that offers an opportunity to get dressed in formal attire and hobnob among the "stars" of the IT field. For many CIO's, within their own company they are taken for granted, while being recognized by their peers and having a chance to meet their fellow hard-working CIO's can be exceedingly satisfying and a topper to their illustrious careers.

CHAPTER 6: THE CIO 100 NOTABLES

We watch the Olympics to see who the world's best athletes are and how good they are. If you are an athlete or an aspiring athlete, you especially watch the Olympics to gauge how you are doing and whether you are at the top of your game or not. Likewise, for CIO's, there are some important recurring ways to gauge who the world's best are and how good they are.

One of the most well-known Olympics-style competition for CIO's is the annual CIO100 awards program that is undertaken by CIO.com (many of you might be familiar with CIO.com or at least the CIO Magazine which for many years ran in print and was popular among CIO's to see who made the cover each issue; it is now available only in online format). If you are an existing CIO, the CIO100 is a handy way to measure yourself in comparison to your peers. If you are an aspiring CIO, the CIO100 is a means to see how high the bar is set for those that rise to the top of the CIO profession.

Even if you are not a CIO and just an observer of CIO's and IT, or maybe a vendor selling to CIOs, being up-to-speed with what and who makes the vaunted annual CIO100 list is worthwhile to explore. Let's cover some useful insights about the CIO100 and offer lessons learned that you should consider thoughtfully about CIO's and these kinds of awards and acknowledgments.

BACKGROUND ASPECTS

The CIO100 is both a listing of the annual top CIO's and also a yearly awards event. Each year, CIO's that opt to submit various IT related business systems and projects that they undertook under their watch are assessed by a team of judges selected by CIO.com. The judges weigh various factors and then identify which submissions are the winners. Notice that the key here is that the selections are based upon the submissions provided. In other words, this is not an overall list of the top 100 CIO's per se, but instead a list based upon those CIO's that decided to make a submission that particular year.

This is an important distinction in that rather than the list being a comprehensive assessment of all CIOs, it is actually a culled list from those that self-selected themselves to make a submission. It is said that those that receive the Nobel Prize supposedly do not "run" for the prize and are selected by the Nobel committee based upon their reputation and accomplishments. That's not how the CIO100 list works, in that only those that happened to submit were even in the running to be chosen.

I know it might seem that I am overly emphasizing this point but it is worthy to emphasize, because when you look at the list make sure to realize it is not somehow a fully comprehensive list. Plus, if you are a CIO, keep in mind that someone is not going to be knocking on your door in the middle of the night to proclaim you on the CIO100 list, and instead you need to take action and provide a submission to have a chance of getting onto the list.

In fact, sometimes CIO's that aren't aware of this facet are prompted by a vendor that does know of this aspect, and the vendor will urge the CIO to provide a submission. A vendor doing so is typically one that is already providing services or its products to the CIO, and hopeful naturally that their service or product will be mentioned as part of a winning submission. Some vendors even go further and tout that they supported a winning CIO.

Each year is different in terms of who happened to make a submission and which ones the judges thought were worthy. So, you really need to look at the list year after year, rather than looking at it once. In that sense, unlike say a ranking of the world's top universities, a list that hardly varies from year to year, the CIO100 list will be quite different from one year to the next.

Furthermore, the CIO100 is usually theme-based each year, such as this year the theme was around the race for innovation. Submissions normally try to aim for something within the ballpark of the theme, though it does not necessarily need to be an effort that was solely focused on that year's particular theme. The themes are broad enough to allow for pretty much any kind of standout kind of system or project.

That's another important facet to consider too, namely that it is a system or project that the CIO led or undertook. As such, the system or project is really a team effort and not somehow a one-person crusader effort by the CIO. At the same time, assuming that the effort occurred under the watch of the CIO, and if they were the champion that drove the system to fruition, it is befitting that they should get acknowledged for it. Most of the winners usually bring their key team members, some from IT and some from the business, in order to spread around the glow of having won. Doing so as a winner can be a great morale booster for the CIO's IT team and the business. They get a chance to be publically acknowledged for their hard work. The awards ceremony even has a formal attire and a party like atmosphere reminiscent of the Academy Awards.

Back at the company of the CIO, some firms will tout within their enterprise the winning aspects and further boost morale throughout the firm. Plus, they will sometimes connect with their external marketing and corporate communications to promote the fact that their company won a CIO100 slot. This can aid the brand image of the firm.

For CIO's that are constantly striving to get top talent, being on the CIO100 can be a booster. Potential IT employees are likely to be impressed by such a winning company and want to come work there. Also, for firms that are not already household names, being on the CIO100 list can make them known to potential IT employees and spark interest.

Are there topnotch CIO's that aren't on the CIO100 list? Absolutely. Some CIO's aren't necessarily of a mind to try and get onto the CIO100 list. Some CIO's don't have a system or project in-hand that they believe would qualify as a potential winner. Some CIO's are in firms that don't want them to go around touting what they do with their systems, perhaps believing it gives away secrets or tips their hand to their competitors.

This then takes us to the other facet about the CIO100, namely the Hall of Fame. Each year, while at the CIO100 event, there are a half dozen CIO's named to the CIO.com Hall of Fame. These are CIO's that have stood the test of time and have over many years established themselves at the top of the CIO profession. It is considered a lifetime achievement award, akin to the same kind of award given at the Academy Awards for a director or actor and their body of work over their career.

I will next describe some of the recent CIO100 winners and CIO Hall of Famers, doing so to highlight aspects of what they did to win. This can be handy to reflect upon what you are doing in your own organization. Are you keeping up? Are you falling behind? In today's world, simply keeping the lights on for IT is not enough. Companies expect that IT will stretch the boundaries of what the company needs to do to properly leverage IT and systems. When you look at some of the winning projects, there are some that will knock your socks off. At the same time, there are some that are not especially moonshots in terms of going way outside the realm of possible. I say this because there are some CIO's that have potentially winning systems or projects that accidentally underplay the value of those systems or projects.

In other words, some CIO's see themselves as "just doing their job" when producing some very outstanding systems. They are modest and don't think that there is a need to go outside their company for recognition. Though their personal judgement on this modesty is perhaps laudable, it does not take into account that they need to also be thinking in a wider scope, thinking about their IT team, about the business, about the image of the company. Even if a system within the company seems tame to the CIO, it might nonetheless be a rock star to others, and provide benefit to others too.

Any CIO with even a semblance of an interesting system or project should consider making a submission. The submission should be carefully reviewed with the company corporate communications group, since the

CIO might otherwise inadvertently step into a company landmine. In fact, some CIO's have indicated that they weren't able to provide a submission because other senior executives were upset that the CIO was trying to gain some limelight. In that circumstance, it might make sense to include the other senior executives and make them winners too, though the internal politics might make it a quagmire.

SELECTED CIO100 WINNERS OF THIS YEAR

I am going to cover just a few of the CIO100 winners of this year here. I encourage you to take a look on-line to see the full listing at the CIO.com web site. You might also consider taking a look at the various published writings of Maryfran Johnson, Editor-in-Chief at CIO.com, as she provides her "insider" insights about the CIO100 and also serves as the main moderator and facilitator at the event.

I offer next some special highlights that caught my attention this year while participating. I also should properly mention and acknowledge that many of these winners I already know. And, those that I did not already know, I met with during the event and chatted about their efforts and how they achieved the CIO100 list. So, here are my special picks.

VMware

Bask Iyer, CIO and General Manager of the Internet of Things (IoT) at VMware, shared how he and his IT team have created mobile applications for seemingly internal uses of the firm, such as approving employee travel and expenses, locating and booking conference rooms, doing a people search within VMware, having a quarterly sales booking tool, and so on. At first glance, you might be thinking that these are mobile apps that could be adopted by using existing off-the-shelf apps from say Concur or BrassRing. Were they reinventing the wheel, and if so how did they win at the CIO100? The answer is that they did these mobile apps not only for internal use, but also so that VMware can sell the apps to other enterprises.

I am going to linger on that point for a moment. It used to be that most firms tended to see their IT group as being internally focused only. There is a trend now toward firms wanting the IT group to also help with systems that fit into the products and services of the company, providing external facing systems. Bask's realization that he could readily create mobile apps that fit to internal needs and that could be added to the product offerings of the firm provided that kind of double whammy that CEO's are looking for. Bask describes these apps as providing "mobile moments" for employees of an organization. Two birds with one stone.

UPS

Kim Felix, Vice President of IT at UPS, shared the background about a new system she oversaw the development of, a system called NRT for Near Real-Time service and reporting. UPS generates an enormous amount of data and has around 100 terabytes of data at any point in time. She indicated that there are 8,700 events per second being recorded every second of every day. This is being collected across 1,800 facilities in 220 countries worldwide.

The new NRT is a business intelligence tool that mashes together both structured and unstructured data. She indicated it provides a "single pane of glass" from which UPS managers can discern the status of packages and their shipment. The system also incorporates predictive analytics. By using weather data and other environmental conditions, NRT can help to reroute shipments before they get bogged down. Essentially, this is a real-time status monitoring platform for some four billion packages shipped annually via UPS.

One of the reasons I have opted to mention this particular winner here is due to not only being an example of the rise of Big Data and predictive analytics, which continues to win the hearts and souls of businesses, but it also highlighted the arduous nature of pulling off these kinds of systems. During the presentation, it was evident that trying to get the data from the numerous other legacy systems was one of the biggest hurdles to this project.

Oshkosh

Dave Schecklman, CIO at Oshkosh, described the efforts he has undertaken to moved away from silos of systems to a single integrated system. What caught my attention was that he has been at Oshkosh for 21 years, having risen up in the IT ranks to become the CIO there about 5 years ago. First, as we all know, long tenure at companies today is a thing of the past. His having been at the same firm for over twenty years is rare these days. Secondly, the aspect that he was able to shake-up the firm and move toward an integrated system framework is something that usually would require an outsider CIO to undertake. Usually, a new CIO brought from the outside is able to see what needs to be done, and becomes a change agent as part of their reason for being brought on-board. A long-time insider can have a harder time making such changes.

Dave says he cleaned house when he got anointed to the CIO slot. This willingness to clean house can be hard on an insider and is usually "easier" with a new CIO that does not know anyone in the firm can make difficult choices without feeling the personal pain per se. On the other hand, Dave's insider status gave him the stature and trust internally to make these arduous choices. One especially clever line was that he indicated you should use your goodwill while at a firm, and there's no sense in having leftover goodwill for your career grave.

Rodan+Fields

Ralph Loura, CTO at Rodan+Fields, described his firm as the Uber of skincare. This is a clever way to describe a firm that we might not otherwise recognize the name, and connect it with something that can be instantly understood. He mentioned that having an extremely high availability of their app and web site is crucial to the company. Any disruption to their online platforms would be the digital equivalent of a stock-out (a clever way to phrase this), and he emphasized and discussed how they have adopted DevOps to reduce the risks of such issues.

Clorox

Manjit Singh, CIO at The Clorox Company, discussed the advent of this well-known product goods company now entering into the Internet of Things (IoT) marketplace. He discussed a Clorox provided water pitcher that contains a reordering device for water filters, and works akin to the Amazon Dash, though built directly into the water pitcher itself. This is another example of IT getting involved in customer facing products and services.

It was also interesting due to the challenges that you might not at first glance be aware of. Since the water pitcher contains water (of course, you say), you need to make sure that the electronics of the ordering device are not going to somehow get fried and mix with water. And since the pitcher is typically being stored in a refrigerator, the question arises as to how to deal with communications aspects once in the refrigerator. Furthermore, you want to make sure that the device does not start ordering multiple filters wildly, and have a dismayed consumer see a hundred of them suddenly arriving at their doorstep.

Domino's Pizza

Kevin Vasconi, CIO at Domino's Pizza, another winner of the CIO100, pointed out that Domino's is now the 8th largest restaurant chain. Even more startling perhaps is that they are so involved in leveraging technology that you could almost say they are a technology company that is made out of pepperoni and emoji's (a funny line, but also one worthy of serious contemplation). He pointed out that there is essentially a zero switching cost for their customers when it comes to online ordering, and so you need to make sure that the online systems are always at the ready (they never want to drop an order).

Kevin remarkably has a sales goal jointly with his CMO, which is a sign of a CIO that is considered an essential and integral part of the customer facing side of the business. We will gradually see more of these kinds of linkages between compensation for CIO's and demonstrative business outcomes. He has instituted agile methods to quickly rollout new updates to their online platforms. One expressed downside of this by an attendee at the event was that he was at risk then of letting something buggy get into the hands of their customers. He deftly pointed out that it also gives him the approach of being able to quickly fix any such bugs, and that by having frequent updates they are able to continually surprise and delight their customers.

Bloomin' Brands

Donagh Herlihy, CIO at Bloomin' Brands, discussed how their restaurant chains are now embarking upon home delivery. Some within the firm were concerned that by providing a home delivery capability that it would undercut sales at the restaurants since consumers might start to decide not to go out to eat. In contrast, Dongah pointed out that it has tended to help sales of the restaurants, including increasing awareness of their restaurants. This is an example of how IT is not just about the technology, but also about the business and business impacts of the adoption of technology.

Southwest Airlines

Randy Sloan, CIO at Southwest Airlines, discussed various aspects about the arduous nature of running IT systems for an airline. He also described a kind of boot camp that he does for his team on how to communicate with business leaders. Many CIO's are not as thoughtful in terms of making sure that their team is versed in how to communicate with the business. Sadly, there are some CIO's that have a kind of sink or swim mentality and just assume that their team will figure out how to do confer with business leaders. Randy's willingness and initiative to guide his team and take the time to run his boot camp is laudable.

Vail Resorts

Robert Urwiler, CIO at Vail Resorts, described his journey during the ten years that he has been with Vail Resorts. The business has expanded greatly during his tenure there, gathering up more and more resorts, and now sells on the order of 500,000 ski passes annually. He pointed out that they need to not only think about the ski passes, but also think of themselves as a resort destination, needing to consider the whole experience while coming up to ski, including getting food, getting equipment, being safe, having fun, and so on.

Their impressive system called EpicMix allows skiers to have an RFID tag that can be scanned when getting onto the lifts and can then be used to keep track of your skiing efforts. You can keep your ski pass in your jacket rather than the old way of having it dangle out of your apparel. They also tie social media into their systems, and enable skiers to earn electronic pins, similar to pin collecting that you might do at say Disneyland. One especially interesting approach by Robert is his use of Maslow's hierarchy of needs as a means of describing how IT needs to get the basics right in order to move up the food chain to more "exotic" and overall strategically compelling systems.

General Electric (GE)

Jim Fowler, CIO at GE, and one of the most notable contemporary and business savvy CIO's, provided a fascinating indication of how GE has been transforming to become a fully digital company. The immense size of GE makes it a daunting task to transform. With approximately $130 billion in annual revenue, getting such a mammoth enterprise to change would seem nearly impossible. Jim showed how it is being done.

GE had earlier gone toward massive outsourcing of IT, and now Jim is pulling it back into GE via a large-scale insourcing effort. He points out that doing so will enable him to have greater flexibility and accountability in what IT does. Jim described an approach that he calls "teams of teams" within IT to foster increased communication and collaboration. He indicated that today GE sells about $6 billion worth of software and that by the year 2020 they are aiming at $10 billion from selling software. He has also signed-up to provide $1 billion of productivity improvement at GE by his efforts of merging together IT and Operations Technology (OT).

The wide sweeping scale, and the notable aspect that Jim is on-the-hook for specific business outcomes, is a remarkable indicator of a CIO at the forefront of what CIO's should be doing, and certainly warrants his being a CIO100 winner.

The aforementioned examples of the CIO100 winners will hopefully give you a representative sense of what and who they are. As mentioned, take a look on-line to see the full list.

THE CIO HALL OF FAMERS

I next mention this year's CIO Hall of Fame winners. By any measure, they are all incredible CIO's. Each has stood the test of time. They have each made their mark on their companies and the IT industry. They have each generously given back to the CIO community at large, doing so by mentoring others and by participating in CIO associations and other related efforts. I will briefly mention each here, indicating their most recent position, and encourage you to consider looking them up to see the full breadth and depth of their accomplishments. I list them in alphabetical order.

Mike Benson, former CIO AT&T Entertainment Group, and formerly CIO of DirectTV. Known for having a strong sense of believing in and supporting his people, and for being the kind of leader that others want to work with. Friendly and a people person when meeting him in-person.

Stephen Gold, CIO at CVS Health. Known for having led multiple major business transformations. Had led the creation of the world's largest Internet pharmacy. Approachable and a keen listener when meeting him in-person.

Donagh Herlihy, CIO at Bloomin' Brands. Described some of his recent efforts above. Welcoming and a big smile when meeting him in-person.

Albert Hitchcock, CTO at Pearson PLC. Helps to lead the digital transformation of this major publisher and education company. Charismatic and easy to meet in-person.

Suresh Kumar, CIO at BNY Mellon. Changing the workplace to become truly a digital one, and instituting an agile culture and digital platforms. Magnetic in-person.

Randy Sloan, CIO at Southwest Airlines. Described some of his recent efforts above. Down-to-earth and a remarkable candidness in-person.

Robert Urwiler, CIO at Vail Resorts. Described some of his recent efforts above. Compelling in-person.

You might have noticed that for each new member of the CIO Hall of Fame, I have indicated something about how they are in-person. I did this intentionally. When you at first hear about CIO's that oversee vast legions of IT teams into the thousands and budgets into the hundreds of millions of dollars, it is easy to forget that they are everyday folks like the rest of us.

I often get asked, what are these "celebrity CIO's" like in-person? You would probably assume that they would be full of themselves, and be pumped up by those around them as being supremely powerful and high flouting. In my experience, these "top of the top" CIO's are usually warm and inviting. They have honed their people skills over the years and it shows. They are not some kind of techie automata that have randomly made their way to the top. Instead, via their attention to caring about people, they have been able to lead and manage their way to great success. It is an important lesson for those that are aspiring to be the top CIO's. You don't necessarily need to be a louse to get there.

Overall, I have tried to cover some of the key highlights about the CIO100. If you aren't paying attention to it now, start doing so. You should be aware of what your peers are doing. One way or another, you are going to be compared to them, either via by those within your firm or by outsiders. It is safer to be aware of what's going on and who is whom, rather than getting blindsided.

Lance B. Eliot

CHAPTER 7

DEVOPS: DEVELOPMENT AND
IT OPERATIONS

PREFACE

DevOps is a buzzword or buzz-phrase that refers to the improved blending and interaction between the development side of the IT function (referred to as the Dev side) and the operations (referred to as Ops) side of the IT function. Dev is responsible for the designing, building, and testing of systems, along with the maintenance and upgrading of the systems. Ops is responsible for the infrastructure and underlying platforms that the systems run upon.

These two sides of the IT house, Development and Operations, have historically been treated as two separate and distinct entities. This has led to a gap between them. The gap creates troubles such as lack of coordination, excessive costs in fielding of systems, and can be disruptive to the delivery of systems to the business.

Like a squabbling brother and sister, Dev and Ops even at times pull each other's hair and duke it out in terms of infighting. CIO's need to rein this in. Doing so by edict alone is insufficient. There is bad blood that often has been festering for years, and the CIO will need to overcome the cultural barriers along with putting in place processes and technology that can aid in their IT function embracing becoming a caring and beloved brother and sister of Dev and Ops.

———

CHAPTER 7: DEVOPS: DEVELOPMENT AND IT OPERATIONS

One of the little known secrets about business applications in companies is that just like the old saying about the making of sausages, it is better not to see them being made. If you peeled back the onion and took a look, you'd invariably discover that there is a large chasm between the Development side of an IT function and the Operations side of an IT function. These two halves of the IT function are responsible for ultimately delivering systems for an enterprise, and doing so in a manner that will meet business needs, will run properly and appropriately for the organization, and be done in the most efficient and effective means possible.

Many CEO's and other corporate executives instead discover that the business systems delivered to the firm are off-target of business needs, seem to take forever to be completed, cost an arm and a leg, and seem to work sporadically, sluggishly, and be error prone. These maladies can be often traced to the gap between the Development side of IT and the Operations side of IT.

The IT developers warily eye the IT operations staff and mistrust them, usually believing that IT operations will fail to properly setup and run the systems infrastructure such as the networks and computers upon which the applications rely. Simultaneously, the IT operations staff looks warily at the IT developers and mistrusts them, usually believing that the developers will create applications that won't work correctly on the enterprise IT infrastructure.

If the company CIO does not overtly take action to prevent this bifurcation, the gap between the Development side and the IT Operations side will widen and grow increasingly dire. Anyone that thinks that the Development side and the IT Operations side will somehow magically work together in harmony is mistaken and will find themselves facing a big mess. In this chapter, I explain why this chasm exists and offer a framework and approach that will overcome the gaps. As a seasoned CIO, I know well this gap and have had to time and again create bridges that get the Development side ("Dev") and the IT Operations side ("Ops") to work together hand-in-hand.

BASIS OF THE DEV AND OPS GAPS

The basis for the gap between Dev and Ops is partially due to tradition. For sake of simplicity, we'll group the various sub-functions of IT into the

Development portion and the IT Operations portion:

- IT Function = Development + IT Operations, consisting of:
    - Development = Systems analysis, design, coding, testing, etc.
    - IT Operations = Networks, architecture, servers, PC's, etc.

Looking back to the early days of IT in business, the developers were often the hotshots that wanted to do their heads-down programming and whip out code, and then toss it over the cubicle walls to the IT operations team. Given the vagaries and low reliability of networks and computer hardware, the IT operations team already had their hands full trying to keep the network running and keeping the hardware up. Tossing applications onto that already flimsy infrastructure just further exacerbated the situation.

A caste system emerged over time within the IT functions of businesses. Some perceived that Dev was the righteous side of IT, having all the creativity and being the closest to the business in terms of understanding what the business is about. The perception of Ops was that it was where those that couldn't cut it in Dev had gone, being nothing more than hardware jockeys that would be happiest only when nobody touched the networks or the computers.

They each grew their own professions, having separate certifications, separate titles, separate ways of thinking about IT, and even separate management and hierarchies. This cleaving of IT can be readily seen in most IT organizational structure charts, wherein the only aspect that connects Dev and Ops is the CIO. Otherwise, they are utterly separate branches of a tree.

Business users of IT are likely well aware of this gap. How many times have you heard the Dev programmers blame the Ops side when a crucial company application is not available? Likewise, how many times have you heard the network administrators and Help Desk blame the application developers when a major piece of software goes down? The blame game can really get out-of-hand. Users get caught in the middle. Dev then refuses to speak with Ops. Ops refuses to work with Dev. A vicious death cycle of worsening conditions just makes things go from bad to terrible.

Some might characterize it as a shotgun marriage that takes out the fractures on the children. Of course, in this case, if the children are the end users, the business will suffer by having systems that won't work and that the users won't want to even use. Many CEOs get tired of hearing complaints from the business and harangue the CIO to do something and get things fixed.

A less seasoned CIO or head of IT won't recognize this dysfunction in terms of what is the root cause. They will think that maybe they need to do something to improve just Dev, or do something to just improve Ops, or maybe get some new-fangled IT tools and it will make the world a better place.

Fundamentally, if the Dev and Ops gap is not recognized and carefully mitigated, no amount of window dressing is going to make things much better. There might be some momentary quiet when the two forces decide to call a temporary truce, but in the end the two see each other as bitter enemies and a few choice sparks will get the arguing and disruption going again. There are various levels of gap size between Dev and Ops, which we'll define as:

- **Gap 0**: No gap, Gap impact = fully functional, Gap Resolution = monitor and encourage

- **Gap 1**: Minimal gap, Gap impact = mostly functional, Gap Resolution = engage to close gap

- **Gap N**: Significant gap, Gap impact = partially dysfunctional, Gap Resolution = urgent

- **Gap Z**: Debilitating gap, Gap impact = fully dysfunctional, Gap Resolution = reconstruction

The nearly ideal gap is a gap that is nonexistent, the no gap level, which I will call Gap 0. This rarely exists, but it is possible to exist. There is the minimal gap level, which I call Gap Level 1, and is the amount of gap that a CIO working hard to deal with the gap can ultimately achieve by taking overt actions.

There is the Gap Level N which is a sizable gap and most IT groups tend to fall into. This kind of gap ebbs and flows toward a lower bound and an upper bound, often stoked by say the new release of an application or the upgrade of the network. When such a moment occurs, the gap widens and becomes more noticeable. After the gap and its crisis subside, it will recede, but nonetheless will still be there, and often now is a tad wider at the lower bound than it had been before. This is the evolution of the gap growth steps over time.

Finally there is Gap Level Z which is the widest kind of gap and one that when present will become so debilitating that something radical will eventually give way (sometimes leading to a wholescale ouster of IT, such as opting to outsource all of IT rather than dealing with the internal gaps issues that are at the core of the problems).

CLOSING THE DEV AND OPS GAPS

How can we get the Gap Z to become Gap N, and how can we get Gap N to become Gap 1, and how can we get Gap 1 to become Gap 0? There are actions to be taken in three areas, namely in People, Process, and Technology.

The CIO will need to make sure that the Dev and Ops sides realize that there is a gap, and that the gap is to be narrowed, and that it will require diligence and attention to achieve. This cannot be some edict from on-high and must instead be done with aplomb. On the People area, the IT organization needs to reflect that the Dev and Ops portions are part of the same overall IT unit, and there should be cross-sharing and cross-functional IT positions that help ensure that the Dev and Ops are working together.

Keywords are collaboration and communication. This is not as easy as it sounds, and will take a lot of concentrated effort and attention to achieve. The IT managers within both Dev and Ops need to first learn to work closely together, since if they are at odds then almost no amount of coaching or intervention below them will overcome the divide.

Explicit training and HR-related sessions need to be crafted and put into use, showing both Dev and Ops how they can work collaboratively and communicate with each other. The Myers Briggs kind of awareness of personal styles can be used. But, the training and sessions cannot be generic and must tie specifically to IT aspects such that the Dev and Ops participants can readily see how this pertains to them. Needless to say, doing these sessions by separating Dev into one set of classes and Ops into a different set of classes is not going to make much progress. I mention this because (believe it or not), this has happened and it was one of those "duh" moments when I pointed out that it might make more sense to combine them in the sessions.

In addition to overcoming the People aspects of the gaps, there is also a need to overcome the Process aspects of the gaps. Within IT, there are various processes involved in terms of hand-off's throughout the system development life cycle. There is a hand-off during the ongoing maintenance and upkeep of systems. In a well-managed IT function there are defined processes that indicate what the steps are for each of these processes. Furthermore, a well-managed IT function has metrics that can be used to gauge how well or how poorly the processes are working. When the larger gaps exist in Dev and Ops, the processes are often either nonexistent, or existent but ignored, or existent and purposely abused. It is important to review the internal IT processes and make sure that those processes are smartly designed, fit to the needs of IT and the business, and are implemented and followed.

The other aspect of dealing with gaps in Dev and Ops involves the Technology aspects. Many IT groups lack the needed internal tools to do their work. Like the cobblers children that lack shoes, there is often a resistance of allowing IT to spend precious corporate funds on "internal IT" tools, but those tools can dramatically impact and improve the speed-to-market of the IT function. This though does not mean that just any tools should be tossed into IT, which is a frequent misstep undertaken when a less seasoned IT head thinks that providing tools alone will fix the People and Process problems too.

OTHER DEV AND OPS ASPECTS

The effort to drive together Dev and Ops in IT has become trendy and often is expressed as "DevOps" meaning that we should be thinking of not just the separate "Dev" and the separate "Ops" but instead should be thinking about the combined and integrated "DevOps" (some have also used the phrasing of "Dev-Ops" with a hyphen, but this perhaps suggest a kind of hyphenated gap between the two sides and so is less frequently employed). In many respects, this is going to be a cultural shift in the IT ranks. Techies that are used to the technical side of things are usually less amenable to the "soft" side of business and will at times resist a cultural change. It is crucial that the CIO and the business be aware of the cultural shift that occurs within IT, and know why it is taking place, and be a participant in the change. Here are some added aspects to be keeping in mind.

Not Just Tools

There is a big push toward tools that are "DevOps" friendly and tie together the work of IT into a "tool chain" that includes say coding, building, testing, packaging, release, configuration, and monitoring of applications. This is certainly advantageous and also overcomes the prior disparate set of tools which were distinct from each other and so were part of the silent killer that kept the Dev and Ops side of IT separated from each other. By having a newer set of tools that work together in an integrated fashion, it reduces those jumps between Dev and Ops, and streamlines their joint efforts.

A tool only though is not the solution to the Dev and Ops gaps. Any selection and adoption of tools must be timed with and aligned with the needed changes from a People perspective and from a Process perspective. It is the proverbial three-legged stool that if one leg is the "right" length and yet if the other two are not then the stool will continue to wobble.

The Instigators

There are sometimes IT members that are so bigoted in their views of the other side that no matter what you do they will still continue to instigate problems. It is like a religious fervor. I always want to give IT members the benefit of the doubt that they sincerely want to work together and so I start with that assumption. Unfortunately, in spite of that viewpoint, there are bound to be some instigators that just won't change. A tough decision will need to be made about trying to give them enough time to adjust, and if not then they are the proverbial bad apple that if you keep them around will spoil the barrel further.

Agile Methods

Development in many IT groups has evolved to embrace agile methods of systems development. These agile methods often mean that there are quick iterations of versions of an application. This then can put added strain on the IT Operations side, since rather than an occasional new release that there are now very frequent new releases. Think about continuous deployment as becoming the everyday approach in IT.

Indeed, it is the agile method that has greatly led to the increasing visibility of the Dev and Ops gaps. If your IT group is moving toward agile, you can anticipate that any already existing gaps of Dev and Ops will be further tested and so you should be on the watch for a widening. Hopefully, knowing that this can occur, you will be prepared beforehand and be in the midst of undertaking resolutions before it becomes a more noticeable issue.

INTERNAL BECOMES EXTERNAL

When you go into a restaurant to eat, you probably don't want to know how they cook the food, and you figure that the restaurant has their act together and knows what they are doing in the back of the restaurant. Likewise, many business users in organizations would like to assume that IT has its ducks in order and that whatever is happening behind the scenes is the right thing. Regrettably, many IT groups do not have their ducks lined-up and therefore either the CIO needs to take a hard look and fix the internals of IT, or if not then invariably the resulting gaps within IT will be felt outside IT and throughout the organization.

Just as restaurants have become more transparent and showcase how they do their cooking, we are seeing a trend in IT that the IT function also opens its doors and windows so that the business users can see how the systems are being developed and fielded. DevOps is something that every IT group should strive toward.

CHAPTER 8

HUMAN-COMPUTER INTERACTION (HCI)

PREFACE

When you get into your car and start the engine, you probably don't put much thought into your actions. You nearly subconsciously know to put the key in the ignition and start the car, perhaps you also need to have your foot on the brake and the car must be in Park when you do so. Most of the time, you likely ensure that these are all properly done in the proper sequence. In nearly the blink of an eye, you take these various steps and the car starts, and away you go.

Think about a teenager that is just first learning how to operate a car. For them, the series of steps might seem bewildering. They are unsure of what to do. For you, their confusion is mildly humorous because it all seems so easy. When thinking about the interaction between you and your computer, you can likewise think about some of the software that seems very easy to use, while other apps that you find difficult to use. The difficult to use ones you would most likely avoid if you could.

The interaction between you, the human, and the computer is a very important element to ensuring that you, the human, will want to use the computer and be able to do so readily. More vital is that you also use the computer in a productive manner and do not inadvertently use it in a destructive manner. Imagine if you confused the brake pedal for the accelerator pedal, and the kind of destruction that you could inadvertently wrought. It is incumbent upon the designers and builders of computer systems to be mindful of the Human-Computer Interaction (HCI) facets.

CIO's need to ensure that the systems they are building or acquiring will have the proper HCI fit for the end-users and customers of their business.

––––––––

CHAPTER 8: HUMAN-COMPUTER INTERACTION (HCI)

Humans and computers are at times mixing together like oil and water (a bad match), meanwhile at other times they are combining like peanut butter and jelly (a good match). The good matches are great when they happen and often go unnoticed by us humans due to being frictionless and seamless between the human and the computer. On the other hand, the mismatches can be aggravating and sometimes downright deadly.

Let's look at a few examples of an aggravating or exasperating human-computer interaction. Imagine that you are interacting with a banking ATM machine and you become confused and inadvertently transfer $500 to someone else's account. Ouch, a few bucks that might be hard to get back. Or, imagine that you are buying via Amazon that pair of shoes that you wanted and while making the purchase on your smartphone you mistakenly order 10 pairs rather than 1 pair of shoes. Guess you'll be walking around for a while with a lot of shiny shoes on your feet.

Our daily lives are increasingly becoming dependent upon our interaction with computers, whether those be smartphones, tablets, PC's, or the emerging Internet of Things (IoT) which will make computing ubiquitous and we will be immersed and surrounded by computing everywhere. As an invited CIO participant in a forum put on by the Center for Digital Transformation (CDT) at the University of California Irvine (thanks goes to CDT's Vijay Gurbaxani and Ed Trainor), I interacted with the keynote speaker and provocateur Nicholas Carr, Pulitzer Prize finalist and author of "The Glass Cage: How Our Computers Are Changing Us," which is his latest book and provides a sobering look at the consequences of our growing dependency on computers.

The discussion prompted me to further examine the topic of Human-Computer Interaction (HCI) and offer some insights that might be helpful for those interacting with computers and for those that design and field computers that interact with people. Similar to studying how humans interact with say animals or even each other, it is equally crucial to understand how humans and computers interact. The field of Human-Computer Interaction focuses on understanding the ways in which humans and computers interact, and strive to advance our understanding so that computers and humans can work more closely in harmony with each other.

The gap between what a human is doing and what the computer is doing when human-computer interaction occurs can be at times quite serious and have dire consequences.

Perhaps the most famous of the dire consequences examples consists of instances wherein a human pilot and a computer-based autopilot HCI-mismatch led to fatal airplane crashes. One such example will be carefully examined to illustrate the nature of the cognitive dissonance that can occur between a human and a computer when the two are interacting with each other. First, let's look at the role of cognitive dissonance in human interactions.

COGNITIVE DISSONANCE

Cognitive dissonance is an important topic in the study of HCI. Imagine that two people are interacting with each other, and envision the cognitive activity that takes place. Suppose two people are involved in the purchase of a car, one is the potential buyer and one is the potential seller. The buyer has in their mind what kind of car they want, how much they are willing to pay, and other facets about making the purchase of the car. The seller has in their mind the worth of the car, and is trying to identify how to sell the car to the buyer. So, the buyer has a mental state about wanting to buy a car, and the seller has a mental state about wanting to sell the car.

Both the buyer and the seller also have mental models about each other. Namely, the buyer has a mental model about the seller, trying to ascertain what is in the mind of the seller as to how much are they willing to come down on the price of the car and how desperate are they to sell the car. Equally, the seller has a mental model of the buyer, trying to ascertain how much the buyer is willing to pay and whether the buyer is serious about making the purchase or just playing around and not a true buyer.

Suppose that the buyer has in mind that she is willing to pay $20,000 for the car, and the seller has in mind that he is willing to sell the car for $20,000. The two briefly discuss the car and then amicably agree to the transaction. This is an example of very little cognitive dissonance, since they both perceived cognitively in quite similar ways the car purchase and selling. Suppose instead that the buyer has in mind that she is willing to pay only $10,000 for the car and that the seller has in mind that the lowest price for the car is $20,000. The two are now at logger heads in that they have a large disparity between their mental models.

Exasperating the matter, suppose further that the buyer is the type of person that likes to have protracted negotiations and relishes the game of bargaining, while the seller is the type of person that hates to negotiate and wants to just get to the point and move on. You can see that this attempt to have the two interact is going to be challenging since they not only have different views about the car purchase but they even have divergent views of how to approach the interaction. We can make this even worse by adding to the interaction that the buyer believes that the seller does not want to sell the car at any price and will be resistant to the interaction, while we can add that the seller believes that the buyer is a hot head and will react adversely to the slightest provocation during the car purchase interaction.

As perhaps is evident, the cognitive mental states of the buyer and the seller are radically at odds, and each has their own views not only about what they intend but also what they believe the other party intends. This cognitive dissonance showcases that the chances of the interaction occurring smoothly is unlikely and there will be an awkward and ultimately possibly dissatisfying conclusion to the interaction. Large gaps in cognitive dissonance can cause the human-to-human interaction to breakdown and lead to adverse consequences. Now, substitute for the human-to-human interaction instead a human-to-computer interaction. The human in the human-to-computer interaction has in their mind a mental model about the task, and also a mental model about what the computer "believes" about the task. Likewise, the computer has a "mental model" about the task, and a mental model of what the human "believes" about the task.

I have purposely put in quotes anything stating a mental model of the computer because I do not want you to falsely assume that the mental model of the computer is somehow akin to the mental model of the computer. Computers are not at all like the mental capabilities of humans (at least not yet, but there is hope for the future!). Currently, the computer has been programmed by a human or humans that have incorporated into the computer various assumptions about the way in which it should "mentally" process tasks and also what assumptions are to be made about the human interacting with the computer.

Anyone that says "the computer did this or that" is falsely ascribing to the computer a human-like quality which is not the case today. The computer as programmed by a human or humans did this or that, and thus it is not the computer per se that has some particular responsibility but instead those that programmed the computer. I do not want to digress and get into the whole topic of whether computers can or will have their own sense of consciousness — and so will just for the moment alert you to be careful when anthropomorphizing computers today.

FAMOUS DISASTER

In 1994, Aeroflot Flight 593 was flying from Moscow to Hong Kong when a sad and frightening example of cognitive dissonance occurred that led to a fatal crash of the plane and killed all 75 on-board the flight. The cognitive dissonance involved a series of cognitive mismatches between what the pilot and co-pilot thought was happening and what the computer auto-pilot "thought" was happening. Do not assume that this is a uniquely odd occurrence as there are many documented instances of cognitive dissonance incidents that have led to planes faltering and on occasions crashing.

The Aeroflot flight was flying along smoothly and the auto-pilot was on. The pilot opted to have his children come visit him in the cockpit, and his son sat at the co-pilot seat to pretend that he was helping to fly the plane. Turns out that the son applied significant force to the flight control column, and, regrettably, via how the auto-pilot worked, this exerting of force was a signal to the auto-pilot to allow the "pilot" to overcome the auto-pilot and switch the ailerons to go into manual control. Notice that at this moment of the flight that the auto-pilot was still overall in control of the plane, but had relinquished the aileron control to be handled by the human pilot (as per how the auto-pilot had been programmed to operate).

Though a silent indicator light came on at the flight dashboard, intending to echo to the pilot that the aileron is now in their control, it did not have an audible alert (which was common in other planes), and unfortunately the pilot and co-pilot did not notice that the indicator light had come on. With the flight control having been adjusted accidentally and unknowingly by the son, the plane started to bank into a 180-degree turn. The pilot realized that for some unknown reason the plane was banking, but for about nine seconds the pilot and co-pilot were baffled by the turn, not being able to figure out why the plane was banking and what the auto-pilot was trying to do. The plane started to lose altitude due to the manner in which the turn was taking place. Nine seconds might seem like a short amount of time, but not when you have a plane flying through the sky at full speed.

The auto-pilot detected that the plane was losing altitude and tried to use the other non-aileron controls to compensate for the problem arising. It pitched the nose of the plane up and tried to do a steep climb, but this led to the plane stalling in air, and another automatic system then pitched the plane downward to get out of the stall.

The co-pilot then took over from the auto-pilot and tried to push the plane upward to get out of the nosedive, but this again caused the plane to stall. Heading into a corkscrew dive downward, the pilot and co-pilot were unable to sufficiently recover the plane and it crashed, killing all 63 passengers and 12 crew members.

Experts that analyzed the incident indicated afterward that had the co-pilot let the plane's auto-pilot try to get out of the final nosedive that it probably would have been able to do so, thus, the co-pilot inadvertently seemed to have contributed to the plane crashing by ironically taking off the auto-pilot and trying to take over the control of the plane. I hope that you can vividly see how the human and computer interaction in this case is a showcase of cognitive dissonance.

The pilot and co-pilot had a mental model of flying, and the flight status, and a mental model of what the auto-pilot can do, and what the auto-pilot was doing during the flight. When the son inadvertently turned off the aileron control of the auto-pilot, the son was not aware that he had done so, and the pilot and co-pilot were not aware that it had occurred (in spite of the light indicator that came on). Notice too that the auto-pilot did as it was programmed to do, namely allowing the "pilot" to take over the aileron controls, even though in this case the pilot did not actually want to take over the ailerons.

The pilot realized that the banking turn did not make sense for his mental model of the flight – the flight should have been proceeding on a level course straight ahead. He could not imagine why the plane was suddenly taking a banking turn. We can guess that he probably searched his own mind trying to think about what would cause such a banking turn. It seems unlikely that he might have guessed that it was due to his son exerting force over the control column. The pilot might have thought it was a mechanical failure on the plane, but if that were the case then he probably was thinking that why didn't he see other indicators alerting him about the plane condition. He probably assumed that the auto-pilot would not have initiated the banking turn because the auto-pilot was supposed to be flying straight ahead.

The auto-pilot was programmed to try and overcome the initial diving action of the plane, and was not presumably aware that the pilot was now trying to take action. Back-and-forth the mental gaps occurred, and we can see that the mental model of the pilot and co-pilot was disparate from the "mental model" of the auto-pilot. This cognitive dissonance created a severe and catastrophic gap over the control of the plane.

One reaction to this incident might be to declare that the pilots were wrong to have allowed the auto-pilot to have control of the plane and they should have never engaged the auto-pilot. This is an extreme perspective in that it assumes that only the human should do the task, and that the computer cannot sufficiently provide assistance.

Another reaction to this incident is that the auto-pilot should be given complete control of the plane and therefore presumably avoid the frailties' of the human pilots. Some would say that had the auto-pilot been fully in control, the son could not have caused the switch to human control, and so the incident would have never occurred. This is another extreme perspective in that it assumes that only the computer should do the task, and that the human cannot sufficiently provide assistance.

This is a false dichotomy. It is a simplistic and myopic viewpoint to assume that in this Human-Computer Interaction that the "solution" to the problem would be solved by pushing everything onto the human or pushing everything onto the auto-pilot. Auto-pilots provide a valuable contribution to the flying of modern day airplanes, and likewise the human provides a valuable contribution to the flying of modern day airplanes. Having the human-only fly the plane is not a reasonable approach in today's world of flight complexities, and having the computer-only fly the plane is not a reasonable approach given the limits to today's computer capabilities.

We must be more mindful about the HCI dissonance and how humans and computers interact.

FRAMEWORK FOR HCI DISSONANCE GAP

To illustrate the HCI dissonance gap, I provide in Figure 1 a four-square diagram that I believe helps to illuminate crucial aspects about how humans and computers interact.

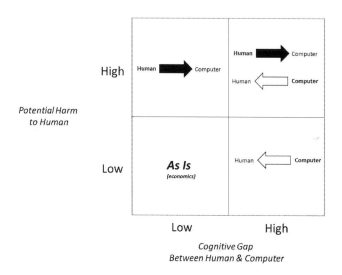

Figure 1: Eliot's Human-Computer Interaction (HCI) Dissonance Gap Chart

On the left side of the four square, there is an indication of the potential risk to humans, ranging from a high risk (such as leading to death, akin to the Aeroflot flight) to a low risk (imagine that your spell checker mistakenly corrects a word that it thinks you misspelled but that you had purposely spelled the way that you intended – this is a dissonance gap, but a likely minor one!).

At the bottom of the four square, there is an indication of the gap distance, ranging from low (when the human and computer are relatively closely aligned) to high (when the gap between what the human is thinking and what the computer is "thinking" are at dramatic opposites). There are four squares, consisting of High-Low on the risk factor, and High-Low on the dissonance gap. Let's take a look at each of the squares.

If the dissonance gap is Low-Low then this means that what the human thinks and what the computer "thinks" are relatively well aligned. Though we could try to push the two toward each other to try and ensure that there is no gap at all, the economics of making that push is probably not of a sufficient cost/benefit ROI (Return on Investment) that making that push is worthwhile to do. Assuming that the Low-Low gap is indeed minimal, we could say that the Human-Computer Interaction can remain "as is" and does not need to be adjusted.

If the dissonance gap is High-High then this means that what the human thinks and what the computer "thinks" are relatively disparate of each other. The likelihood then of problems arising are heightened, and given that the risk to humans is high, we should look carefully at what can be done to close the gap. It is probably the case that we would want to push both parties closer toward each other. We would want to adjust the computer so that it is better aligned, and we would want to somehow "adjust" the human so that they are better aligned. The economics of doing this are probably worthwhile, and especially when you consider incidents like the Aeroflot flight (in other words, circumstances where the gap can lead to death and destruction).

If the dissonance gap is High for risk to humans and Low as a gap, the High-Low square, typically the economically viable solution is to push the human toward the computer in terms of alignment. This might involve added training for the human or taking some other steps to ensure that the human is more mentally aware of and engaged in the task with the computer.

If the dissonance gap is Low for the risk to humans and yet High for the gap, typically it is more economically viable to push the computer toward the human in terms of alignment. This might involve some kind of re-programming of the computer or otherwise altering the nature and involvement of the computer in this task with the human.

Remember the mentioning earlier of the false dichotomy of some believing that only the computer should do the task or only the human should do the task? In Figure 1, I imagine that the upper right quadrant and the lower left quadrant do not exist, leaving us with just the upper left and lower right quadrants. This is a false dichotomy. It is crucial to avoid the trap of falling for the false dichotomy.

Imagine the same four square framework with "As Is" noted in each of the squares. This is indicative of circumstances whereby there is misalignment between the HCI and yet there is no action taken to deal with the misalignment. The chances are that this head-in-the-sand kind of approach is going to ultimately lead to something disastrous, since for the High-High, High-Low, and Low-High squares we are sitting on the edge of the razor and at some point something bad is probably going to occur. This is the proverbial "don't know what you don't know" which sometimes happens when there is not a proper analysis done of a human-computer interaction.

Next, re-imagine the four square framework and put the dual Human-to-Computer and Computer-to-Human couplet into each square. The notion is that we would try to push the human more toward the computer, and the computer more toward the human. Though this is an ideal approach, it is economically often not viable. The costs involved to push the human toward the computer, or to push the computer toward the human, might not be ROI attractive to do, and usually the risk to the humans will help to ascertain what this economic trade-off is like.

When HCI is slanted or skewed toward the computer, we always need to be aware of and generally suspicious to make sure that the human is not overly far out-of-the-loop. The reason to be suspicious is that we need to ask whether the computer can really handle the full range of circumstances that might be faced in the task, and whether it can sufficiently handle those circumstances.

Let's take the example of self-driving cars, an exciting and emerging use of computers. The intent is to ultimately relieve the human of having to take any action of driving the car. During our efforts to get to that pot-of-gold at the end of the rainbow, we need to be careful that we don't falsely believe that the computer can do more than it can really do, and that if we carve out the human entirely then to what degree we are creating risks for the human. This is not to suggest that we will not likely eventually get to the point of having no human involvement in a self-driving car, but we need to be careful to not jump ahead of ourselves and omit the human entirely prior to the point at which doing so makes reasonable sense.

When HCI is slanted or skewed toward the human, the human becomes the dominant performer of the task and the computer plays only a minor role. Humans are not infallible, and so having the computer be more involved might be beneficial as it can possibly mitigate the human foibles of the task. Or, it could even be simply that we want to relieve humans of performing the task for purposes of letting the human do something else or not be concerned about the task.

Self-driving cars are trying to alleviate the human of having to drive a car. This can be beneficial because the human could possibly use the driving time to instead focus their cognitive efforts on something else, maybe on their work efforts as they are heading into the office, or maybe for entertainment if joined in the car by fellow passengers and wanting to act as though they are in a cab that has a driver taking care of the driving task. In addition, self-driving cars are being justified on the basis of the number of car accidents that occur when driven by humans and the potential for reducing such incidents, saving lives and reducing costs associated with our driving of cars.

ALIGNMENTS OF HUMAN-COMPUTER

Nicholas Carr had brought up the example of radiologists, medical doctors and related medical professionals, and the examining of X-rays and MRI's for trying to diagnose diseases such as when looking for indications of say cancer. Prior to the advent of computer analyses of X-ray images and MRI's, the human radiologist would need to look at the images and try to on-their-own figure out what maladies might be indicated. Computers have been increasingly used to also undertake these same kinds of analyses.

Some studies indicate that radiologists are reluctant to either use or even trust the computer analyses and so will at times ignore of discount whatever the computer analysis shows. One solution voiced to this misalignment was to not allow the radiologist to at first see the computer analysis, and thus have the radiologist do their own image analysis first. Presumably, after doing so, the radiologist could then take a look at the computer analysis and use it as a kind of "collegial" second opinion.

This approach tends to border on the false dichotomy that has been have discussed earlier in this piece. This idea of having the radiologist do their own analysis first, and then distinctly and separately use the computer analysis, will have other potential adverse consequences. Studies show that often an expert will anchor to their own opinion, and so the radiologist upon seeing an image might form an opinion that then no matter what the computer analysis secondarily indicates they will ignore or discount.

Furthermore, it is already well known that radiologists are often faced with mind numbing caseloads, along with urgency for doing the analysis, and that they often suffer from radiologist fatigue. By shifting the computer to the back-seat of this task, we are not likely helping to overcome any of those factors of vast caseloads, urgency to analyze, and fatigue. If anything, it would probably just make those factors worse, since the radiologist would be essentially doing the task twice, once on their own, and then again but then with the use of the computer.

A more satisfying approach would be to consider how to help seamlessly align the human and computer in this Human-Computer Interaction. For example, we might have the computer showcase its analysis on the image so that when the radiologist first sees the image that it does not dominate the image and allows and makes the radiologist perceive that they (as the human) are performing the task, but that it also is being augmented by the computer in a more subtle fashion.

We could even add a dose of serious gamification by perhaps having the radiologist consider the computer as a type of "game" in terms of what the radiologist discovers in the image versus what the computer discovers. When I say the word "game," be aware that I am not suggesting this is not a very serious task, and I fully acknowledge and agree that this task has the potential of great risk to humans (imagine a misdiagnosis that fails to detect cancer, and yet the patient has cancer and so is not aware to take action accordingly). The use of gaming techniques can be done in a serious way, and actually be quite beneficial since it can increase the human engagement involved.

Besides the potential for a false dichotomy perspective when trying to solve HCI dissonance gaps, another approach that some are advocating is a forced engagement between the human and computer on a randomly activated basis. For example, some might suggest that with the pilot and auto-pilot, we ought to have the auto-pilot periodically and randomly hand control of the flight back over to the pilot. This is being done solely to keep the pilot engaged, and not because the auto-pilot has reached a point wherein it cannot properly control the flight.

Though at first glance this maybe seems sensible, kind of like a wake-up call for the pilot, this approach will have adverse consequences. The pilot will be on-edge as to when that next random hand-over is going to occur, and so it will be unlikely that any reduced stress on the pilot is going to happen during the auto-pilot efforts. Also, imagine that the auto-pilot does purposely want to hand over the flight because of some anomaly that has occurred, and the pilot might become momentarily confused or even lulled into less attention because they are expecting the next random handover to be taking place (which is not an emergency situation).

Carefully consider too the cognitive load that we are placing onto the pilot. One moment their mental processes are not especially on the flight, and the next moment by surprise (due to the random prompting) they have to mentally engage. This on-again and off-again effort of mental exertion might actually produce heightened pilot fatigue, ultimately leading them to be even worse at piloting once the flight is entirely handed over to them such as perhaps when landing the plane.

We need to be watchful of seeking overly simplistic solutions to complex HCI arrangements.

HCI AS THE SILENT KILLER

The lack of general awareness about the importance of HCI in today's computer systems is alarming because we are all increasingly becoming dependent on computers. Often, the rush to get a new computer system out-the-door does not incorporate sufficient attention to Human-Computer Interaction. Even if there is some attention, it is frequently performed by programmers that are not necessarily trained in the HCI facets. They then believe that they have done a good job of encompassing HCI, but then often upon fielding are horrified to discover that there are misalignments that they never envisioned.

Economics comes to play in this HCI focus too, since there is "added" cost to being careful and thoughtful about the HCI aspects, though the benefits of that added cost can often well exceed the added costs. Firms that find themselves being sued and giving up large monetary awards for systems that did not have thoughtfully prepared HCI find out afterwards that they underestimated the value of HCI. There are often programmers that wanted to deeply do HCI, but the budget for doing the system did not include the needed expenditure.

Often a new app or computer system will land like a dud in the marketplace and a retrospective often shows that it is due to a poorly done HCI. In contrast, good and really good HCI's are being increasingly expected by consumers and businesses, and so the poorly designed HCI's won't last. Part of the tremendous success of Uber has been partially attributed to the HCI that they put in place, and which allowed humans to more easily and in a frictionless way call for cab-like service in a manner that had not been made available widely before.

Next time that you are engaged in an interaction with a computer, think about what the computer is "thinking" and what you are thinking, and see if there is a dissonance gap in that HCI. Then find a way to deal with the HCI dissonance gap, thoughtfully and with purpose.

CHAPTER 9

RANSOMWARE AND
DIGITAL EXTORTION

PREFACE

You are undoubtedly familiar with computer viruses and likely have some kind of anti-virus software on your computer that strives to detect and prevent a virus attack. The creators of computer viruses are continually finding new ways to exploit potential holes in your computer and find a means to get their virus into it. Usually, the result of a successful attack by a computer virus is that your data on that computer gets corrupted and/or possibly deleted. We all know that to be safe of such a loss that we are supposed to regularly do back-up's of our data, though many are lazy about this and fail to do regular back-ups.

A computer virus can be launched at your computer by someone that has nothing to do with the actual creation of the computer virus and possibly knows almost nothing about how it works. Computer viruses are readily available on the open market and just about any nitwit or evil doer can get their hands on them. Why do the computer virus makers and attackers do their evil deeds? Historically, they did their deeds out of just the sheer evil joy or challenge of doing it, while in some cases they are more clearly motivated and do so for revenge or purposeful malice (such as an embattled country attacking another country's systems due to hostilities between the two countries).

These cyber-attacks are becoming more commonplace, partially due to the ease of doing them and partially due to the rise of the vast number of computers and devices connecting together on the Internet. There are some attackers that want to try and monetize what they do. Thus, one form of attack involves trying to hold hostage the data on the computer. By potentially freezing and denying access to the data of a business, these money hungry cyber crooks use digital extortion to try and profit from launching these special kind of computer viruses, known as ransomware. CIO's need to ensure that the systems of the enterprise are well protected, including being able to detect and hopefully prevent a ransomware attack. Even if such an attack occurs, there should be a bona fide and readily available back-up so that the ransom demands can be spurned and the firm can be quickly restored to ongoing business conditions.

<hr>

CHAPTER 9: RANSOMWARE AND DIGITAL EXTORTION

According to recent FBI reports, cyber-extortionists were paid $209 million in Q1 2016 by companies that were hit by a type of computer virus called ransomware, and that it could amount to a payout in all of 2016 to the tune of $1 billion. In short, ransomware is becoming the hottest digital crime of the modern age and readily is eclipsing prior forms of business extortion such as threats to contaminate a business's products or reveal a company's deepest secret formulas.

The term "ransomware" comes from a mash-up of the words ransom and malware, and denotes a circumstance wherein a computer malware (a type of computer virus) is used to infect a computer so that the extorter can then try to extort something from the victim. As you will shortly see, it is sometimes also called scareware, since it tries to scare the victim into paying a ransom. Sometimes the ransomware is more puffery than harm, but it tries to scare a business into paying, either because the business does not realize that the ransomware really hasn't done much but they fear that it has, or the business wants to keep hidden that it got attacked and so is willing to pay hush money.

Unlike the more commonly known destructive computer viruses that we all dread and hate, a ransomware infection is not particularly used for destructive purposes as much as it is used for obstructive purposes. Obstructions include making various business files and data unusable (but with the chance of turning them back into being usable), and/or obstructing access to a computer. Refer to Figure 1 for a helpful framework of ransomware typology.

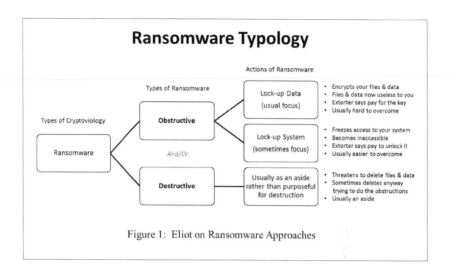

Figure 1: Eliot on Ransomware Approaches

Do not though be misled into thinking that ransomware cannot be destructive. It can be. Sometimes the ransomware deletes some of the files and data, perhaps inadvertently at times, or even intentionally as a show of strength by the extorter to impress the victim about what power the extorter has over the situation. You might think of this as a variant of kidnapping and the extorter decides to shoot the kidnapped hostage in the leg to prove they are willing to play rough.

The extorter might even provide a snippet of the data to you, doing so as proof that they have it or can unlock it, which might be analogous to say cutting off a kidnapped person's finger and mailing it to prove that they have the hostage in their possession and for pressuring to get a ransom.

To-date, the largest volume of ransomware victims are tending to be the computers of individuals rather than business computing per se (i.e., business computing consisting of business servers and networks), but the attention by extorters to aim at the business realm is rapidly rising, mainly since the pay-out from a business tends to be higher than what an individual would pay to the extorter. According to statistics published by the FBI's Internet Crime Complaint Center (IC3), the average pay-out by individuals is around $300 while the average pay-out by businesses is around $10,000. Some individuals and businesses aren't reporting what they have shelled out to the extortionists and so it is difficult to accurately gauge how large the payouts are.

As a sense of the magnitude of this problem, reports indicate that there are 753,000+ computers already having a form of ransomware on them, even though only a fraction of those infections have been activated to enliven the ransomware infection. Yes, that's right; you might already have ransomware on your computers and not even realize that it is there. Surprising? Well, some anti-virus software packages don't look to find ransomware.

Some ransomware is so well hidden in your computer that anti-virus fails to detect it. In fact, ransomware programs are continually being updated and modified by the perpetrators so that the anti-virus community has a hard time keeping up with the cat and mouse game of virus hide-and-seek (there is an entire field of study known as cryptoviology that focuses on computer viruses).

You might think that businesses would be a much harder target since presumably businesses would be better protected than the average individual, and unfortunately you would tend to be wrong in your assumption since businesses are sadly often ill-prepared for ransomware. I provide next some key background about ransomware and describe how businesses should try to prevent themselves from becoming victims, and also what to do if a business does fall victim to ransomware.

As the old saying goes, an ounce of prevention is worth a pound of cure. If you get your business in shape to prevent becoming a victim of ransomware, you can save a ton of headaches and potential loss of company money, data, and reputation.

Most businesses sadly won't undertake the right precautions upfront and only after-the-fact will they devote the needed resources toward IT security that can reduce their chances of a ransomware infection. It is like earthquakes and not doing anything to prepare for one, but after one hits and causes damage and havoc that only then will precautions be put in place for the next earthquake that comes along. You have been forewarned!

UNDER-THE-HOOD OF RANSOMWARE

Let's get into the inner workings of ransomware. The cyber-extortionists send out their infecting programs trying to find victims that they can take electronic hostage of, and will sometimes do so on a "spray and pray" (or "spray and prey") basis that blankets a wide range of businesses and individuals randomly. In rarer cases, they target a particular business or on some occasion a particular industry. Currently, hospitals are a prime target since regrettably hospitals have traditionally been lax at protecting their computers, and also relying on the aspect that workers at hospitals tend to be more likely susceptible to the behavioral or social engineering tricks that some of the extorters use to get in the door (more about this in a moment).

Most commonly the infecting program is an attachment on an email that tries to fool someone into activating the attachment. Known as the Trojan horse attack, the email might seem real to the receiver and so they unknowingly go ahead and open the attachment, which then activates and tries to start the digital infection. If an individual does this at home then the infection might only encompass that person's specific PC at home. In contrast, while at work, the infection might not only infect that employees PC but then try to climb along further and infect other employees PC's. Keep in mind that the employee is typically on the inside of the protective firewall that is built to keep out intruders, and so by unknowingly unleashing the infector on the inside of the firewall then the infecting program can try to make its way throughout the inside of the company network (thus, the Trojan horse moniker).

Why would an employee be foolish enough to open an attachment on an email that has a cyber-extortionist infecting program? The employee can be fooled several ways. One is that the email sent by the extorter uses phishing, which is a means of making an email seem like it has come from an email address that the employee trusts, such as the email address of a fellow employee. Or, the email might appear to come from a governmental agency and the employee might think that they had better open the attachment since it came from the IRS or the FTC or some other agency that perhaps the firm does business with.

There are even instances of employees opening email attachments that are on emails that glaringly look amiss, but afterwards the employee insisted that since the company had anti-virus software installed on their equipment that they assumed any such adverse email would have already been quarantined or at least shunted to their spam folder. And there is the other potential of the employee just being so busy that they don't look carefully at an email and in a rush to get through what might be dozens of awaiting emails that they open one that they should not have.

On a so-called social engineering basis, some of the emails try to tug at the heart of the receiver. Maybe it is an email from what seems to be a laudable charity and the employee then is fooled into thinking that they can help that charity by opening the attachment. For industries where there is a greater preponderance of being aware of charities and of employees that want to help others, this kind of email can be especially effective. Hospitals tend to be in that category, as are non-profits. Extorters at times think about who is the easiest mark and go after those the most.

Extorters will also try to infect servers that are part of the business network. A company network and server administrator might not have established the security precautions that would prevent such an attack from succeeding. There are continually loopholes discovered in servers and operating systems, and these gaps are often posted onto the "dark web" (the part of the web that is considered the criminal side of the Internet) and even onto the security web sites as a warning to everyone (but that the crooks use to their advantage and exploit).

Companies are continually being bombarded by hundreds and thousands of attacks by a vast cacophony of cyber-criminals. Unbeknownst to most employees, businesses that have computer security precautions in place are constantly fending off these attempts to crack into the business's computers. There is a famous saying in the IT security realm, namely that a digital intruder only has to be right once, while the company computer security has to be right ALL the time. OK, so let's assume that the ransomware gets activated by an employee, by one means or another. Let's take a look at what happens next.

SYSTEM HOSTAGE TAKING

Ransomware will typically undertake one of two attacks, either it will try to lock-up the computer and take it hostage from access by the business, or it will try to encrypt the data on the computer and take the data hostage so that even if accessed by the business it will be unusable.

Usually, trying to lock-up the computer is not going to be very effective and can be more readily overcome by IT security specialists. Indeed, the lock-up attack is usually more scare tactic than serious per se, and it is an attempt to intimidate those that rely upon that computer. The hope by the extortionist is that the user will get frightened and then be amenable to paying a ransom to have the computer become unlocked.

An employee that gets one of the lock-up infections might try to pay the ransom so as to hide from the company that they had made the mistake of opening an evil attachment. The employee figures that if they keep things low-key and just pay, no one else in the company will know and they won't get in trouble (fearing perhaps being fired). This is one reason why it is crucial that a business should ensure to inform employees about what to do when they see such an infection, and assure employees that it is better to fess-up than to keep quiet and attempt to resolve the situation themselves.

Often, in lieu of the lock-up attack, the other attack involves encrypting the files on the computer. The infecting program uses some form of encrypting to encode the data on a disk drive, and the key that could decode the encoded data is presumably known only by the extorter. A ransom is then sought from the user to presumably buy the key that will decode the data.

Notice that the extortionist is usually not "stealing" the data, and instead is just locking it up. Stealing the data would involve taking it, which either involves making a copy and then threatening to release it or distribute it, or making a copy and then deleting the data from the original location so that you then no longer have that data available. The extorter could certainly seek to steal the data, but more often they just lock it in place. One of the latest ransomware viruses, Crysis, does the data lock-up and a stealing of the data too.

You might wonder why the extorter would not always want to steal it. One reason is that trying to copy the data would usually involve pulling lots of data across the network and this could not only take a lot of time, increasing the chances of the infecting program getting detected and stopped, but it could also reveal the infecting program by detection mechanisms that would realize the PC is sending out a huge chunk of data. Companies today often have security precautions in place to purposely prevent their own employees from copying large gigabytes of company data, and those same mechanisms would likely become alarmed if the extorter tried to copy the data.

In terms of locking the data in place, the extorter will usually make use of an encryption algorithm to do so. Encryption algorithms are readily available these days and very easy for the extorter to make use of (in the past, encryption algorithms were hard to use and required smarts on the part of the extorter, but nowadays it is trivial to invoke an encryption algorithm). Popular encryption algorithms include DES (Data Encryption Standard), RSA, AES (Advanced Encryption Standard), Blowfish, Twofish, and others. Generally, they make use of keys that are used to encrypt and then later decrypt the data.

The size of the key is usually significant in terms of the longer the key, expressed in number of bits such as say 128 bits, the harder it is to guess what the key was. Imagine for example the PIN that you use for your ATM card. A 4-digit PIN code is not very hard to guess, if you were allowed to try all possibilities of codes of 4 digits and could use a computer to make the guesses for you. But with the encryption algorithms and when using a 128 bit key or 256 bit key, the amount of time it would take for even a computer to try all combination is astronomically high and would take years or even centuries or longer to crack.

Some extorters will use "weak" encryption which is relatively easier to crack, while some will use "strong" encryption which is much harder to crack. There have even been instances whereby the extorter stupidly left the key inside the infecting program and so the IT security specialist was able to find it and unlock the data readily. The point being that there are many varieties of ransomware, some reports suggest perhaps 120 separate types of strains of ransomware viruses, and so it is important to figure out which one has hit you (if you are struck), as will be explained further shortly.

Once the infection takes hold, the extorter needs to let the user know that the infection has occurred and then ask for the ransom. Believe it or not, some of the ransomware is so poorly written that it at times fails to ask for the ransom. It can also be the case that the ransomware itself gets disrupted while doing its evil work and thus does not present the ransom demand. In some instances, the ransomware reports back to the extorter that the hostage taking has occurred, and then the extorter sends a separate message to notify about the ransom demand, rather than having the infecting program do so.

Indeed, the extorter wants to know that a hostage has been taken, and thus they usually require that the user contact them to start the negotiation process. Yes, I said negotiation process. The extorter will make a demand, and the company will need to decide whether to pay it or not. This is more complicated than it might at first glance seem.

The demand by the extorter will usually start high. For example, in the case of the Hollywood Presbyterian Medical Center, the ransom was first set at $3.4 million. Ultimately, the Hollywood Presbyterian Medical Center decided to pay, but paid $17,000 rather than $3.4 million. Why would the extorter settle for "only" $17,000? Because they realize that getting something rather than nothing is likely better than holding out for their higher demand.

To push along the negotiations, most extorters will provide a time limit. They will say that if you don't pay within 48 hours that they will never provide you the key. Or, they might say that after 24 hours the price doubles for each next 12 hours. Similar to what you have seen in TV show plots and hostage scenes of movies, this is old fashioned extortion at this point. The digital part of it is the new twist in terms of taking a hostage, but the rest of it is the same kind of blackmail tactics that have plagued mankind from the start.

Of course, even if the extorter says they will provide the key when paid for, you have no assurance that they will ever provide the key. Kansas Heart Hospital made a payment that the extorter said would get them the key, and then the extorter made a second demand saying that they now wanted more money. At that juncture, Kansas Heart Hospital decided to stop playing the extortionist game. This is, as I suggested before, part of the "concern" that the extortionist has, i.e., the company will decide not to pay and so the extortionist needs to figure out how much the fish on the hook can take before it will no longer let itself get reeled in.

Suppose you do get the key? This does not guarantee that you can fully decrypt your data and nor that all of your data is still there. During the infection process, some of your data might have been deleted or changed by the infecting program, and so the key only decrypts some of your data or there isn't even your data left to be decrypted. It is doubtful that the extortionist will provide you any guarantee that the key will work and that your data still exists. Overall, I think you get the idea that once you've been infected by ransomware, all bets are off as to whether you will be able to reclaim your data.

This can be disheartening since the data might be those important spreadsheets that contain vital financial numbers, or maybe crucial text documents about your latest research breakthroughs, or maybe video that was costly to make, or pictures that were collected and that are nearly priceless. The infecting program doesn't care what kind of data it is, and the extortionist just hopes that whatever data it manages to take hostage will be of value to you.

RANSOMWARE RESPONSE

A business is faced with a lot of ugly choices when it gets infected by ransomware. Thus, the first recommendation is don't get infected by ransomware. Sounds simple, I know. Preparation and prevention are crucial. Refer to Figure 2 for an illustration of the response stages.

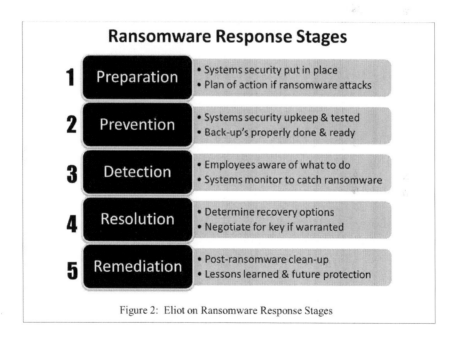

Ransomware Response Stages

1 Preparation
- Systems security put in place
- Plan of action if ransomware attacks

2 Prevention
- Systems security upkeep & tested
- Back-up's properly done & ready

3 Detection
- Employees aware of what to do
- Systems monitor to catch ransomware

4 Resolution
- Determine recovery options
- Negotiate for key if warranted

5 Remediation
- Post-ransomware clean-up
- Lessons learned & future protection

Figure 2: Eliot on Ransomware Response Stages

You will need to invest sufficiently in IT security so that you are well protected. Multiple layers of protection are the best practice. Imagine that at your home you maybe live in a gated community (that's one layer of protection), and you have a fence around your property (second layer), and you have a lock on your door to your house (third layer). Likewise, you need to have multiple layers of systems security on your network, your servers, your PC's, and so on.

Besides trying to detect ransomware in the same way that any anti-virus software will try to catch other kinds of computer viruses, there are other telltale signs of ransomware that can help detect it once it starts its actions. The ransomware needs to run its encryption algorithm and so will likely use your own computers to do so, which can potentially be detected by being a process running on your system that is unknown to the system and chews up a lot of your computing power. Another is that it will be writing lots of data onto your hard drive, doing so can be potentially suspicious behavior that can be detected. It might be deleting data, which could be suspicious, and it could be generating "bad data" errors and also be taxing your network.

In some respects, the ransomware is doing things on your computers that other normal activity might also be doing, and so it is not necessarily readily detected. On the other hand, if your systems are suddenly being very active at 2 a.m. and if normally there is little activity on your systems at that time, it certainly can be a sign to send up a red flag and get someone to take a look.

Another vital form of preparation and prevention involves doing back-ups. Your computer systems data should be regularly backed-up. If so, you can presumably just treat the ransomware attack as nothing more than any other kind of disaster that has wiped out your systems, say like an earthquake or tornado, and then use your back-ups in lieu of trying to un-hostage your data.

Here though there are a number of caveats. Some companies make a back-up of their data say once per week on a Sunday night. If you discover mid-week that you got hit by the ransomware, and assuming your back-up's are actually any good, you will then have lost the data that occurred subsequent to the Sunday back-up. How much data that is, and hot important it is, and how hard it is to recreate it, varies from business to business. Your back-up frequency should fit to your business needs.

Another aspect about the back-up is that sometimes a business makes a back-up and then deletes the prior one. The danger here is that suppose that the ransomware was not detected and thus at the Sunday back-up you piled the hostage taken data onto your back-ups and deleted the prior ones that were not encrypted. Your back-up is now useless and equally hostage taken. It is important to make sure that you have versioning of your back-ups so as to prevent this kind of foul-up from happening.

Some companies properly have back-ups and they do them frequently and they have versioning. But, they have never tried to actually recover their data from their back-ups. So, when a crisis happens, they struggle to see whether they can actually use the back-ups and sometimes discover problems in doing so. It is best to periodically do checks of the back-ups and practice doing a recovery from them.

Besides the above preventions and preparations, you also need to have an awareness campaign among your employees regarding watching out for activating ransomware. You need to have policies in place and make sure that employees are familiar with the policies. You need to have a means for employees to readily report when they think an infection has occurred, such as calling a special hotline or Help Desk. The employees need to believe that they can report an infection without potential repercussions to them; else they will be afraid to report it and likely take actions that will worsen the situation.

BUSINESS ACTION IF ATTACKED

No matter how much preparation and prevention you do, there is still a chance of getting hit by ransomware. You should have a process for responding to the advent of ransomware. Some companies think "it is an IT problem to fix" but they would be taking a very myopic and endangering viewpoint.

A ransomware attack can be very debilitating to a business. If the data is really crucial to day-to-day running of the business, the business might come to a halt. If word leaks out about being caught by ransomware, it might severely damage the reputation of the business. If the company is regulated by government agencies, it might be a violation of law that the business has allowed the ransomware to take hold. These are just some of the adverse consequences that can hit a business.

Some companies will try to keep the whole attack tightly known by only a handful of company employees. This can be a good approach, but you need to be prepared for it to leak out, and if so, what will you do then. Also, employees themselves that rely upon the data might already realize something is afoot, and so if you try to hide from them what is happening it can create added confusion and then also lead the employees to distrust the company when they feel they aren't being told what is happening.

For all of these reasons, a best practice involves having at the ready a Ransomware SWAT team that consists of not only the IT security specialists but also your corporate legal team, your corporate communications team, your HR team, and essentially representatives from each function of the business. This is because the ransomware can impact all functions, including accounting, finance, operations, etc.

Besides invoking the Ransomware SWAT team, there are then prescribed steps that should be undertaken. It is best to have those steps already identified and not be scrambling during a crisis to figure them out. This is why a Disaster Recovery plan is important for businesses. How widespread is the ransomware? Did it hit just a few PC's or many? Did it hit the servers? Is it still infecting or did it stop? What variant is it? Are their known solutions to it? How did it get in? Can the hole be plugged so that more cannot get in? Is it doing a lock-up approach? Is it doing a hostage taking of the data? How much data? How important is the data? How harmed is the business? Can we use our back-ups? What else will be missing? What will be our communication internally? What will be our communication externally? Does this impact our suppliers? Does this impact our customers?

By the way, another sneaky way that ransomware gets into your business is via your other trusted business partners. You might have a vendor that supplies you with say paper supplies, and maybe have an electronic ordering system that connects your computer and their computer. Suppose the ransomware infects their computer, and then piggybacks over to your computer since the vendor is considered a trusted partner. Something to watch out for!

Some companies have cyber-crime insurance, providing a form of insurance similar to other kinds of insurance for business losses. If your business has this, you'll want to see whether ransomware is covered, and if so what the coverage limits and stipulations are. This would need to be considered during the process of dealing with ransomware and if you aren't careful in your approach it can invalidate your cyber-crime insurance. This is yet another thing to watch out for.

DEALING WITH RANSOM DEMANDS

The company Ransomware SWAT team needs to be ready to deal with the ransom demands. Even if you determine that you will not need to seek assistance from the extorter, you will potentially still need to decide what communication if any to have with the extortionist. And, you need to consider the legal aspects too. In some jurisdictions, you might be required to report the ransomware, and failing to do so might be a criminal act on the part of your business. Some firms are reluctant to get law enforcement involved since they perceive that it will just make the situation more public and harmful to the brand and reputation of the firm. You will need to carefully consider this aspect since it can have potential legal consequences by not reporting it to the proper officials.

Law enforcement might also be able to assist in dealing with the circumstance. Increasingly, at federal, state, and local levels, there are cyber-cops that can help in dealing with the circumstances, either aiding on the technology level, or aiding in dealing with the more traditional ransom aspects of the crime.

Suppose you reach a point wherein you believe that you did not do sufficient preparation and prevention, and have no means to recover your data, or that the recovery would take a long time and be tremendously costly, and that you believe you now have no other recourse than to negotiate with the extorter and hope that you can buy a key to unlock your data.

This is the classic: "To Pay, or Not to Pay, that is the question" dilemma. As earlier mentioned, there is no guarantee that even if you pay that the extortionist will provide the key. Nor that the key will properly work. Nor that the data is even still there intact. Etc. On the other hand, the amount you are willing to pay and if the amount that the extortionist is willing to accept is low enough that you might think it is worth a chance of getting the key, even in spite of the aspects that it might not work. This is all part of the cost/benefit analysis needed to be determined by the SWAT team of your business.

On a more macroscopic scale, some say that you should never pay the ransom, since it will help the extortionist to stay in business and then continue their nefarious efforts, it will embolden the extortionist and they will continue trying, the extortionist might think your business is sucker and then try again or try to go wider against you, and that you are rewarding the extortionist and saying to the world of extortionists that they can make a buck doing this and so you are perpetuating their criminal activities globally.

Another part of the cost/benefit calculus involves what your customers and the marketplace might think too. If you are able to recover your data with the key, but if your customers know that you paid a ransom, will they think less of your firm? Will the market ding your stock more so for paying or for not paying? I can bet already that there will be some executives in your firm that will urge to just pay the extortionist and make the problem "go away" – and though this can seem alluring, I believe you can also see that it is a likely simplistic hope and a large bet even if the ransom amount itself is low.

What does the FBI advise? In what became a somewhat famous quote, Joseph Bonavolonta, Assistant Special Agent in Charge of the Cyber and Counterintelligence Program in the FBI's Boston office, while speaking at a conference on cyber security was quoted as saying: "The ransomware is that good. To be honest, we often advise people just to pay the ransom." This is not though the official position of the FBI. One published statement by the FBI has been this: "The FBI doesn't make recommendations to companies; instead, the Bureau explains what the options are for businesses that are affected and how it's up to individual companies to decide for themselves the best way to proceed. That is, either reverts to back up systems, contact a security professional, or pay."

There will be some gut wrenching hand wringing in your firm as you wrestle with what to do. The time limit imposed by the extortionist will cause things to get very heated in your company. You will be watching the clock tick, frantically making decisions and trying to figure things out, doing so hurried and possibly hastily. This is by design in that the extortionist wants to force your hand and not allow you to be able to readily and systematically decide what to do. They are hoping that you will be so frazzled and tense that you'll just acquiesce and pay that ransom.

The emotional toll on the company can be as much damage to the firm as is the ransomware itself. There will be finger pointing, angry bursts, accusations, and usually heads will roll. As I say, it is ugly, and the HR fallout alone can be tremendously hurtful to a company. If you decide to pay, the method of payment then becomes an issue. The extortionists don't want to get caught and so they realize that the method of payment can be a means to catch them (you know, the famous "follow the money" credo). In the past, they might have had you do a wire transfer of the money, but this can be readily traced and it is therefore not the most attractive route nowadays by the extortionists. They usually now ask for Bitcoins. Bitcoins are a form of digital currency and it can be easier for the crooks to turn it into actual cash without so readily being found.

Speaking of being found, some of you might wonder why these extortionists are able to get away with these ransomware crimes without getting caught. Usually, they sit in a country that does not care that they are doing these crimes, or cares but not enough to do something about it. And, there are even some countries or at least locales that somewhat encourage the practice, since the locale can benefit financially too.

The "beauty" of ransomware is that it appears to be a crime without any real harm to actual person. It can be portrayed as a crime against those companies or even individuals that have money and so why is it any big deal to take some money from them. A billion dollar company that pays a $17,000 ransom can be seen as either a token amount or maybe even heroic for the extortionist that they got some "greedy" company to pay them. All those kinds of rather askew reasoning has been given for those that do these acts.

GROWING THREAT OF RANSOMWARE

Ransomware is a burgeoning industry. Cyber-crooks can easily purchase ransomware kits on the web via the black market. Though you might think these extortionists must be incredibly smart computer scientists, they actually don't need to know much at all about computers. Basically, any idiot can now be a cyber-extortionist. I am not calling them idiots; I am just saying that it has become an easy crime to commit. Just go and buy a ransomware kit, make use of the already existing means to spam it out, and it is a volume business wherein they gamble that statistically only maybe a fraction of their ransomware attacks will succeed, but the cost to distribute and then deal with the ones that grab a fish is pretty low. Then take payment in Bitcoins, remain hidden and avoid getting caught, and turn the Bitcoins into cash or use it to buy goods.

The Internet of Things (IoT) is going to further help them out. More and more devices are going to be connected onto the web. More and more data is going to be generated. This provides a feeding frenzy for the cyber-extortionists. You might find of further rankling that some of the ransomware kits are even available as free open source software. For example, one of the kits, EDA2, got posted as an apparent educational approach to informing about how ransomware works. Some cyber-crooks then hijacked it and modified it to further their own nefarious ransomware pursuits.

Social networks are also now becoming an increasingly popular way to spread ransomware. Rather than relying on email as a Trojan horse delivery method, social networks provide another avenue. It is an attractive avenue since so many millions and now billions of people are interconnected by social media.

What should your business do? As emphasized, do the appropriate preparation and prevention. Be the less likely target and hope that the cyber-extortionists put their attention elsewhere. Watch out for your trusted business partners not being as diligent as you, and guard accordingly. Be ready to detect ransomware, and have a response process that is well articulated and practiced. Respond as befits your business and circumstance. After an attack and once the dust starts to settle, use the hard lesson learned to make your business more resilient and hopefully less likely to become a double-dipped ransomware victim.

CHAPTER 10
HYBRID IT

PREFACE

The word "cloud" has become a common way to refer to the Internet. We store our files "in the cloud" and we access YouTube videos via the cloud. The phrase "cloud computing" is a variant phrase that means we are accessing and using computers via the cloud. For many businesses, when cloud computing first appeared, they were reluctant to move their proprietary systems onto the Internet (becoming part of the cloud), often due to concerns over security (wanting to keep their systems off-the-grid and accessible by only other private networking means).

Meanwhile, major software providers began to offer their software available via the cloud, rather than having to install the software on your own system. Plus, vendors that wanted to offer online storage to consumers and to businesses began to spring up on the cloud, along with vendors that offered computer servers so that you would not need to buy your own computer hardware for your business.

In the IT field, the term "hybrid IT" has arisen to suggest having an IT infrastructure of hardware and networking that is not only of a private off-the-cloud nature but also commingled in some fashion with the cloud. Companies have often already heavily invested in their computer hardware that they purchased, and so question to what degree they should switch over to cloud computing. There are also accounting questions to be answered since making an investment in buying hardware and systems is considered a capital expense, while making use of the various cloud computing services is usually considered an operating expense. CIO's needs to take a look at what their mix of cloud and non-cloud use is, and decide on an ongoing basis what the right mix is for their business.

CHAPTER 10: HYBRID IT

One of the most frequent questions that I keep getting asked is "what in the world is hybrid IT?" The word "hybrid" evokes images of some kind of Frankenstein IT that maybe has various oddball pieces cobbled together. Is it systems, is it people, what is it? Furthermore, the phrase "hybrid cloud" is floating around quite a bit these days in the halls of IT and so there is confusion about whether hybrid cloud and hybrid IT are the same thing or different from each other. Let's clear up the confusion and explore an explanation about hybrid IT and also about hybrid cloud. It is also essential to consider key insights about how to manage both.

Let's start with hybrid IT. It should probably be rephrased as "hybrid IT infrastructure" because the phrase "hybrid IT" refers to the infrastructure side of the IT environment in a business. The infrastructure consists of the various hardware servers and networking equipment that act as the host and plumbing for applications and data. The reason that the word hybrid is tossed into this infrastructure stuff is due to the mixing of the cloud into what was previously non-cloud infrastructure.

We first had non-cloud IT infrastructure that often consisted of equipment on-premises in a business, perhaps having its own Data Center that housed the equipment. Some companies not only had their own on-premises equipment but they also put some of their equipment into vendor-hosted sites, such as colocation facilities (these "colo's" provide the racks, electrical power, air conditioning, and space for a business to then house its equipment, and many different companies would put their equipment into these colocation sites).

Now that the cloud has come upon us, many businesses not only have their legacy infrastructure but they now also are putting some of their systems into the cloud.

Take a look at Figure 1.

Hybrid IT: Overall Depiction

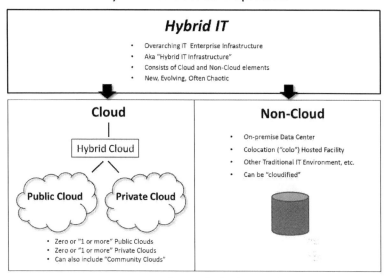

Figure 1: Eliot – Hybrid IT framework

As shown in Figure 1, hybrid IT consists of two major components, namely cloud based infrastructure and non-cloud based infrastructure. Hybrid IT is then a mixture of infrastructure that contains some infrastructure that is in the cloud and some that is in the traditional non-cloud infrastructure. The reason that it is useful to give this a new name is to remind us that the cloud and non-cloud portions should be managed on a unified basis. Some IT groups allowed the cloud portion to grow separately and apart from the rest of their existing infrastructure, and then realized after-the-fact that they ought to be looking at the totality of the infrastructure to make sure it is entirely and comprehensively well managed and maintained.

HYBRID CLOUD

Hopefully you now have a sense of what hybrid IT is and why it is important. Let's next discuss hybrid cloud. As shown in Figure 1, the cloud consists of two subcomponents, namely the public cloud and the private cloud. Note that a business could make use of numerous public clouds, if it wanted to do so, and likewise a business could make use of numerous private clouds. When thinking about both the public cloud and the private cloud, those two are considered a hybrid mixture and so the phrase "hybrid cloud" refers to making use of both public and private clouds.

We hear all the time about "the cloud" but you might be wondering what is a crisp definition for infrastructure that is in the cloud. I like to use the NIST definition which can be found at this governmental URL http://nvlpubs.nist.gov/nistpubs/Legacy/SP/nistspecialpublication800-145.pdf. According to NIST, the cloud is "a model for enabling ubiquitous, convenient, on-demand network access to a shared pool of configurable computing resources (e.g., networks, servers, storage, applications, and services) that can be rapidly provisioned and released with minimal management effort or service provider interaction."

So a cloud can be viewed as IT infrastructure, just like the infrastructure that good old traditional legacy IT has had, but the cloud has some added characteristics, especially that the infrastructure in the cloud is available on-demand and can be rapidly setup and taken down.

This can be very handy. Suppose a business puts up a web site in its own internal infrastructure. Maybe the web site is so exciting that tons of consumers want to visit it. This might cause the web site to go down or respond slowly to users.

Having to quickly procure additional infrastructure to handle the volume of web visitors is bound to be arduous for an IT group. On the other hand, if the web site is hosted in the cloud, the cloud provider presumably has lots of extra infrastructure available at a moment's notice and can allow the company to make a request for cloud bursting (rapid infrastructure increase to handle a burst of web traffic).

Clouds then are intended to provide elasticity and scalability, allowing a company to readily be able to shift up or shift down in terms of the amount of infrastructure that they need. The agility of being able to quickly have added infrastructure is crucial in the fast paced business environment of today.

At the same time, once things slow down, suppose the web site fades from popularity, the company is not stuck with lots of expensive infrastructure equipment that they might have bought to bulk up. Instead, the company would tell the cloud provider that some of the bulked-up infrastructure should now be released and would presumably become available for other customers of the cloud provider.

A public cloud is a cloud that has been setup for general public use, and the cloud provider has multiple clients such as many different businesses that use the cloud (a well-known example is Amazon Web Services or abbreviated AWS). Thus, the cloud services are being shared. Usually, even though the infrastructure is being shared, there are various ways in which the different clients are kept apart from each other during the use of the cloud infrastructure.

A private cloud is a cloud that is exclusive to a specific organization. This is somewhat rare right now, and most businesses tend to use a public cloud. Nonetheless, some companies are looking at wanting to have what they consider a more focused environment for their specific needs, a private cloud, and believe that a public cloud does not provide the necessary security and exclusivity for them (maybe due to say regulatory demands).

VARIATIONS OF HYBRID IT

We have now covered the overall explanation of hybrid IT and hybrid cloud. Hybrid cloud consists of a combination of public clouds and private clouds. Hybrid IT consists of a combination of the hybrid cloud and the traditional non-cloud IT infrastructure.

There are some interesting and important variations of the hybrid IT model. Take another look at Figure 1, and imagine that the lower left box containing the "Cloud" was not there, leaving just the "Non-Cloud" box to its right. In that sense, a business that has only the non-cloud IT infrastructure is really not the full mixture of what hybrid IT is all about. We would think of this circumstance as a quite limited variant of hybrid IT since it lacks any cloud elements. This is pretty much what IT has been managing as infrastructure all along.

Look again at Figure 1, and imagine that we crossed out the "Private Cloud" portion in the "Cloud" box, and thus have just the "Public Cloud" portion remaining. Now we are getting into the proper sense of hybrid IT. We have a business that has both the non-cloud traditional IT infrastructure and also has opted to make use of a public cloud. Many businesses are doing this today.

The public cloud and the non-cloud are typically considered separate and distinct from each other. They do not have any particular interconnection. If we added a network connection between the public cloud and the non-cloud portions of the infrastructure then we would have the next evolution of the hybrid IT. By adding an interconnection, we are allowing applications and data to flow among the public cloud and non-cloud portions of the IT infrastructure. Some businesses are just now getting to this level of evolution in hybrid IT.

For some businesses, they have the circumstance of a business that has no non-cloud infrastructure, and instead has entirely cloud-based infrastructure. For their cloud based infrastructure, they are using both public clouds and private clouds. And, they have connected their public clouds and private clouds. They are thusly using a hybrid cloud approach, and interconnecting their hybrid clouds. Businesses that are doing this kind of a hybrid IT are usually newer firms, start-ups that didn't have any legacy IT infrastructure. They started fresh and went entirely with the cloud.

The furthest evolution would be interconnecting them all, namely the Public Cloud, Private Cloud, and traditional IT non-cloud. This would be considered a full hybrid IT. There is the true hybrid cloud, consisting of public and private clouds, which are also interconnected, and there is the non-cloud portion, and which is also interconnected to the hybrid clouds. Very few businesses are at this level of hybrid IT. It will probably be a few years from now before we see much of this kind of hybrid IT.

LEVELS OF HYBRID IT ADOPTION

The hybrid IT approach has been shown as graduating from the simple to the complex. In the simplest case, we saw the instance of almost no particular hybrid aspects involved, such as an entirely non-cloud circumstance and no clouds at all. There was the quite complex hybrid IT consisting of fully interconnected non-cloud and hybrid cloud infrastructures. Take a look at Figure 2.

Hybrid IT: Levels of Adoption

	Level	Non-Cloud	Public Cloud	Private Cloud	Connected
			Hybrid Cloud		
Not Hybrid IT	Level 0	■			
	Level 0		■		
	Level 0			■	
Low Hybrid IT	Level 1	■	■		
	Level 1		■	■	
Medium Hybrid IT	Level 2	■	■		■
	Level 2		■	■	■
	Level 2	■		■	■
High Hybrid IT	Level 3	■	■	■	■

Figure 2: Eliot – Hybrid IT Levels of Adoption

Here in Figure 2, we describe hybrid IT in terms of levels. There is Level 0, the simplest variant of hybrid IT. Level 1 is slightly more involved and is considered a low level of hybrid IT adoption. You can see that for example a circumstance of having a non-cloud and a public cloud is in Level 1. Level 2 is the meatier variant of hybrid IT. The interconnectedness now comes to play. Finally, Level 3 is the most complex and involves all the elements, which then constitutes a high level of hybrid IT.

Please notice that the Figure 2 does not depict all of the possible combinations and permutations of the factors, and offers the more significant variants as a means of typifying the levels of adoption. For each successive level of hybrid IT adoption, the requisite attention by the IT function increases. The IT team needs to be increasingly involved in brokering the cloud services to be used. Overseeing and managing the hybrid IT becomes vital, since otherwise the pieces will become less effective and more inefficient without a comprehensive approach.

The enterprise will suffer without the appropriate management over the IT infrastructure in the more complex hybrid arrangements. Applications won't be able to share, or loads won't get balanced and applications will falter. Same for data too. There are economies of scale to be had when the hybrid IT infrastructure grows in size. If the infrastructure is being treated as piecemeal, the economies of scale will not be adequately leveraged.

In many businesses today, they are trying out the cloud and making initial forays into the public cloud and/or the private cloud. Sometimes a shadow IT group emerges that has opted to just suddenly strike a deal with a particular public cloud service, doing so because it is easy for this non-official IT end-users to do so. But, they might be opening a can of worms. They might not be aware of and have made sure that the proper security precautions are established in their public cloud use. They might have signed a contract with the public cloud provider that lays open company data or that has severe restrictions that will be costly to overcome.

An enterprise perspective of a comprehensive nature needs to be undertaken for a company's IT infrastructure. The hybrid IT moniker is a handy indicator that we are veering quickly into an environment that is a combination of the cloud and the non-cloud. CIOs need to make sure they are ready for this environment and must press the case that IT needs to help ensure that the business does hybrid IT in a strategic and sound manner.

CHAPTER 11

CONSUMERIZATION OF IT

PREFACE

As a consumer, we are pretty much spoiled that when we use a mobile app we expect it to be easy to use and maybe even fun to use. Think about using the Uber mobile app. The ability to readily indicate that you want to have a car come pick you up is very easy to do. Watching the car on your smartphone screen as the vehicle makes its way to you via the little car icons as they turn streets and head to you is almost like watching a Frogger game (a once popular video game involving getting an animated frog across a busy thoroughfare).

In companies today, most of the applications that the end-users access are not like Uber in that the screens to be used are confusing and jam packed with info. The applications often do not connect with each other and so you need to log into one application and yet another application to get your job done. The Finance team has a multitude of applications and databases that contain needed financial information and must try to navigate across them. Each application has a different looking interface, requiring differing commands and having differing capabilities. This mess of disparate applications, interfaces, and data is likewise for Human Resources, Operations, Marketing, and the rest of the business.

CIO's are now confronted with end-users that are used to having pleasing and easy to use mobile apps while outside of work as everyday consumers, but then they come into the office and find themselves seemingly stepping back into the dark ages. In the IT field, the phrase "consumerization of IT" has arisen to suggest that the IT systems of a business should be just as responsive, just as easy to use, just as fun to use, and otherwise on the same footing as consumer accessible mobile apps and web sites. This is harder than it might seem. Nonetheless, there is tremendous pressure to get there, and CIO's need to know how to move their firm in that direction.

CHAPTER 11: CONSUMERIZATION OF IT

Consumerization of IT. Within the halls of the IT leadership ranks there is a battle cry to either embrace or to reject the consumerization of IT. Business executives and leaders are often unaware of what the consumerization of IT is, and probably have never even heard about it.

Surprisingly, some CIO's give it little notice too, while others are touting it as the best new paradigm for a dramatic shift in delivering contemporary IT services in modern organizations. In this chapter, I take a close look at what "consumerization of IT" means and the impact that it can and will continue to have on the IT function of businesses, and examine how IT leadership and the CIO should seriously and swiftly adopt the principles of IT consumerization.

DEFINING CONSUMERIZATION OF IT

Succinctly stated, the consumerization of IT has to do with the changing mores of technology and of technology-use outside the company, and the infusion of those changes into the inner workings of a business and its IT function. For example, today's consumerization of IT outside enterprises involves consumers being able to readily use their mobile device to get their tasks undertaken, perhaps using their mobile device to order up an Uber ride or buy movie tickets via say Fandango. Consumers use their mobile device to text with fellow consumers, and interact extensively via social media such as Facebook and Snapchat.

In business, many firms provide IT services to their employees in a manner and form that is quite different from the consumer world. Employees get issued laptops, hefty devices, and are instructed to use official company email to communicate with each other, often eschewing texting or online chats. Additionally, the employees need to have company software that gets loaded onto their laptops by IT, rather than being able to use an iTunes-like store, and it is often difficult to use the applications and equally arduous to access the applications. And so on.

Employees working in companies often find themselves puzzled that the consumer world they live in is so much easier to deal with from an IT perspective than is the company environment of IT that they deal with. Puzzlement often turns into anger and disgust that the internal IT is seemingly so bad in comparison to what they see and use the moment they walk outside the walls of the company buildings. As such, there is an increasing clamor by employees to make their company's IT more akin to the consumer world of IT. They are asking sensible questions. Why can't company apps be readily downloaded like doing so from iTunes? Why can't they use social media apps to communicate within their company? Why can't they use a mobile device instead of using a heavier and clunky laptop?

In some companies, the clamor is relatively low key and barely heard. Murmurs occur around the water cooler and end-users make occasional off-hand remarks during meetings about how hard it is to use IT at the company. Meanwhile, in some companies there is an outright expression of disgust with the existing IT approach.

Traditional internal IT is seen as producing systems that are:
- Ease of Use = Difficult
- Systems Shape = Cumbersome
- IT Devices Used = Heavy and arduous
- Timeliness of Systems = Outdated

While modern consumerized IT is seen as producing systems that are:
- Ease of Use = Friendly
- Systems Shape = Streamlined
- IT Devices Used = Quick and lite
- Timeliness of Systems = Current and trendy

CIOs are embattled and confronted constantly about how the existing systems are outdated and antiquated in comparison to what their fellow executives and the rank-and-file employees deal with everyway outside the office. Knowing this discontent, software vendors often successfully go around the IT function by whispering to the rest of the organization that the cloud-based applications they are selling are already "consumer certified," so to speak, and when users see the demos they instantly fall in love with what they see.

CIOs that refute or resist the consumerization of IT are likely to find themselves on the wrong side of the drive and will undoubtedly find themselves gradually being edged out, either by the rise of shadow IT efforts that will occur behind their backs, or by an overt struggle to root out the CIO so as to make way for a new wave approach to IT. Essentially, conventional IT has lagged behind the progress of IT outside the company in the consumer marketplace, and the outside-the-company experience by employees as consumers is increasingly becoming a movement within companies to reshape their company's internal IT.

COMPREHENSIVE APPROACH

Some CIOs tend to view this as just a matter of embracing mobile devices inside the firm (i.e., the tech side of things), or maybe adopting something like Yammer to help the enterprise become more social network oriented. These are important aspects of the consumerization of IT, but are often piecemeal and only address random parts of it or do so in a peripheral way. In turn, this partial tech-only approach is usually seen by business leaders as a half-hearted attempt by IT, or worse as an inept and incompetent attempt.

IT leadership would be wiser to look at the consumerization of IT on a more comprehensive basis. The overarching "enterprise IT strategy" should include the consumerization of IT aspects, incorporating explicitly the timing of the adoption and how the adoption will occur for consumerized IT. This is also definitely more than just a one-time indication and will need to be included in ongoing long-term and short-term IT plans on an ongoing basis. The external consumerization of IT will likely always be ahead of where the internal company IT is, and so it will be an ongoing struggle to keep up by the IT function. As shown in Figure 2, the consumerization of IT is not only about the Technology, but also about the People and the Processes of IT and the business. All three aspects need to be considered and coordinated.

In terms of the more obvious aspect, the Technology, the IT function needs to figure out how to make the company's legacy applications be more like the types of apps that consumers use. The user experience (UX) needs to be as easy and simple to use, apps need to be readily available for download and use, and mobile devices beyond just laptops need to be utilized. That being said, it is not an easy task, and those that shout at the CIO to make the changes are often unaware of the costs involved in doing so. Resources by the company will be consumed to make the consumerization of IT shift. Can the firm afford it? And/or should those resources be used for other purposes and goals of the company instead?

Even seemingly simple aspects such as the adoption of mobile devices raises many crucial questions. Should employees be encouraged to use their own mobile device, the Bring Your Own Device (BYOD) notion? But if so, in what manner should employees be compensated for the use of their own mobile devices? There are important legal ramifications too, as to whether and when an employee uses a mobile device and how it might be construed as a work related usage versus a personal use. This can then impact employee pay and also legal responsibilities for the firm.

From a People perspective, the IT function needs to adjust to a consumer serving mindset. IT employees need to perceive themselves as service providers. In some firms, there is an "us versus them" mindset by IT and a lack of appreciation for and proper service attitude toward the end-users of the firm. This is why some firms went the route of outsourcing IT, hopeful that it would send a message that IT needs to think of themselves as a service provider, and act accordingly.

Imagine that a consumer is using their American Express card and has some troubles in doing so. The consumer can contact American Express in a variety of ways, including via email, phone, and even online chat. Within companies, when end-users have troubles using a company system or application, they often must fill-in laborious internal IT-request forms to make a request, or they call an internal Help Desk that puts them on-hold and at times is incapable of answering their questions.

Consumerization of IT would sharpen the focus of the IT function toward providing the same kind of Help Desk support that an American Express would for consumers. This entails a more efficient and effective support approach via multi-modes, including email, phone, and online chat. IT would need to likely change-up the technology used for support, would need to instill in the IT support staff a consumerization mindset, and change the processes so that the manner of making requests and being served were more like those of a consumerization perspective. In short, there needs to be a marriage between the People, the Process, and the Technology, in order to achieve a balanced consumerization of IT.

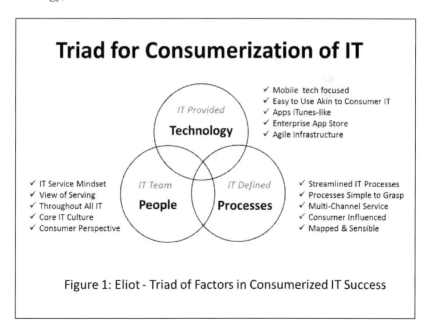

Figure 1: Eliot - Triad of Factors in Consumerized IT Success

LIMITS OF CONSUMERIZED IT

This comparison though between an internal consumerization of IT and an external consumerization of IT is somewhat fraught with difficulty because American Express has for example the need to satisfy their card holders in a manner that one might say is not equivalent as to meeting the needs of internal end-users.

In fact, I've often seen CFO's that disregard the consumerization of IT in organizations, and will insist that the cost of "coddling" employees is not worth it. The CFO accepts the notion that American Express needs to "coddle" consumers in order to keep them as loyal card holders, but does not see that a similar analogous situation exists within the enterprise. This will of course vary from firm to firm as to whether or not the cost to provide consumer-like IT services and products internally is worthwhile (or at least perceived as such) for the end-users of the firm.

In the consumer world, consumers can opt to walk away from a business that does not provide appropriate consumer IT services and products to them. They vote with their feet and their wallets. In terms of end-users in an enterprise, it could be argued that they are not quite in an equivalent posture within a firm and cannot "walk away" in that same sense as consumers do (employees are akin to "captives" rather than consumers), though it could also be argued that a firm will lose its employees perhaps due to lousy or poorly provided IT products and services, or that at least end-users that are contending with such IT services and products will become less efficient or less productive, ultimately causing an adverse impact of one kind or another to the business. And, this in turn could ultimately impact the external customers of the firm.

One way to deal with the consumerization of IT is to gradually shift in the direction of the IT consumerization aspects. A gradual approach might be better served than a "big bang" all at once transition. In a gradual approach, any new systems should try to ensure that consumerization characteristics are included during the building and fielding of the new systems. The legacy systems could do likewise when they undergo maintenance or upkeep. Thus, rather than an explicit overhaul overnight, there is a gradual incremental shift that softens the blow in terms of added costs towards adopting an IT consumerization approach.

The consumerization of IT can be measured on a scale of 1 to 10, ranging from a 0 meaning no consumerized IT and rising up to a 10, full consumerized IT. Using this scale, gauge what score your firm has today, and ascertain what score it needs to have. Based on a carefully considered ROI, you then should be making moves toward a goal that fits your firm.

CHAPTER 12

BIMODAL IT

PREFACE

Bimodal is a word often used in statistics to refer to something that has two modes, such as a bimodal statistical distribution that has two distinct peaks (imagine two camel humps, side by side). In the IT industry, a major research think tank has come up with a somewhat controversial idea that they call Bimodal IT, suggesting that there are two modes of an IT function.

This Bimodal IT consists of one part of IT that is slower and more sluggish to get things done, while the second part of IT has to be fast and agile. Some see this as consisting of the legacy systems of the business (the slower part) and the newer hip systems of the business (the faster and more agile part). Depending upon your perspective, some ageism possibly creeps into these discussions because some would also say that it is the older generation of IT as the "slower" side and the newer millennial generation of IT as being the "faster" and more agile side.

Whether you like the idea or hate it, nonetheless Bimodal IT is making the rounds and a CIO needs to know what it's about. Furthermore, a CIO needs to take some kind of position on the matter because invariably someone will ask them where they stand on Bimodal IT. In some respects, regardless of the specific merits, at least the discussion and debate helps to bring up the overarching point that an IT function often needs to contend with older systems while also contending with building and fielding newer systems. Trying to have those two "sides" of IT be able to work together is crucial, and the CIO and IT leadership team need to figure out how to make sure their IT team works cohesively in doing so.

CHAPTER 12: BIMODAL IT

Bimodal IT is it a savior or scourge? The IT industry has been abuzz about a trending topic known as Bimodal IT and there are some CIO's that think it is the next best thing since sliced bread and are adopting it as though it is the grand savior for IT ilk's, while there are many other CIO's that consider it to be a terrible idea and an appalling approach that is going to reverse years of progress in the evolution of the IT function.

I hope to be able to enlighten you about Bimodal IT and have you make the right choice for your particular organization. Bimodal IT is a term coined by the research group Gartner in 2014 and refers to the notion that CIO's ought to recognize that today's IT function needs to be divided into two halves, thus the "bi" part of the bimodal, and the two halves are referred to as Mode 1 and Mode 2. Mode 1 is considered a form of IT delivery that offers stability, while Mode 2 is considered a form of IT delivery that offers agility.

For Mode 1, notice the use of the word "stability" which some believe is a kind of tricky word game and it actually means "traditional" IT, namely the IT that most companies are used to is the IT function that builds and fields large-scale systems for the enterprise and that does so in a very regimented way. This is typically undertaken on a time scale of many months and years to arrive at the systems that the company needs.

Development is performed via the so-called waterfall model, taking each step from the start of identifying requirements to then design, and then to programming, and then to fielding of the application in a waterfall metaphor manner. This is accompanied by a high level of "ceremony" (an IT term meaning lots of documentation, reviews, and traceability), such efforts are often shaped around reducing costs in a company and are justified based on cutting heads and making operations more efficient.

In contrast, Mode 2 is oriented toward rapidly building new systems that are innovative and help drive revenue for the business. Rather than using a development methodology that is one laborious step at a time, a more agile approach is used that quickly moves from step to step, doing so in a continuous or sometimes considered spiral manner. There is not a lot of planning involved and the level of ceremony is low, presumably keeping the development efforts slim and trim. Some would say that these are projects and systems that are business-centric rather than IT-centric of Mode 1.

Gartner refers to Mode 1 as the marathon runner and that Mode 2 is the sprinter (some say Mode 1 is the business suits or traditional IT, and Mode 2 is the T-shirts or agile IT).

Let's suppose we have an IT function that has the two modes:

Mode 1, traditional IT is considered:
- Conventional systems
- IT-centric
- Long cycle times
- Plan-driven
- High-ceremony
- Waterfall model
- Cost justification focus
- Uses enterprise suppliers
- Stability is key

Mode 2, agile IT is considered:
- New & innovative systems
- Business-centric
- Short cycle times
- Continuous driven
- Low-ceremony
- Agile & spiral models
- Revenue justification focus
- Uses small/new suppliers
- Exploratory is key

CONTROVERSIAL ASPECTS

You might be saying to yourself that so far this all seems to make a lot of sense. Why not put together an IT group that deals with the traditional IT stuff, and have a separate part of the IT group to deal with the newer IT stuff. This seems like specialization and putting your eggs into the right basket for the right kind of job to be done. Let's take a deeper dive.

The perception of the Mode 1 group is pretty much that it is those within IT that are the "old timers" and are relegated to keeping the legacy systems up and running. They are perceived as stodgy, difficult to deal with, are dull and get things down really slowly, and essentially have no future other than to bide out their time until their nearing retirement.

The perception of the Mode 2 group is that they are the uprising millennials that want to punch out new mobile apps and use the cloud and otherwise dazzle the business with the latest in hot technology. They are perceived as eager, smart as a whip, and move fast in terms of generating system after new system. Some would proclaim them as "The" future of IT, meaning that all of IT will eventually be like them and it is just a matter of time until the Mode 1's are replaced and put out to pasture.

Admittedly these perceptions are a bit over-the-top and perhaps in reality a bit more muted, but the point is hopefully clear that the two modes are perceived in vastly different ways. In Figure 1, I provide a handy chart that lists the various key characteristics of Mode 1 and Mode 2, along with the key perceptions about those that are considered Mode 1 type of talent and those that are considered Mode 2 type of talent. I have generally abided by the Gartner characteristics, though with my own poetic license, and also I have added anew the perceptions aspects.

Bimodal IT		Mode 1: Traditional	Mode 2: Agile
CHARACTERISTICS	Systems/Applications	Conventional systems	New & innovative systems
	Culture	IT-Centric	Business-centric
	Cycle Times	Long cycle times	Short cycle times
	Governance	Plan driven	Continuous driven
	Approach	High ceremony	Low ceremony
	Models	Waterfall model	Agile & spiral models
	Value	Cost justification focus	Revenue justification focus
	Sourcing	Uses enterprise suppliers	Uses small/new suppliers
	Talent/Viewpoint	Stability is key	Exploration is key
PERCEIVED AS	What They Work On	Only legacy apps	New/hot apps
	Who They Are	"Old Timers"	Millennials
	How They Are	Stodgy	Eager
	Their Mental State	Dull	Smart
	Pace of their Work	Slow	Fast
	Presumed Future	No Future	The Future

Figure 1: Eliot - Bimodal IT Chart of Characteristics and Perceptions

We are now ready to revisit the question earlier posed as to why would there be any concern or qualms about the Mode 1 and Mode 2 grouping of IT. The major objection is that this cleaves IT into two halves, each of which will most likely resent the other, maybe even hate the other, and will tend toward either undermining the other half or at least not playing well with the other half. This can produce bad outcomes for IT and for the business.

Most of the time, new systems that the business wants to build and field will rely upon the existing legacy systems, doing so for example to obtain transactions data from large-scale ERP systems. Without a cohesive connection and the bounding of new systems and old systems working hand-in-hand, the new system will likely be incomplete and not very useful, and those using the old system will likely find themselves hampered by limits of the old system that could have been overcome by the new systems.

You can imagine that if we have two halves of IT that are fighting each other bitterly, the chances of them coming together to jointly and seamlessly bind together the old systems and new systems is fraught with great difficulty and angst. Put yourself into the shoes of a programmer that has been maintaining the company legacy system for ten years and that has a million lines of code written in an older programming language and sits on older kinds of hardware. The programmer is obviously in the Mode 1 group. Meanwhile, imagine a fresh out-of-college hotshot programmer hired into the Mode 2 group. The hotshot wants to use the latest programming language and tools, and wants to swing for the fence in developing almost overnight a killer app for the firm.

Oil and water. They are probably not going to mix together very well. Furthermore, in terms of pay scales and promotions, the odds are that the Mode 1 group and the Mode 2 group are going to have radically different pay scales and promotion ladders. Mode 1 will eye the Mode 2, which would tend to have higher pay scales and faster promotions, and those Mode 1 team members will be ready to pick-up protest signs and march back-and-forth outside the IT area and scream for better pay and better opportunities.

Think also about recruitment. When hiring someone into the Mode 1 group, the IT job ads will need to emphasize that there is little of anything new about the jobs, else there might be candidates applying that once they come on-board would feel ripped-off. By getting hired into Mode 1, they are pretty much stopping their career growth.

How do you think morale amongst the IT function will fare? Rotten. The Mode 1 team and the Mode 2 team will likely not only avoid working together but they will probably also not associate with each other, whether at the workplace or even outside the workplace. Getting the entire IT department together for a lunch would be like a United Nations get together, reminiscent of the Cold War era and having Russia on one side of the table and the United States on the other side of the table. Two superpowers that are preoccupied with dinging each other.

Unfortunately, this infighting will most likely lead to Mutually Assured Destruction (MAD), the terminology used during the Cold War of the potential impact once the two superpowers might unleash their nuclear arsenal at each other. In the end, they would both destroy each other. The same concern is seen about the Mode 1 and Mode 2 groups, namely that their fighting with each other would so undermine the totality of the IT function that the company would need to take drastic action and probably fire the whole lot (or outsource them all).

The CIO will be continually trying to balance the tension between the resources that need to go toward Mode 1 and Mode 2, and the power struggles will be ongoing. Managers in Mode 1 are naturally hopeful of progressing someday to the top job of IT as CIO. Managers in Mode 2 are equally hopeful of progressing someday to the CIO job. They each will want to make their own mode seem the best and the best performing.

Schizophrenic IT. That's what some critics of Bimodal IT are calling the approach. Another is Bipolar IT (suggestive of the psychosis from being divided into two halves).

OLD WINE IN NEW BOTTLE

Another oft lobbed criticism is that IT functions in companies have always had this same issue of trying to balance the old with the new, and so this Bimodal IT is nothing more than a rebranding of an issue that is already well known and being dealt with every day by IT.

Like the old wine in a new bottle, some CIOs believe that this Bimodal IT is a fancied up way of trying to pretend that there is something incredibly insightful in something that is otherwise pretty much routine. It is viewed as a hype cycle wanting to get IT attention for purposes of gaining consulting toward helping IT departments revamp themselves into Bimodal IT.

Critics of the critics say that they have failed to deal with the balancing of the old and the new, and so this refreshed way of bringing up the topic is at least bringing light to something that has been languishing in the shadows and not yet solved. Yet, Forbes magazine came out and supported those that are criticizing Bimodal IT and said that it is a recipe for disaster. Those CIOs that seek to actually implement Bimodal IT will find themselves creating many more problems than are solved. The CIO might as well sign their own death warrant.

Some would argue that the Bimodal IT is actually a dodge, avoiding the real work of getting an IT function to do both old and new systems work, and do so in a coordinated and cooperative fashion. It is incumbent upon the CIO to make sure that all of IT works together as one cohesive team. They are relegating their duty to do so by simply tossing in the towel and setting up two separate IT groups within a shell called IT. Where is the management acumen that a CIO is supposed to possess, they ask. What else might the CIO do that is being done to avoid actually acting like a true executive and leader? Will the CIO be nothing more than a figurehead and not actually take hold of IT.

TO DO BIMODAL OR NOT

You can choose to either go along with the Bimodal IT approach and adopt it, or reject the Bimodal IT approach and shove it aside. There is also an in-between approach of considering some kind of dual track within IT, trying to do so in a blended manner.

The belief that IT needs to be divided into the Mode 1 and Mode 2 halves is seen by critics as a false dichotomy. The in-between approach seeks to avoid having two distinctly separate IT groups for Mode 1 and Mode 2, and instead have parallel aspects that give career paths for the so-called legacy team onto the new systems, and gets the new systems team onto the legacy systems. There are of course potential difficulties in doing so, and prior solutions such as using back-fill on the legacy systems efforts to help the legacy team branch over to the new systems, along with having special training for the legacy team to get up-to-speed on the latest tools and techniques is also often used.

In fact, rather than Bimodal IT, one might say that there should be Multi-Modal IT, providing multiple avenues within IT and an IT org structure that provides opportunities on several dimensions. Others say that it should be Unimodal IT, offering one overall path and that all of IT funnels into and is supported by the single overarching mode of IT.

You might liken this to a factory whereby we have the factory workers that have long toiled in the factory and feel that they helped to make the company where it is today, coupled with the new workers being brought into the factory and that don't know what came before them.

The claim that the old systems can only be built and maintained by older methodologies and large time cycles is considered another false assumption about the Bimodal IT. Similarly, the claim that new systems can always be built with very fast cycle times and without much attention to planning and ceremony is also a seemingly false assumption.

If Mode 1 is so-called "stability" then does this imply that Mode 2 can create systems that are unstable and error prone? These presumed fallacies in the Bimodal IT argument lead toward undermining the argument's validity and soundness. In the end, time will tell whether CIOs opt to adopt Bimodal IT, and the results thereafter will provide proof (or not) of the pudding.

By and large, most CIOs are not adopting Bimodal IT, and many aren't even particularly familiar with the tenets of what Bimodal IT is, and so the Bimodal IT notion continues to bump along as an idea that is floating in the sea. In the sea there are lots of suggested ways to improve IT, and the Bimodal IT approach is one that has more recently been bobbling along.

Some would say it will hopefully get lost at sea. Others say it is handy to occasionally see it floating along, and serves as a reminder to be ever vigilant in finding a balance between the new and the old of IT, regardless of whether a CIO is actually willing to swallow full gulp the Bimodal IT pill.

There is no doubt that the balancing of the old and new of IT will be perennial issue, and even the newest systems will eventually be considered legacy systems (then to be eclipsed by even newer systems, and so on). Bimodal IT might come and go as a solution, but meanwhile the tension of the old and new in IT will always continue to persist.

CHAPTER 13

SHADOW IT

PREFACE

Most companies have an IT department that provides various IT services to the organization. In some cases, the IT department is on the same level as all other functional departments such as Finance, Human Resources, Marketing, and so on. One of the attractions to those that work in IT is that they provide a service to all other functions of the company, and so you might be working on a system for Finance one day, and the next day be working on one for Marketing, and otherwise have an opportunity to work across the breadth of the company. This is exciting and few other functional areas get the chance to be involved in all aspects of the business.

Sometimes, if the formal IT function is not readily available (or desirable), another functional group might decide that it will launch its own miniature IT department. Let's say that the Finance department opts to put in place its own IT staff. This can be done in conjunction with the formal IT department and be considered as a branch or offshoot of the formal IT team, or it can be done under-the-table and without the explicit awareness of the formal IT group. In cases where the mini-IT is without formal connection to the official IT department, they are often referred to as Shadow IT.

A shadow IT element could be as simple as one person acting in an unofficial IT capacity. Shadows usually start small and then tend to grow over time. Once they grow large enough, their resultant size tends to attract attention and there is usually a head-to-head showdown between the official IT and the budding unofficial IT group. What should CIO's do about a shadow IT group? Should they stop it in its tracks, or should they force it to become part of the official IT department, or maybe try to alienate it and make it into a pariah? We will explore the various approaches and consider the consequences and impacts of dealing with a Shadow IT element.

———————

CHAPTER 13: SHADOW IT

You might be familiar with a famous line from an old-time radio show called The Shadow: "Who knows what evil lurks in the hearts of men? The Shadow knows!" Any sizable company will have its official IT department and will likely have other "shadow IT" groups that often exist on their own and without official sanction by the enterprise. Living in the shadows, these unofficial IT groups are frequently hidden from view.

A local Business Unit (BU) or Line of Business (LOB) might foster its own IT group and account for the costs by burying the spending into their overall BU or LOB budget. This allows the BU's or LOB's secret IT army to void detection by not even labeling their unofficial IT members as IT people. The Operations function might have its own IT team and hide the costs within their spending on warehouses and distribution centers. A Marketing department might create its own IT team and keep them secret by setting aside part of the advertising dollars they are scheduled to spend and put it toward their unofficial IT staff.

Notice that shadow IT is distinguished by its unofficial status. An organization might have lots of official IT people throughout the firm and stationed at outposts of the company, serving as part of an official collective of IT. These official IT people are not considered part of shadow IT. Instead, shadow IT is when there are people in the organization that have taken on an IT role and yet are doing so without being a part of the official IT department.

Note that a typical end-user that happens to do IT types of work and that confers with official IT people would also not usually be considered shadow IT. How does shadow IT arise? Often, a part of the organization will find themselves frustrated by the official IT department's efforts and so decide to take matters into their own hands. If they were instead to try and get the official IT department to changes its ways and be more helpful, the odds are that there would be a huge political battle within the company. The IT department would likely argue that these unofficial IT people should be wrapped into the official IT department. A big stink could result as the tug of war takes place. Desirous of avoiding the politics of such a situation, the rogue part of the organization will opt to start their own unofficial IT group.

Realizing that once they have gone down this path of being "off the reservation" that there is a risk that the official IT department might try to rope them in, these unofficial IT people are purposely hidden from corporate scrutiny by the rogue entity, giving them non-IT titles and sneaking the costs into other non-IT sounding spending buckets. Hopeful of not getting caught, the rogue part of the organization will often start small with their unofficial IT and then if it seems like they are able to get the proverbial one cookie out of the cookie jar (without getting slapped), they might enlarge their unofficial IT efforts.

Besides IT people being in this unofficial IT capacity, the entity might also decide to purchase hardware of its own, buy software, setup a computer network, and otherwise expand toward becoming a real-sized IT group. Thus, the unofficial IT can consist of people, hardware, software, and so on.

A company might have an official IT function and then have one or more of these shadow IT elements. The shadow IT elements can range in size, sometimes being small, sometimes medium sized, and sometimes becoming quite large. They can have arisen completely independently of each other. Or, sometimes, one shadow IT element will form, and then other parts of the organization see that this is feasible to do, and then in a snowball like manner there will be other shadow IT elements formulated.

There have even been circumstances wherein the shadow IT eventually become larger than the official IT, and they banded together to ultimately become their own "official IT" — ultimately swallowing whole the other official IT department. It can be a dog-eat-dog world out there.

Are these shadow IT elements indeed "pirates" and do they need to be stopped? Some CIOs feel very strongly that any shadow IT is bad. Such CIOs ruthlessly seek out and squelch any shadow IT. Meanwhile, there are many non-IT executives and managers that believe equally strongly that shadow IT is a necessity and must be allowed to exist. Let's take a look at the arguments opposing shadow IT and those arguments favoring shadow IT.

THE GOOD AND THE BAD

Those opposing shadow IT emphasize that these rogue IT elements suffer many maladies that are bad for the business. Take a look at Figure 1.

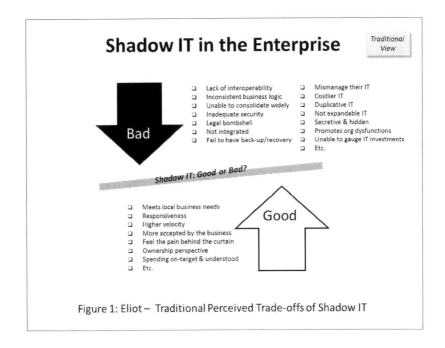

Figure 1: Eliot – Traditional Perceived Trade-offs of Shadow IT

The systems in a shadow IT group are often lacking in interoperability with other systems of the company. This prevents sharing across the enterprise and so data and information often gets trapped within a part of the company. As a result, the larger synergies that could have been had are lost.

Business logic used in a shadow IT system will usually tend to use non-standard ways to account for important metrics of the business. Such inconsistent business logic can confound the ability to have enterprise wide metrics and can also confuse customers that deal with the company and seem to get one answer from one part of the firm and an entirely different answer from another part of the company.

Another concern is the potential security risks of the shadow IT. A shadow IT group might not have the same expertise about systems security that the official IT department has. As such, valuable corporate information might be at high risk of being stolen or compromised.

A shadow IT element might also not be aware of the legal ramifications of IT systems and information. They often will sign contracts with outside computer vendors and not be aware of the pitfalls of the contracts. The official IT department likely works with legal counsel that understands how to negotiate for contracts that best protect the enterprise and does so many such contracts that they know the in's and out's.

Shadow IT typically does not consider aspects of performing regular back-ups. Without doing back-ups, if the unofficial systems get corrupted then the shadow IT will be without the potential for proper recovery. The official IT department usually is quite versed in performing back-ups and regularly does so, along with periodically doing recovery drills to make sure that recovery will be feasible when a disaster hits.

Other criticisms of shadow IT include that it is often mismanaged, it tends to be costlier than the official IT, It is often duplicative of official IT and so in that sense the company as a whole is paying more for its total IT services then it needs to do so (losing out on any economies-of-scale). Shadow IT sometimes is not readily expandable because the manner in which it was formed and developed did not anticipate the need to grow, which then can become limiting for that part of the business and the company as a whole.

Shadow IT often twists and turns trying to keep itself hidden from the rest of the company. This can be bad for the morale of those shadow IT staff since they need to be secretive and avoid sharing with other fellow IT people, and it can lead to overall organizational dysfunction. This dysfunction can occur because one part of the company might resist working collaboratively with other parts of the company because they are trying to hide their shadow IT.

Finally, another concern about shadow IT is that it involves spending on IT that is not fully accounted for in a holistic sense of the company. A company should know how much it is spending on IT. Firms often say that they are spending X dollars on IT and yet if they included the shadow IT spending it would often be much larger. Some estimates suggest that shadow IT often is perhaps 30% or more of the official IT spending. Without top management knowing how much is truly spent on IT, they are not able to effectively ensure that IT spending is being done in an efficient and effective manner.

That's the bad of shadow IT. Why would shadow IT exist if all of those bad aspects are true? Here's some of the reasons why shadow IT exists, taking a look again at Figure 2a. I earlier mentioned herein that shadow IT often develops due to dissatisfaction with the official IT. This dissatisfaction arises in many guises.

One is that a BU or LOB might believe that the official IT does not understand and is not able to satisfy local business needs. Frequently, the official IT is centralized in an organization and a local BU or LOB perceives that those corporate headquarters IT staff are oblivious to the true local needs. It becomes an "us versus them" kind of situation. Of course, this is not limited to just IT, and often a BU or LOB will spawn a shadow HR group, or a shadow marketing group, and other such shadow functions too.

Another reason that shadow IT exists is that the official IT might not be considered sufficiently responsive. Requests by the rogue part of the company are perhaps put on the back-burner by the official IT, and so their IT needs are not adequately dealt with or dealt with on a delayed basis. The BU or LOB is being held accountable to get their job done, but without a responsive IT department they find themselves seemingly having no choice but to start their own shadow IT to make sure they meet their BU or LOB goals.

Even if the official IT is responsive, the official IT might not have the high enough velocity to get things done in the time frame and pace desired by the BU or LOB. Sometimes the official IT works on the basis of months to get things done, while the BU or LOB believes it needs a time scale that is based on weeks and days. Shadow IT is often more readily accepted by the BU or LOB because it is perceived as more on-target and that they are part of that rogue entity. It is the "we want things that are invented here" mindset, which can be valid in some cases, but in other cases only a mantra and not truly of substance.

The management overseeing the shadow IT often tends to take a stronger ownership of the IT elements than they do when IT is provided by an official IT department. This can be partially due to having had a more intimate hand in the IT aspects, and can also be due to having more responsibility to make sure that the IT works. Often the official IT is considered "not their responsibility" and so they do not embrace IT as strongly.

This then covers many of the bad and good aspects of shadow IT. There are other facets that come to play in the trade-offs of shadow IT but hopefully you get the overall notion of the bad and good. Use caution in assuming that these good and bad aspects are true in all cases. These good and bad aspects are generic and for a particular company they may or may not apply. In some instances, I have seen first-hand shadow IT that was very well managed and only suffered from a few of the bad aspects. I have also seen shadow IT that claimed that the official IT was not responsive and yet the official IT was very responsive. There are circumstances where a rogue entity is going to be rogue regardless of any true rationale and will take shots at the official IT but are not backed-up by the true facts of the situation.

SHADOW AWARENESS AND ACTION

Let's assume that the official IT is being led by a CIO or equivalent. Take a look at Figure 2 to see a taxonomy of shadow IT awareness and action recommended for the CIO. There are five categories, consisting of Unaware, Ignores, Cuts Off, Co-Exist, and Wrap-in. Let's explore each of these categories closely.

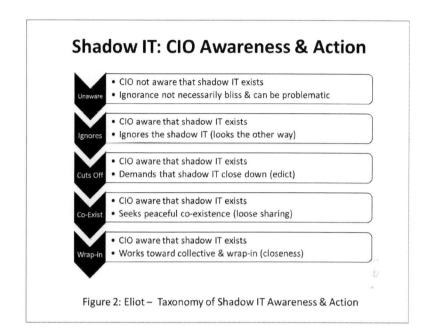

Shadow IT: CIO Awareness & Action

Unaware
- CIO not aware that shadow IT exists
- Ignorance not necessarily bliss & can be problematic

Ignores
- CIO aware that shadow IT exists
- Ignores the shadow IT (looks the other way)

Cuts Off
- CIO aware that shadow IT exists
- Demands that shadow IT close down (edict)

Co-Exist
- CIO aware that shadow IT exists
- Seeks peaceful co-existence (loose sharing)

Wrap-in
- CIO aware that shadow IT exists
- Works toward collective & wrap-in (closeness)

Figure 2: Eliot – Taxonomy of Shadow IT Awareness & Action

Unaware

In some cases, a CIO might be utterly unaware of a shadow IT element. This lack of awareness is usually not good, and means that there are IT efforts afoot that the CIO does not even know are taking place.

A CIO that goes out of their way to work with the rest of the company should ultimately be able to find out about the shadow IT elements. If the CIO does not overtly try to find the shadow IT, that is a sign that the CIO is either not familiar with shadow IT or otherwise does not realize the importance of being aware of shadow IT. Ignorance is not bliss.

Ignores

The next level in the taxonomy is for a CIO that is aware that shadow IT exists, but the CIO chooses to ignore the shadow IT. This act of looking the other way can be at times purposeful. The CIO might be silently planning to someday seek to work with the shadow IT, but has decided that the timing right now is not right for doing so.

If a CIO is ignoring a shadow IT and has no basis for choosing to ignore it, they might be making a mistake in that now that they know that the shadow IT exists, but are not formulating some kind of plan or action about it, in a sense, one might argue that the CIO is not properly exercising their fiduciary duty to the company.

Cuts Off

The next level in the taxonomy is for a CIO that is aware that shadow IT exists, and the CIO then seeks to close down that shadow IT. There are some CIOs that take a very dictatorial approach and jump on the throats of the rogue managers that are undertaking the shadow IT. Though in some companies this edict method might work, often it can backfire and the shadow part of the organization takes shots at the official IT, causing disruption and distraction to the official IT.

Co-Exist

This next level is for a CIO that is aware that shadow IT exists, and the CIO seeks to peacefully craft a co-existence with the shadow IT. A loose sharing of IT people and IT systems is put in place.

This approach usually requires two-to-tango, in the sense that once the CIO extends the olive branch that the management of the rogue entity needs to be willing to meet half-way. If there has been bad blood already between the CIO and that entity, this attempt to co-exist might go awry. Or, it can turn into a Cold War like arrangement whereby both sides eye each other warily.

Wrap-in

This final level involves wrapping shadow IT into the fold of the overall official IT. This sometimes occurs after the co-exist level has taken place for a while. The wrapping in of the unofficial IT people can be good for the unofficial IT people because it can bring them closer to their same "birds of a feather" profession, allowing them to learn from and share with their fellow IT people. Of course, if there has been bad blood already between the two IT factions then the attempt to blend them together can lead to angst and difficulties.

PORTFOLIO OF SHADOW IT

I've heard some CIOs say that shadow IT should be wiped from the face of the earth. They often characterize the shadow IT as a single monolith, failing to recognize that there are different amounts and levels of shadow IT that might exist in an organization. It is seen as on or off. Good or bad. This is a false dichotomy and fails to see shadow IT as multiple instances and each of which has its own goodness and badness. I therefore prefer to think of shadow IT as a portfolio. You might have a shadow IT instance that you are currently unaware of, meanwhile another shadow IT that your purposely ignoring, simultaneously one that your trying to cut-off.

Each of the three shadow IT elements in terms of levels of small, medium, large, should be considered in their own right. For each one, we need to consider into which of the taxonomy levels each fits into currently. For example, suppose that there is a small instance that is unknown to the CIO, suppose there is a medium instance that is being pursued by the CIO to cut it off, and suppose there is a large instance known to the CIO but being ignored. The CIO should be contemplating the future status for each of the shadow IT elements.

The process involved in dealing with shadow IT consist of these four crucial steps:

1. Find Shadow IT
2. Assess the Shadow IT
3. Determine appropriate action about the Shadow IT
4. Perform the appropriate action
5. Continuous loop to Step #1

Here are some aspects about each of the four steps.

Find

The CIO and the business need to find all of the shadow IT in the company. Look across all BU's and all LOB's. Look within the functional departments. Look across all geographies of the firm. It is better to know that it exists than to be caught completely off-guard. Also, looking just one time a year will not be sufficient. You need to routinely be looking for shadow IT, as it will spring up quickly and the best circumstance involves knowing about it sooner rather than later.

Assess

Once they have been identified, assess each shadow IT to ascertain what its status is. Does it pose a danger to the firm? Or is it being run reasonably well? What is the underlying cause or reason for its coming to existence? Is there something about what the official IT is doing that leaves a gap that is being filled by the shadow IT? The assessment should be done without raw emotion coming to play.

Some CIO's are prone to charging forward angrily that anyone dared to seemingly encroach on their turf. This kind of a quick fuse can end-up backfiring on the CIO, since calmer heads might see this as the CIO being unreasonable and galvanize support for the shadow IT.

Determine

The next step involves determining what action to take. Here the taxonomy can be used, and a portfolio should be prepared. Which of the approaches will be best used in dealing with the shadow IT, namely, should you use the Unaware, the Ignores, the Cuts Off, the Co-Exist, or the Wrap-in. Identify what the first approach will be. Plan ahead and anticipate what you want to do as the next approach, and figure out the timing of when it can most likely occur.

Action

The last step involves performing whatever action has been ascertained. The most amount of effort will be undertaken to carry out the Cuts Off, the Co-Exist, and the Wrap-in. Indeed, you should carefully ascertain which of the official IT resources you can spare toward the reigning in of the shadow IT. The effort will involve not only technology aspects, but also involve project aspects and other non-tech considerations. Internal politics and management attention to the action will most likely be key to the successful carrying out of the action.

Continuous Loop

Notice that there is then a loop that takes us back to the first step of finding the shadow IT. This is important because in any sizable organization there will likely be new shadow IT continually being formed. Taking a snapshot at a particular point of time will only be valid for a short period of time.

Organizations are like a forest of living fauna and continually changing. The business needs to be frequently reviewing how it is undertaking its IT in the enterprise, and make sure that the official IT is keeping up with the needs of the firm. Shadow IT is often a barometer that the official IT is not robustly meeting the company needs, since the shadow IT tends to form or even flourish when official IT is inadequate in some manner or another.

We cannot solely blame official IT though. In some companies, the manner of how IT is treated by the top executives and how it is funded will lead to the formation of shadow IT, regardless of what the official IT might do or want to do. Shadow IT often lurks in the shadows. This suggests a kind of evilness, but it can really be just an expression of frustration with the official IT or a failing by business to look at IT comprehensively.

CHAPTER 14

TO WHOM SHOULD THE CIO REPORT

PREFACE

One of the most vexing structural issues facing organizations is where should the IT function be placed. Assuming that there is a CIO heading the IT function, and since that the IT-head title says the word "Chief" in it, one might assume that therefore the IT function should be considered on the same level as the rest of the C-suite and report accordingly to the CEO of the firm. That's an overly simplistic view and by-and-large it is rare that the IT function reports directly to the CEO, and also the title of CIO is not quite as readily conferred as are other C-suite titles such as the CFO title and the COO title.

Specialists in organizational design will tell you that deciding where IT should report is a somewhat difficult matter and that the history of a firm and what it intends to do with IT are key factors in making such a decision. They are right about that. It is a difficult decision. Some in IT would assert that IT should always report to the CEO. How could any modern firm put IT anywhere else, given the importance of IT in the age of digital businesses?

Others would claim that IT is not well suited at the C-suite level. They view IT as subordinated to something else, such as Finance or perhaps Operations. Another complication is the person that heads IT and whether they are a suitable match for wherever IT reports. Some firms have put in place a less-than-CIO caliber person into the CIO role and then discovered "shockingly" that they were mistaken to put in place a CIO. The deck was stacked against success there before they even got it underway. In any case, it is important to understand the trade-offs involved in where the CIO reports and realize that it can be a crucial make-or-break of IT within that firm by that decision alone.

————

CHAPTER 14: TO WHOM THE CIO SHOULD REPORT

An age old question about the IT function involves its placement within an organization. Usually IT is headed by a CIO or equivalent (such as a EVP/SVP/VP of IT), and I will refer to the CIO role when I am discussing the placement of IT in an organization. Sadly, the IT function has been akin to an orphan child that does not seem to have a clearly defined home. Each company tends to use a bit of tradition and magical dust to figure out where to put IT. There are often internal debates about where IT should be placed. Indeed, sometimes IT gets seemingly placed into a "final resting stop" in the organizational structure and then months later it gets moved again.

Having consulted with many companies in a wide range of industries, and having been a sitting CIO, I know well the angst that companies and their executive team have about where to put IT. There are many business functions in addition to IT, and so it is important to realize that there are also debates about where each of the other business functions should reside too. In that sense, it is not just IT that is the only "problem child" in terms of organizational placement. That being said, there does seem to be a greater infusion of ambiguity into the IT placement topic and also it seems that IT tends to bounce around more so than most of the other major business functions.

Let's take a close look at where IT has and might be placed, and consider key insights as to the tradeoffs of both advantages and disadvantages of the placement. Generally, a specific company will need to consider the specifics of their situation to ascertain the "best" choice of where to place IT, but in so doing should consider the facets illuminated in this blog. I say this because the placement of IT is at times done by semi-random means within a firm, and if an organization was asked why they put IT where they did; the answer is often rather slim and lacking in much reasoned logic.

REPORTING RELATIONSHIP

When referring to the placement of the IT function, I will do so by indicating the reporting relationship of the CIO. As the head of the IT function, the CIO represents the official IT resources and capabilities of the firm, and so to whom the CIO reports is effectively where IT reports. By far, the most common reporting position of a CIO is to the CFO (we'll label this as "CIO-CFO"). There are several reasons why the CIO-CFO reporting arrangement is so often used.

First, historically, much of the crux of IT and systems was devoted to keeping track of the financials of the firm. ERP systems were of such newness and importance that firms opted to put IT under the Finance realm. Secondly, many heads of IT were considered "nerds" or techies and so it was viewed that a presumably more polished senior leader such as a CFO should be overseeing ultimately IT. Third, IT is often a substantial part of the internal operating costs of the business and frequently is a big chunk of the capital costs, and so again it was perceived prudent to have Finance watch over IT and manage the costs aspects of IT.

Though this might have been OK in the past, and even though many firms still carry on the tradition of having IT report to Finance, there have been disadvantages that often accrue with this approach. In terms of disadvantages, the IT services and products tend to be preoccupied toward financial-only types of systems. It makes sense that this might happen either overtly or even by happenstance, when you consider that since the CIO reports to the CFO and since all of IT perceives that their destiny is shaped by the Finance Department, they naturally all will focus on financial systems aspects in hopes of gaining favor for advancement. This is the nature of organizational hierarchies. This unfortunately can be damaging to the rest of the firm in that other business functions are essentially starved of IT services and products.

In fact, when shadow IT aspects emerge, involving unofficial unsanctioned pockets of IT, it often is due to the aspect that when IT reports to Finance, and has starved attention of those other business functions, those other business functions take matters into their own hands and start-up their own mini-IT groups. One way to counteract this preoccupation with Finance in a CIO-CFO arrangement is to ensure that the CFO is mindful of the potential for this finance-only kind of blinders. If the CFO is explicitly aware of this potential, and takes explicit action to avoid its pitfalls, there is a chance that the finance-only emphasis can be overcome. But, notice that it takes awareness and also ongoing action by the CFO, and in conjunction with the CIO, in order to mitigate this tendency (i.e., it is not mitigated by simply saying it exists and instead requires direct and ongoing action to overcome).

Another disadvantage of the CIO-CFO arrangement is that IT can be perceived by the company as not particularly strategic in nature. If IT was truly important, the assumption is that IT would report to the CEO, which whether you believe this to be a valid perception or not, it nonetheless often is the perception. In other words, even if the CFO believes that IT is strategic, and even if the CIO believes IT is strategic, if IT sits anywhere other than with the CEO, the rest of the firm is likely to not believe that IT is considered truly strategic since why would it not otherwise be at the highest possible point in the enterprise and be reporting to the CEO.

I realize these above points often rankle a CFO that has IT reporting to them, and I have known CFOs that went out of their way to ensure that IT was readily available and used by the entire firm and that the CFO did everything they could to elevate IT to a strategic stature. Even in those instances, the scuttlebutt amongst the rank-and-file still persisted about my above points. You can shake off the points as just the usual organizational rumor mongering, but it is still something to be considered.

One less oft discussed potential disadvantage of the CIO-CFO reporting relationship is whether the CIO can really blossom when reporting to the CFO. As earlier mentioned, one reason for the CIO-CFO relationship is that the CIO was previously seen as not ready for the big chairs at the top executive suite. Nowadays, there are many that would argue that CIOs today are ready and able to sit at the top. Does putting the CIO under the CFO suppress that capability? Will CIOs never reach their full potential by being underneath a CFO?

In fact, some argue that firms that try to hire a CIO and that are only willing to place the CIO under the CFO are unlikely to get the true world class CIO. The true world class CIO would presumably see this CIO-CFO arrangement as a demotion of placement and a backward step in their career. And so a firm will get only what it can get, namely a CIO willing to be under a CFO. That being said, there are many CIOs that are in a CIO-CFO arrangement and would vehemently disagree that they are somehow not true world class CIOs. They would argue that it is insulting to suggest that simply because they report to the CFO that they aren't able to be world class.

CIO-CEO REPORTING ASPECTS

The next most popular reporting relationship is the case of the CIO reporting to the CEO (labeled herein as CIO-CEO). This is less common than the CIO-CFO, and is also a somewhat more modern tendency and a departure from past tradition. Amongst CIOs, this is usually the most sought kind of reporting relationship, and one that advocates of the CIO role say should be the standard. Presumably, by reporting to the CEO this is a bold statement that IT is vital to the firm and that the CIO will have directly the ear of the topmost executive. This suggests that IT will be considered strategic to the firm. This implies that the CIO will be able to participate in the top executive suite and be elbow-to-elbow with the other top executives. There are disadvantages lobbed at the CIO-CEO reporting relationship.

In terms of disadvantages, some argue that the CEO might become distracted by having the CIO reporting to them, taking their eye away from more strategic aspects. This criticism assumes that IT is not strategic to that particular firm and particular CEO, which maybe is the case or maybe is not the case.

Next, along the same lines of distraction as an issue, the argument is made that the CIO will bother the CEO will bits and bytes. This criticism assumes that the CIO is unaware of which topics to bring to the CEOs attention, which maybe is the case for some CIOs and maybe not the case for others. Furthermore, some argue that the CIO is not business savvy enough to report to the CEO. Though there are certainly CIOs that are not ready for the CEO reporting relationship, making a blanket statement that all CIOs are not ready or that they have not already done so successfully is quite mistaken and naïve. I've had sometimes someone mention a specific instance of a CIO-CEO relationship that went sour as a basis for claiming or suggesting that all CIO-CEO reporting relations are frail and doomed. Again, this is faulty reasoning and a false and misleading argument.

To clarify, are all CIOs ready and apt for the CIO-CEO reporting relationship? No. Is it the case that then no CIOs should ever report to the CEO? No. Are there some CIOs that are a great fit to reporting to a CEO? Yes. Are there some CEOs that would well benefit by having the CIO report to them? Yes.

CIO-COO REPORTING ASPECTS

The next reporting relationship to take a look at is the CIO-COO. Take a look at Figure 4. It is somewhat rarer that a CIO would report to a COO (rarer in comparison to the CIO-CFO and the CIO-CEO reporting relationships). Similar to some of the criticisms of the other reporting relationships, some would say that a CIO reporting to a COO will tend to be focused upon operations-only, and that the IT function will be preoccupied with operations. This might mean for example that the IT for manufacturing and the warehouses is top priority, while IT for finance, HR, and other business functions is starved. Likewise, some would say that this relegates IT to being considered less strategic because it reports to the COO rather than the CEO.

I have seen some companies that are insistent that IT not report to the CEO, and so a political battle brewed between the CFO and the COO in terms of trying to grab up IT. The tug of war led to first the CFO having IT, and then after a while when Ops complained bitterly then the CEO moved IT under the COO. Musical chairs, for sure.

OTHER REPORTING RELATIONSHIPS

Another reporting relationship involves the CIO reporting to the head of Administration, i.e., the CAO. This is rare partially because relatively few companies tend to have a CAO anyway. In cases where there is a CAO, typically the CAO might already have Finance, HR, and other such business functions, in which case, it makes logical sense to put IT in there too. Of course, many of the same concerns as mentioned above are possible, and one might argue that it buries IT. This is contingent on the importance of IT to the particular business.

Yet another reporting relationship involves the CIO reporting to the head of Marketing, i.e., the CMO. This is quite rare. It is a newer notion. It started to arise when the Marketing side of companies began to get a great deal of attention, especially with the rise of digital marketing. Some pundits said that for a company to really exploit digital marketing that IT should report to the CMO.

The usual disadvantages mentioned above are still the case. Namely, IT can become shaped only for Sales and Marketing, and starve the rest of the firm, etc. Another concern sometimes expressed is that the head of Marketing is often a "people person" while the head of IT is more of a "tech person" and so there is an inherent mismatch involved in doing this kind of reporting. The Marketing head has wild ideas, big plans, and wants to turn on a dime, while the CIO needs concrete specifications, lead times, and wants to make sure that systems are safe and secure.

Of course, one might say that this kind of gap would exist regardless of whether the CIO reported to the CMO or not. The difference is that by reporting to the CMO, the CIO is somewhat trapped since their boss is now calling the shots, rather than dealing with the CMO as a colleague. In any case, this CIO-CMO is quite rare and one would need to look at the specific situation to ascertain whether it would make sense or not.

Yet another rarity is the notion of the CIO reporting to the head of HR. I refer to the head of HR as the CHRO, even though few use that acronym now. Nowadays there are lots of various titles for the head of HR, such Chief Talent Officer, but for convenience sake let's use CHRO. Once again, the same concerns as before will apply to the CIO-CHRO reporting relationship. Systems and IT attention goes toward HR only. Other business functions get IT starved. And the chemistry between the head of

HR and the CIO might be amiss.

SPLINTERED APPROACH

So far, we have looked at the CIO reporting to a particular executive such as the CFO, CEO, COO, and so on. Some argue that IT should not report to one area only, and should report to multiple areas. In this case, the notion is to divide up IT and have it report to say the CFO and the CAO and the CMO. This might either be on a matrix approach or might involve actually splitting IT into separate pieces.

Some organizations split their IT by Line of Business (LOB) or by Business Unit (BU), and create a federated model of IT. The notion of splitting by business function is a bit different and quite rare in comparison to splitting by LOB or BU. Also, even in a typical federated model of LOB or BU, IT often still has an overarching centralized IT function.

Criticism of the idea of splitting IT among the business functions is that it can lead to a lack of any single point of responsibility for IT. It can dilute IT, and produce a mishmash of systems. There is less likely any reasonable chance of gaining economies of scale of their IT resources. Some would say it is an absurd extreme. Imagine that IT is divided entirely among all business functions. There is no longer anything particularly called IT per se.

Pundits calling for this structure are claiming that as the millennials eventually become the dominant employee base in companies that they are so tech savvy that no IT entity in a company will be needed. This seems farfetched and omits the aspects of IT that no matter how savvy an employee might be with using technology does not translate into being able to ensure that an organization's IT resources are well selected, maintained, and so on for the entire organization. Maybe this will work magically a hundred years from now. Guess we'll hold our breath and wait and see.

STRATEGIC MATIX OF CEO OR CFO

Let's concentrate for a moment on the CIO-CFO and the CIO-CEO reporting relationships. I pick these two reporting relationships because they are the most prevalent. Figure 1 is a handy matrix about these two reporting relationships. Various research studies have tended to show that when the CIO-CFO relationship occurs that the firm has a Cost-of-IT focus, while when the CIO-CEO relationship occurs that the firm has more of a Strategic IT focus.

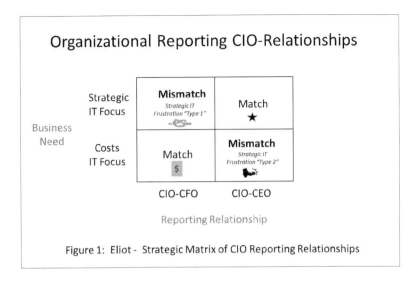

Figure 1: Eliot - Strategic Matrix of CIO Reporting Relationships

One can question whether this is a chicken-and-the-egg kind of reasoning. In other words, a firm that is using the CIO-CFO had a cost focus for IT and therefore overtly chooses the CIO-CFO reporting relationship, or whether a company that opts to do a CIO-CFO reporting relationship will be driven toward a Costs-of-IT focus. We won't fight that one for the moment. Instead, take a look at Figure 10 to see how this plays out.

If a firm has a Costs-of-IT focus, and if they are using a CIO-CFO reporting relationship, it probably would work out well since the CIO-CFO pairing tends to have that kind of mindset and direction. I label this quadrant as a match, and use a dollar symbol to indicate that the match emphasizes the focus on costs.

If a firm has a Strategic IT focus, and if they are using a CIO-CEO reporting relationship, it probably would work out well since the CIO-CEO pairing tends to have this kind of strategic mindset and direction. I label this quadrant as a match, and use a star to indicate that it is considered by many to be the best kind of reporting relationship for modern day firms that rely so significantly on IT.

We then have two quadrants of potential mismatches. For a firm that has a Strategic IT focus and has a CIO-CFO reporting relationship, this is potentially a mismatch and the creation and use of IT will likely not achieve the strategic level of attention and success. I call this a "Strategic IT Frustration" and label it as a Type 1. Firms that cannot figure out why their IT is not being strategically deployed will often fall into this Type 1 category. They would need to relook at whether the CIO-CFO reporting relationship is the right one for their circumstance, or whether it is holding back IT from being strategically positioned.

For a firm that has a Costs-of-IT focus and has a CIO-CEO reporting relationship, this is potentially a mismatch too. If the firm is mainly concerned about keeping IT costs down, it might not be willing to invest in IT appropriately and might also be so risk adverse that it won't take chances on innovative IT.

This will be again of a Strategic IT Frustration nature, and I call it Type 2. Here, the CEO and CIO can potentially overcome this frustration since they are likely to have the willpower and clout to do so, but they need to first be aware of the mismatch in that case. I have seen CIO's that got booted out of their job because the CEO was frustrated by the CIOs preoccupation with costs, and maybe that CIO would have been better served in a CIO-CFO relationship.

CEO AND CIO COMPATIBILITY MATRIX

Given that there is a desire by the CIO community to drive towards the vaunted CIO-CEO reporting relationship, I have put together an easy to understand CIO-CEO Compatibility Index that I have used from time-to-time. Take a look at Figure 2. There are of course maybe parameters that might be considered in the CIO-CEO relationship. To make things easy, I have boiled it down into four major characteristics.

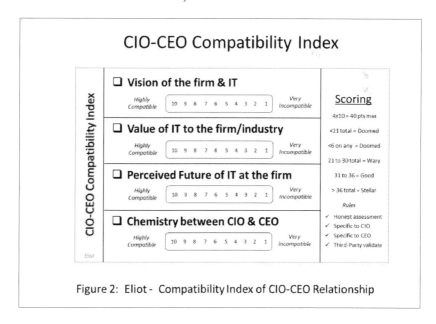

Figure 2: Eliot - Compatibility Index of CIO-CEO Relationship

Vision of the Firm and IT

Using a scale that ranges from 10 (highly compatible) to 1 (very incompatible), I rate the CIO and the CEO as to whether they see eye-to-eye on the overall vision of the firm and also their vision of IT's purpose and role in the firm. If the score is less than 6, I would say that things are likely doomed for the company in terms of IT and its use at the firm. I use a color coding scheme to help illustrate the nature of the numeric coding.

Value of IT to the Firm/Industry

Using again the 10 point scale, I rate the CIO and the CEO on their compatibility by their views on the value of IT to the firm and to their industry.

Perceived Future of IT at the Firm

This 10 point scale rates the CIO and CEO on their perception of how IT will be treated and used in the future at the firm. This is important because even if the IT is coming along well now, if they have differing views of the future of IT at the firm it will eventually and inextricably lead to problems.

Chemistry between the CIO & CEO

Some might say that this characteristic of compatibility is the most important of them all. Even if the other three parameters are good, if the chemistry between the CIO and the CEO is bad then the odds are that nothing else will turn out well. The two will be at logger heads. Chemistry between the CIO & CEO needs to be sufficient throughout. I could have weighted each of the four parameters and given this one a higher weighting, but for sake of simplicity I am treating all four parameters of equal weight.

If the total score is less than 21 then it is a pretty solid bet that the CIO-CEO relationship is doomed, and so IT at the firm is somewhat doomed too. If any score on each of the parameters is less than 6, the same doom can be expected. I would rate the circumstance as "wary" of a total Index score that is in the 21 to 30 range, while in the 31 to 36 it is rated good, and above 36 is stellar.

A doom score would likely mean that a radical change is needed, normally involving the CIO being let go (since the CEO is less likely to be the one let go). For a wary score, there is a chance of improving things, especially if the low scores are not on the chemistry parameter. With some work, the CIO and CEO can hopefully get on the same page about the vision aspects, the value aspects, and the perceived future aspects. Getting them aligned from a chemistry perspective is often harder. Usually this involves an HR intervention.

For a good or stellar score, this is a great sign for IT at the firm. Periodically, a re-scoring should occur, since over time there is a chance of wandering afield on each of the four parameters. Doing the re-scoring can be a helpful reminder of the big topics that the CIO and CEO need to be aligned on.

One of the reasons that there are concerns about having the CIO not report to the CEO is that there can be gaps in communication about the IT aspects of the firm with respect to what the CEO wants or knows about it. Let's take a look at the various reporting relationship chains.

For example:

- Gap 0: CEO has CIO as direct report

- Gap 1 level: CEO has CFO that has CIO

- Gap 1 level: CEO has COO that has CIO

- Gap 2 levels: CEO has COO has CFO that has CIO

A gap 0 is used to indicate the CIO-CEO reporting relationship. As an aside, there can still be a communications gap even when the CIO reports directly to the CEO, but that is more a factor of how the CIO and the CEO interact with each other. If they interact well then there is no gap. If they are not able to interact well with each other, this is something that can be potentially improved upon. The point being that there is not an intermediary sitting between the CIO and the CEO. Presumably, the CIO has direct and unabated access to the CEO.

A gap of 1 level is usually the case when the CIO reports to the CFO. This means that whatever the CEO has to say about IT, or whatever the CIO has to say about IT, will be funneled between them via the CFO. This can lead to garbled communication. The CFO might misinterpret the CEO and relay a misinterpretation to the CIO. Likewise, the CFO might misinterpret the CIO and relay this misinterpretation to the CEO. It is like the telephone game wherein one person whispers something into one person's ear, who then tells it the next, and what comes out on the other side is sometimes dramatically different than where things started.

A gap of 2 level is even more pronounced. This can happen when say the CFO reports to the COO and whom reports to the CEO. In this case, the CIO-CFO reporting relationship puts the CIO and the CEO at an even larger gap. The reporting relationship chain is a very important element of the CIO reporting aspects and should be carefully examined in any organization. Though I have above characterized the communication chain gap as an adverse aspect, some argue that it can be actually a blessing in disguise. They are suggesting that it is like having someone that speaks German (let's say the CEO), and someone that speaks French (let's say the CIO), and so having an intermediary such as the CFO or COO to translate between them is essential.

This usually again makes the assumption that the CIO will be only comfortable with bits and bytes, and so there needs to be a translator that takes the CEOs business utterances and translates them to what the CIO can comprehend. This makes sense if the type of CIO in-hand is a bits and bytes kind of CIO, but otherwise for most of the modern CIOs it is a miscasting of the modern CIO.

BEST REPORTING RELATIONSHP

I am often asked which is the best reporting relationship for a CIO – is it the CIO-CEO, CIO-CFO, CIO-COO, or any of the other combinations. In theory, given the importance of technology and IT to modern day organizations, the CIO-CEO should be the norm, but, this is balanced by the circumstances of a particular firm and a particular CIO and a particular CEO.

Some CEOs are not ready for the CIO-CEO relationship. Some CIOs are not ready for the CIO-CEO relationship. Trying to force fit a CIO-CEO relationship in a situation where it won't fit is likely to undermine IT, undermine the CEO, undermine the CIO, and undermine the business. For some firms, the CIO-CFO is the best fit. For some firms the CIO-COO is the best fit.

A catch-all statement about the specific best fit is overreaching. It is prudent to consider the trade-offs described in today's blog, and then look at a particular company to gauge what makes most sense for that company. That being said, it is worthwhile to do re-looks from time-to-time because organizations are changing entities and so over time the best fit can shift depending upon how the company is changing

CHAPTER 15
INTERIM TEMP CIO

PREFACE

Turnover at the C-suite can be higher than you might at first assume. In an earlier era, the C-suite tended to consist of long-time devoted employees that gradually worked their way up the ladder into the executive stratosphere. Those days are pretty much gone. Today, there is nearly a revolving door in comparison and firms tend to bring in whomever they think is the "best gun" to serve on the C-suite team. Boards have little tolerance for executives that aren't cutting the mustard. Plus the ease of sharing information about what executives are doing has heightened their external visibility and added to potential pressure on moving out an executive for something they did do (and should not have), or did not do (and should have done).

Most CIO's lament the relatively job-threatening turnover rate they face, which by some surveys say that a CIO will only get a runway of about 2-3 years in their spot before moving along. This can be a good sign in that it might mean that the CIO is getting a chance to move up to a larger firm or larger CIO role elsewhere. It can also be a bad sign in that it could mean that firms have little patient for CIO's and unrealistic expectations that knocks a CIO out of the box just by the time they have settled in (this, unfortunately, seems to be more of the case than the rosier scenario).

Notably, other functional areas like CFO's apparently face similar turnover rates. When I mention this aspect, many CIO's are surprised because they thought it was just the CIO profession that gets the bums rush. Not so. Everyone should be looking over their shoulder. When the

CIO position is vacant, some firms will leave the slot open until filled, but this can have adverse consequences due to having no definitive leadership for IT or having a muddled sense of leadership. As a result, there is a rather robust market for interim CIO's. The interim CIO comes in, takes the reins, and will either continue until the position is filled or possibly become the CIO after the firm has kicked the tires on their candidacy. There are important aspects explored next about picking interim CIO's, along with some handy insights about what to do if you become an interim CIO.

CHAPTER 15: INTERIM TEMP CIO

I am often asked about the increasing use of so-called "temp" CIOs for companies that want to quickly shore-up a Chief Information Officer (CIO) vacancy that they have. Having been both a temp CIO and a perm CIO, I can vouch for the business value in making use of a contingent CIO when an enterprise has the need to do so. In the CIO community, some refer to a temp CIO as a contract CIO, or a consulting CIO, or even sometimes a hired gun CIO.

There is also the use of the word "interim" too, which can be confusing because a firm will occasionally appoint an internal interim CIO, which is considered different than a firm bringing in an external CIO that serves in the interim CIO status. Wanting to avoid getting mired in the wording of this role, I will go ahead and use the formal phrase "interim temp" CIO to refer to an externally provided CIO that sits as the interim CIO in an enterprise on a temporary basis. I will also shorten it at times and just say more informally "temp CIO" and trust that you will know that I mean the same thing as "interim temp" CIO.

That being said, firms will often bring in an interim temp CIO that they want to not only shore-up IT, but also be a potential candidate for the perm CIO role. It is handy for a firm to get a chance to see the temp CIO in action and then be able to judge whether they are the right fit for the firm. When trying to hire a perm CIO, it can be daunting trying to assess after just a few interviews whether the candidate is a good fit. In contrast, by having a temp CIO for say several weeks or even months, the firm gets a close look and can make a more reasoned decision whether to keep that temp CIO or seek someone else for the perm CIO role.

Why wouldn't the temp CIO automatically become the perm CIO? I get asked this quite a bit. There are several sensible reasons. First, the temp CIO might only want temporary CIO positions and prefers to go from firm to firm, kind of a traveling gun, if you will. Second, the temp CIO might live in Topeka and have taken the temp position in Calabasas, and was willing to do so on a temporary basis but did not have in mind to do so permanently. It is important therefore that if the business is considering the temp CIO as a candidate for a perm CIO that upfront there be discussions about whether this is something the temp CIO also has in mind.

Another reason that the temp CIO might not become the perm CIO is that firm could realize during the tenure of the temp CIO that the type of CIO they want on a long-term basis has different characteristics than the facets needed in the short-term. For example, some CIO's are especially good at turning around a sinking ship IT group, but once the ship is righted, they aren't as adept at keeping it on a steady even keel. So, a firm that brings in the save-the-ship CIO would likely realize soon that the person is probably not as well suited for the long-term steady state running of IT.

Please be thinking ahead when you seek out a temp CIO. It is perfectly fine to focus on and be insistent that it is merely an interim and temporary situation, if that's what makes the most sense for your firm.

CIO VACANCIES

Under what circumstances might a firm seek to make use of a temp CIO? I show in Figure 1 the typical vacancy circumstances that I have encountered.

CIO Vacancies: Circumstances of the Vacancy

Reason for a CIO Vacancy	Key Points
CIO was let go	• Prior CIO was not a good fit & let go • Firms grapple finding right CIO
CIO left the firm	• CIO's are in hot demand • Often lured to leave
Never had a CIO	• Considering establishing CIO role • Experiment to see if CIO is good for firm
Tried an exec as substitute CIO	• Appointed a non-CIO to CIO role • Did double-duty & now over-extended
Existing head of IT needs help	• Have a head of IT struggling as a leader • Want to provide coach re: seasoned CIO
Tried IT managers as "oligarchy"	• Firm opted to avoid having a CIO • Assumed IT can self-manage by itself
Thinking about upgrading to a CIO	• Have had a Director of IT as head • Aiming to elevate position to CIO role

Figure 1: Eliot – Typical circumstances underlying CIO vacancies

The most obvious vacancy circumstance is when the CIO has been let go. This can happen for numerous reasons, and does not necessarily imply that the prior CIO messed-up or was somehow not adept as a CIO. Firms change and grow over time, and the type of CIO they need will change over time too. Often, when a new CEO comes into a firm, there are lots of changes made at the CXO executive level, and it is natural that the CEO would want to put in place a CIO of a different nature than was there beforehand. Notably, the fit between the CEO and the CIO is crucial, and it might be that the fit between the former CEO and the existing CIO was great, but now the fit between the new CEO and the existing CIO is not a matching one.

Another relatively obvious vacancy circumstance is when a sitting CIO chooses to leave a firm. Again, this is not necessarily a bad sign and can be that the CIO got lured elsewhere, perhaps being offered a step upward in their career. If your firm is a $1B sized firm and the CIO gets an offer to be the CIO at a $10B firm, it is quite sensible for the CIO to move along.

In the situations where the CIO was summarily booted out or left under a cloud, it is a good idea to very quickly bring in a temp CIO and not allow whatever ill will exists to simmer and soak. Firms tend to discover that when things have gone badly with the prior CIO that the IT function can get twisted out of shape and become highly dysfunctional. I will describe in a few moments the kinds of maladies that can arise during the vacancy period.

Besides the obvious vacancy circumstances involving a CIO that was let go or that left on their own, there are several other more nuanced circumstances. Again, refer to Figure 1. Some firms that have never had a CIO are curious about whether having one will be of benefit to their company. This is another case where having a temp CIO would be handy. Kick the tires and see what having a CIO is like.

Another instance involves cases whereby a firm had a CIO vacancy and had opted to ask a non-CIO executive to step into the role. Perhaps the COO is someone that is savvy with IT or the CMO is a big proponent of IT, and so the firm puts one of them into the CIO role on an interim basis. This usually does not work out, unfortunately. The non-CIO tends to not know enough about IT to adequately perform in the CIO role, and decisions are made about IT that the firm comes to regret. Furthermore, the substitute CIO finds themselves doing double-duty, usually having both their existing role and the CIO role, but they soon discover this is over-extending and they get burned out. When this substitution happens, the organization eventually realizes that they need to get a temp CIO and that the vacancy probably should have been filled with a genuine CIO to start with.

One rarer circumstance of a "vacancy" can involve the situation where there is an existing head of IT, maybe holding a title somewhat lesser than the CIO title, and that is not quite ready for the CIO role, but that the firm wants to ultimately move them into the CIO role. In this case, a firm will make use of a temp CIO to serve as a coach or mentor for the budding CIO. For the firm, this is handy because they don't want to let go of the head of IT and are faithfully trying to figure out how to keep them. The firm does not want to hire a perm CIO since it would crush the hopes perhaps of the existing head of IT. Thus, the temp CIO serves as a non-threatening elbow-to-elbow partner with the head of IT and can be a convenient means to keep and uplift the existing head of IT.

One of the strangest circumstances of a CIO vacancy involves the use of existing IT managers in an oligarchy kind of arrangement. I am sure you are asking, what is that? I have seen firms that decided they would not replace a CIO and instead they asked the existing direct reports to the CIO to take over the reins of IT. In other words, let's say there are three direct reports to the CIO and now all three are supposed to work together as one, doing so in absence of the CIO. Not a good idea.

If you look closely at those direct reports, I am betting you will see that they each have different views of how to run IT. Furthermore, they might perceive that one of them will become the CIO and so they might be purposely trying to outshine each other. Anyway, trying to get them to entirely agree on a direction for IT that brings them in unison is nearly impossible on their own. And, they likely might not yet individually have the seasoning to be a CIO, and so you are going to have more junior-like CIO's do arm wrestling with each other over aspects that they probably don't know and that they cannot agree on. I vote for a temp CIO in that circumstance.

Finally, another vacancy can occur when a firm has a head of IT that the executives do not believe is likely suitable for the CIO role, maybe a Director of IT that has been with the firm for many years, but now the firm has grown and the person is stuck in their old fashioned techie ways. Providing a coach or mentor by a temp CIO is not especially considered valued because the thinking is that the head of IT is not the stuff of a true CIO. The firm is thinking about creating a new CIO position, and wants to fill it to signal to the existing Director of IT that they are not a viable candidate for the role.

Given that it could take a while to find the perm CIO, the odds are that the existing head of IT might begin to falter or feel that they just don't see much need to keep doing things because they are so disappointed about that perm CIO opening that they are not being considered for.Getting in a temp CIO quickly would be wise.

CIO VACANCY BREWS PROBLEMS

I mentioned earlier in this blog that there can be maladies that appear during the time of a CIO vacancy. The world does not sit still, and when there is no CIO the rest of the business wants to regardless continue moving forward. IT and the business can readily get jammed up. Take a look at Figure 2.

IT/Business Problems During CIO Vacancy

Troubles While CIO Vacant	Explanation
Key IT projects stall	• No full IT leadership without CIO • IT projects slow down or freeze
Needed new systems delayed	• Proposals for new apps sit & wait • Confusion about IT approvals
Legacy apps further decay	• Legacy maintenance at minimum • Unsure of investment worthwhile
IT strategic plans waylaid	• Lack of IT strategic executive view • Bump along with existing systems
IT team members jump ship	• IT specialists worried about future • Exit to a stable place elsewhere
IT/Business relationships sour	• Business users upset at IT jam up • Shadow IT starts to emerge
Competitor IT moves ahead	• Competition IT striving forward • Firm without CIO falling behind

Figure 2: Eliot – Typical problems that emerge during CIO vacancies

Here's what I usually see happen after the CIO vacancy lasts for a bit (even occurring in just days and a few weeks). Key IT projects get stalled, since nobody is providing direction from the top of IT. The existing IT project managers are worried that without top approval they will get burned once a CIO finally gets in place (the new CIO might criticize decisions they made, right or wrong).

There is no CIO at the executive level to help shepherd the projects. And so on. Needed new systems sit in the queue, awaiting the arrival of the new CIO. Who wants to green light a six figure project without knowing that the CIO blessed it? And the entire IT approval process gets messed-up without someone that can see the big picture and know whether the budget can accommodate the new initiatives. Etc.

Legacy apps will likely further decay. Should investments in older IT systems upkeep continue or not? Furthermore, any IT strategic plans and discussions will probably be for not, since the existing IT staff might not either know the overall vision of the firm or even know how to forge it into the IT systems.

Most importantly from an HR perspective, the vacancy of the CIO will tend to scare the existing IT team members. Will the new CIO keep them or dump them? Given how hot the market is for IT specialists, they will likely look around in hopes of finding a more stable place to work. Meanwhile, during all of the above, relationships with the business side and the IT side will sour (and were probably already souring).

This usually then leads to the business groups starting their own informal and unofficial IT shadow teams. The longer this occurs, the more that there will be of a mess of disparate systems and probably gapping security holes.

Finally, while the maladies of the vacancy are occurring, you can pretty much assume that your competition is moving ahead at breakneck speed on their own IT advances. Your firm will have not only have not progressed, but your firm is digging itself a bigger and bigger hole with each passing day.

WHAT AN INTERIM CIO DOES

I have put together a list of the typical actions and efforts that a temp CIO will do.

Take a look at Figure 3.

This list is handy not only for the executive team to be aware of, in terms of what a temp CIO can or should do, I have also found it handy for my fellow perm CIOs that want to be temp CIO, since they are often not quite sure of what a temp CIO is supposed to do.

Interim *Temp* CIO: What They Get Done

Goals for Interim Temp CIO	What This Accomplishes
Keep the lights on	• Makes sure IT is running right • Systems up & available
Plug any leaks	• Scours for any security issues • Ensures firm IT protected
Move ahead on IT projects	• Shift from neutral to drive • Gets stalled IT projects going
Tee up or launch new initiatives	• Gives IT/Business proposals air • Setup to start or move ahead
Collaborate with top execs	• Confers with top leadership • Finds out what is needed by IT
Partner with the business	• Meets with business managers • Repairs any soured relationships
Calm the IT team	• Reassures the IT team • Prevents further stampede out
Setup transition to Perm CIO	• Aids firm in clarifying CIO role • Stage set for perm onboarding

Figure 3: Eliot – Interim *Temp* CIO and what they do

Of course, each vacancy of a CIO position will require a careful assessment to properly come up with a list specific to the needs of that particular firm at a particular point in time. Nonetheless, my starter list will be helpful to you when you are considering what the temp CIO is to do.

First and foremost, keep the lights on. This might seem obvious, but I have stepped into IT functions that were barely running IT even at the most fundamental of levels when I first came in the door. Systems were error prone. Downtime was through the roof. Equipment was getting lost. Had the top executives realized how the sausages were being made, they would have been aghast. A firm usually assumes or takes for granted that IT will be running right, and so the temp CIO needs to quickly take a look under-the-hood and then make any tweaks needed to ensure that the engine is running smoothly.

Second, plug any leaks. I am referring mainly to security related leakage. How secure are the networks? The data? The systems? During a CIO vacancy, there can be a tendency to take an eye off the security protections that should be in place. There are other leaks too. For example, I came in and immediately noticed that one firm was paying an exorbitant amount to a vendor for software licenses that the firm wasn't even using at all. Money was leaking out the door in droves. Put a stop to that.

For IT projects, the temp CIO can help get those going again. Plus, tee up for new initiatives. Importantly, the CIO should have the kind of bedside manner and business acumen that they can collaborate with the top executives. During the vacancy period, the odds are that the top executives have had various desires for IT to do this or that, but have not readily had anyone that could understand and nor translate those wishes into reality. That's the temp CIO.

Likewise, the temp CIO should partner with the business. Remember those shadow IT groups that might have formed due to the vacancy maladies, well, now the temp CIO should get in there and find ways to bring them back into the official IT fold. Doing so with aplomb. The temp CIO must make sure that the IT team feels reassured and that the IT group is in good hands. By being a calming influence, the rush to the exit should diminish.

Finally, the temp CIO is going to be a great boon to the later on perm CIO by being able to get a transition ready for the perm CIO. Knowing the in and outs of the IT at the firm, the temp CIO can reduce the onboarding time for the perm CIO and make sure that there is no interruption between the shift from the temp to the perm. As mentioned, there are other facets of IT that the temp CIO might be called upon to help with. Overall, the list provides a rather popular set of tasks for attention.

RISING USE OF THE INTERIM CIO

Firms are realizing that having a temp CIO is important. We have seen that the longer the vacancy period of a CIO being missing-in-action can lead to quite a number of problems and issues. The rapid speed and low risk of getting a temp CIO makes this quite an attractive option for firms to then minimize the vacancy period and reduce the eruption of systems and IT maladies.

The turnover rate of CIOs continues to be relatively high, and so the need to shore-up IT during the transition to a perm CIO is equally increasing. Many executives don't even realize that a temp CIO is a possibility. They mistakenly assume that their business and their systems are so specialized that it would not be viable to bring in a temp CIO. They falsely believe that the temp CIO would need months of reviewing their IT to become active and helpful. The reality is that a good temp CIO can be up and running within days. Consider the temp CIO option and give it serious due. Might just make the difference between your IT faltering when those occasional vacancies of the CIO occur.

CHAPTER 16

SOCIAL INTELLIGENCE AND THE CIO

PREFACE

For many years, CIO's have been branded as socially inept. This has been attributed to their presumed preoccupation with technology. They are a techie more so than a business person. They enjoy the interaction with machines more than they do with humans. They are the type of person that wears the propeller hat.

Admittedly, there are CIO's that fit this description. Unfortunately, it helps to perpetuate the view of "all" CIO's as lacking in social intelligence. There are many IT industry efforts that have been trying to ready the next generation of CIO's so that they are not socially inept or otherwise ill-prepared in being socially adroit. The CIO version 2.0, if you will.

What does it mean to be a socially adroit CIO? I explore next the characteristics of social intelligence and see how that fits to the CIO role. If you are an existing CIO, do a selfie and see how you are doing in terms of being socially intelligent. If you are an aspiring CIO, try to make sure that you don't repeat the mistakes of the past and become or be seen as the CIO without social intelligence.

———

CHAPTER 16: SOCIAL INTELLIGENCE AND THE CIO

Socially intelligent CIOs. Some sarcastic critics would claim this is an oxymoron like saying jumbo shrimp. They assert that CIOs are inept at social intelligence. A recent survey by Deloitte of over 1,200 respondents that were asked about CIO's and their social intelligence capabilities revealed that there is a perceived dearth of socially intelligent qualities in today's CIOs (http://deloitte.wsj.com/cio/2016/06/22/social-intelligence-a-hallmark-of-cio-success/).

Admittedly, the perceived and actual failings of being proficient in social intelligence has been an ongoing issue for CIOs and there are persistent suggestions that CIOs are unable to climb further up the executive ladder due to their lack of social intelligence skills. In one sense, their focus on technology and technological aspects is somewhat at odds with being socially adroit too. Whether the type of person attracted to technology is low on social skills to begin with, or whether once one gets into technology that social skills tend to fall by the wayside, either way it has been a long time tradition that has been the butt of many a joke at the expense of the future of CIOs.

Many IT functions and likewise many academic institutions that are producing the next generation of IT leaders are trying to turn around this social intelligence weakness. Curriculum focused on so-called soft skills is now being targeted at future CIOs. One way or another, it is hoped that future generations of CIOs will not be deficient in social intelligence and then will change to the perception of CIOs as not being socially proficient. It is hoped that CIOs can have their cake and eat it too, namely be top notch in both technology and also be top notch in their social intelligence.

What does it means to say that someone has social intelligence? Generally, social intelligence consists of being proficient at social relationships, being aware of and acting on social beliefs and attitudes, exhibiting self-awareness and self-management, and otherwise being able to seamlessly navigate social ecosystems.

There has been extensive foundational research undertaken on social intelligence. A popular offshoot of social intelligence is the now famous Emotional Quotient (EQ) which has to do with being able to sense the emotions of others. Some place EQ and Emotional Intelligence under the umbrella of Social Intelligence, asserting that it is a subset of Social Intelligence. Others say that Emotional Intelligence is distinct from Social Intelligence.

Biological studies claim that social intelligence and emotional intelligence are tied closely to the neurons of the brain and that early development of human brains evolved and expanded in size due to the need to interact socially with each other over time. For a review of social intelligence and the biology of leadership, see for example this URL http://www8.gsb.columbia.edu/rtfiles/psi/Goleman_et_al_SocInt_BioLea dership.pdf. I am going to avoid this somewhat arcane debate about the differences or similarities of Social Intelligence versus Emotional

Intelligence and focus directly on what I consider the broader notion of social intelligence and how it relates to CIOs.

Social intelligence in the workplace is a key for success as a CIO. As an executive and top leader, the CIO is called upon to represent IT and interact socially with fellow executives, board members, shareholders, business users, vendors, and a slew of other stakeholders inside and outside the enterprise. Without the requisite social skills, a CIO will not get very far, no matter how good the technology might be that they are seeking to deploy.

The world of the CIO is a continuous and unrelenting social ecosystem involving influencing, negotiating, gaining allies, forging support, and the like. Social missteps can quickly undermine the best of IT and lead to attacks by executive colleagues and others.

I recall one strategic steering committee meeting where the CIO openly criticized the COO, catching the fellow exec off-guard, and for which the CIO was not even cognizant of what he had done, and subsequently the COO worked tirelessly behind-the-scenes to get the CIO booted from the firm. The CIO never knew what had hit him. His lack of social intelligence was so profound that it did not even occur to him that he had gotten canned for a socially incompetent reason.

Indeed, some CIOs are like a hiker in the woods that does not know how to read the signs of nature in the forest. Which plants are edible and which are poisonous? Where do predators tend to live and stalk their prey? Just like a hiker that wanders through a forest without realizing the dangers that are all around them, some CIOs wander the halls of the enterprise and are equally lacking a suitable social compass and social awareness of what surrounds them.

SOCIAL INTELLIGENCE ASPECTS

As mentioned earlier, there are some that suggest that CIOs are without any social intelligence. Let's imagine a Venn diagram that might depict the realm of Social Intelligence (SI) and the realm of Chief Information Officers (CIOs). If we had a circle embodying SI, and another circle embodying CIO's, there are some that would say that the two circles do not intersect. This would imply that: (1) No CIO's are SI, and (2) All CIO's are not SI. This implies that no CIOs have Social Intelligence. In other words, all CIOs are without any Social Intelligence.

I think that anyone of a reasonable nature would likely agree that this is a rather wild claim that there aren't any CIOs that have Social Intelligence. It is an easy kind of off-the-cuff claim to make, and will certainly get smirks by executives that have endured CIOs that were lacking in social intelligence. But, it is an extreme position that is without merit. All it would take is for even one CIO to exhibit social intelligence and thus disprove the claim that no CIOs are SI. If you take a look at the top 100 ranked CIOs, you would find that many of them are quite proficient in SI.

I believe anyone reasonable would agree that there is an intersection between the SI realm and the CIOs realm. There are some CIOs that are SI. Not all CIOs are not SI. When I say this, there will immediately be someone that yells out that they know for sure a CIO that is definitely lacking in social intelligence, and thus this seems to undermine my Venn diagram. Well, finding instances of CIOs that are lacking in SI does not undermine the Venn diagram. Clearly, there are some CIOs that are not SI, and not all CIOs are SI.

The larger question is more about how big is the intersection and how big is the remainder of the CIOs that are not SI. It is hard to measure this and the reported numbers are all over the map. Some say that maybe 10% or less of CIOs are SI, and we would then assume that 90% are not SI. Some say it is much lower like 1% are SI (implying 99% are not SI), while others say it is much higher like 50% are SI (implying that half of all CIOs are SI, and half are not SI).

Let's just agree that there are CIOs that are SI, and not all CIOs are SI, and that there are CIOs that are not SI, and that not all CIOs are not SI.

We can move on from there. One implicit assumption about saying that a CIO is SI involves the notion that one is either SI or not. In other words, like an on/off kind of circumstance, you are either someone that is socially intelligent or you are not. This harsh distinction of suggesting that you can only be in one of two states, either socially intelligent or not socially intelligent, provides a naïve view of social intelligence. It would be equivalent to saying that one is either intelligent or not intelligent, and yet I would assert that we in our daily lives encounter some people that seem to have a semblance of intelligence or smarts, and others that seem to have an abundance of intelligence, and some that seem to be pretty low on the IQ scale.

The same kind of gradation for social intelligence is applicable. It is likely that an S-curve could be used to illustrate increasing levels of social intelligence. For ease of discussion, let's divide the social intelligence realm into three levels, namely low, medium, and high. CIOs that are low in social intelligence are the ones that seem to dominate the perception of CIOs. Those in the medium and the high camps often need to fight the perception that they are lacking in social intelligence.

At times, the perception of being low in social intelligence can actually be used in favor of a CIO. In some companies, when a CIO first joins the firm, the perception might be that the CIO is going to be low in social intelligence. If the CIO is actually medium or high, they can exceed the expectations and appear to be of a miraculous nature in that they socially "get it" when the assumption was that they would be always behind-the-eight-ball on social aspects. Don't feel too happy for those CIOs. The other side of the coin is that the moment that something socially goes bad, they will likely get the blame right away as everyone knows that CIOs are socially inept, so goes the perception. The bad rap of being low in social intelligence can follow them no matter what they do, and it is proverbial albatross around the neck of proficient SI CIOs.

When we are trying to assess how socially intelligent a CIO is, we are really comparing them to others. Some would argue that CEOs must have top notch social intelligence skills. They presumably could not have gotten to the vaunted CEO position without having high SI skills. Well, this is not entirely true and there are some famous CEOs that would be considered low scorers on most SI tests. But, anyway, let's for the moment go with the idea that CEOs generally must have high SI.

In theory, the head of HR must also have a high SI, presumably since it is their daily activity of working with and managing the talent in an enterprise. The CMO is usually considered a very socially oriented personality and so we will put them up high on the SI levels (again, this is not necessarily the case for all CMOs). The CFO is sometimes criticized in the same way that CIOs are in that a CFO can be so immersed in the arcane financials of a firm that they are less socially adept, in the same manner that CIOs are immersed in the technology of the firm. In any case, we'll put CFO's relatively high on SI. COOs are also given a high SI, though they too are frequently criticized for being so operations focused that they care more about moving product out the door than the SI aspects.

Overall, the key here is that most perceptions of CIOs is that they are toward the tail end of the CXO suite in terms of SI skills. There is a gap between their level of SI and the levels of SI of their peers. In recent years, CIOs have gradually been closing that gap, but it still exists and still seems like a relatively wide expanse.

CIO SI GRID

We have seen that SI can be subdivided into levels of low, medium, and high. There is another important factor involving social intelligence. The context of when to especially utilize SI is vital to social intelligence. Some say that SI is something that you are always using and always applying. Others say that SI is used sometimes, when needed, in the proper context. It would be akin to describing when one would make use of intelligence. If you are highly intelligent and playing a game of peek-a-boo with a baby, you probably are not especially applying your high intelligence. The context of the circumstance should dictate the application of the intelligence.

Take a look at Figure 1. The vertical axis indicates the contextual aspects of SI, showing that one might always be using SI, or sometimes be using SI, or rarely using SI. The horizontal axis has the levels of SI, encompassing low, medium, and high.

We now have a handy grid to explore the variations of SI and CIOs. In the upper right, we have a level of SI that is High, and a contextual factor of Always. CIOs that are in this box are typically the topmost of SI CIOs. They are always on, and continuously exercising their high SI. The norm for most CIOs is more like the middle box, consisting of Sometimes applying their SI and only having a Medium level of SI capability. For these CIOs, because they are only sometimes exercising their SI, they might at times blunder in SI by not having applied their SI when they should have. Also, even when they rightfully apply SI to the context, since they are only medium rated in terms of SI, they might blunder as they are exercising their SI skills.

Social Intelligence and CIOs

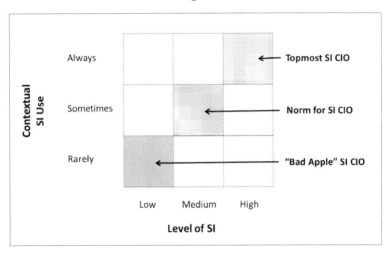

Figure 1: Eliot – CIO SI Grid and CIO Ratings

The worst case for CIOs are those that are Low in their SI rating and that Rarely apply their SI capabilities. For them, they routinely misjudge when they should be applying their SI. And, their SI is low such that even when they apply it, they are likely to do so poorly. You've perhaps seen this happen when such a CIO is so overtly trying to be SI that it is obvious and painful to watch, given that they are doing it awkwardly and often poorly timed. Unfortunately, these CIOs in the lower left box are the bad apples in the barrel. Regardless of their intent (they might be genuinely trying to be

SI), their lack of properly applying SI leads to the furtherance of the perception that CIOs are lacking entirely in SI.

By-and-large, CIOs seem to be in the Sometimes row. Whether having SI at the low, medium, or high level, they are only applying their SI sometimes. This might seem to make sense, given that SI is not necessarily always needed. But, as mentioned earlier, since CIOs are already behind-the-gun by being considered without SI, they're not applying SI all the time provides an opportunity to be again labeled as without SI.

Most IT staff is usually in the bottom four boxes in the lower left corner. The CIO that is SI savvy should be trying to lift their IT team members upward and rightward, getting them to be engaging more of the time with SI and being more proficient at SI.

Let's consider another angle on the perception of CIOs with respect to social intelligence. Let's imagine that we put the CEO into the upper right box, having the Always contextual SI and the High level of SI. In the lower left corner we will put the CIO, meaning those CIOs that rarely exercise SI and that are low in their level of SI. You can quickly realize that there is a large gap between the CIO and the CEO on such a grid.

SOCIAL INTELLIGENCE TEST FOR CIO

There are an abundance of social intelligence tests. Some use pictures of faces that express emotion, and you are supposed to indicate what emotion you believe that the person is expressing. This kind of test is used for both measuring social intelligence and emotional intelligence. Rather than using a pictorial test, there are also social intelligence tests that ask a person to rate themselves regarding various social intelligence factors. One downside of this self-rating is that the person might believe themselves to be rated higher than they really are. Or, the person might know they are lower in rating but just don't want to admit it.

Anyway, if you seriously and honestly want to gauge your SI level, I have provided in Figure 2 a quick version of a social intelligence test. Some of the social intelligence tests are lengthy, requiring you to rate yourself on dozens of factors. Some are carefully researched and have been subjected to the rigors of proper research methods. The version I am providing is more of a quick and easy variant, and not meant to be scientifically backed per se. If you want to take a more involved and extensive social intelligence test, there are plenty to choose from.

Take a look at Figure 2 for the simple 14-question CIO-SI test.

Social Intelligence and CIOs: 14-Question CIO-SI Test

	Strongly Disagree				Strongly Agree	**CIO Self-Rating Social Intelligence Test**
	0	**1**	**2**	**3**	**4**	
1.	o	o	o	o	o	I well motivate others
2.	o	o	o	o	o	Others well motivate me
3.	o	o	o	o	o	I actively listen to others
4.	o	o	o	o	o	Others willingly listen to me
5.	o	o	o	o	o	I drive social relationships
6.	o	o	o	o	o	Others include me in social relationships
7.	o	o	o	o	o	I socially persuade others
8.	o	o	o	o	o	Others socially persuade me
9.	o	o	o	o	o	I coach and mentor others
10.	o	o	o	o	o	Others coach and mentor me
11.	o	o	o	o	o	I well lead others
12.	o	o	o	o	o	Others well lead me
13.	o	o	o	o	o	I team well with others
14.	o	o	o	o	o	Others team well with me

Scoring

Any 0 = Concern

All 0's or 1's = Flunk

<23 = Low SI

24 to 39 = Medium SI

40> = High SI

Figure 2: Eliot – CIO Social Intelligence Test

For each statement or question, answer honestly and with careful introspection where you sit on the scale from strongly disagree to strongly agree. There is a scoring approach depicted on the test.

You can cheat the test by noticing that a strongly disagree gets you a score of zero, while the strongly agree gets you a score of 4, and so you could just blindly put yourself as a score of 4 on each statement in order to get the maximum possible score on the test. I could have switched around the scale and varied the statements to make this harder to cheat, but again this is a simple version and I am assuming that you won't want to cheat it.

Assuming you do this test honestly, I would say that if you get a score of 0 on any of the 14 questions then you ought to carefully rethink your SI capability, and figure out how to improve it.

Likewise, if you get all 0's and even all 1's, or any combination of 0's and 1's, you are scoring pretty low and would want to consider doing something constructive about it. Some would say that a very low score would make you "toxic" in terms of your social intelligence, while if you get a very high score you are considered a "nourishing" socially intelligence person.

A medium SI level is probably in the 24 to 39 score range, and a high would be 40 or higher.

Even if you are a high scorer, the thing about social intelligence is that you can always be improving yourself in being better at SI, so don't become complacent even if you genuinely have a high score.

For now, the perception of CIOs as low on SI is undoubtedly going to continue. Anyone seeking a career in IT should be pursuing whatever reasonable means they can to enhance their SI. The expectation by top executives is that CIOs should be getting better at SI. Success as a CIO is dependent on your SI, not just on your technical prowess. Boost your business acumen and your chances of success by aiming to improve your SI and make use of SI in whatever work you do.

CHAPTER 17

CIO AND THE BOARD OF DIRECTORS

PREFACE

In the past, the CIO was generally considered not suitable for meeting directly with Board members of the company. The thought was that the CIO was overly technical and did not have the appropriate business acumen to be able to be in the big leagues, so to speak. When Board meetings happened, the CIO was often crucial in preparing materials for the Board, including contributing a sizable chunk of crucial materials for the Board briefing book put together for the Board. But, when it came to making a pitch to the Board or explaining what had been put together, the CIO was on the sidelines, relegated to sitting outside the Board Room and simply being available if another C-suite executive came out to talk with them.

This trepidation to have the CIO able to participate actively and directly in Board meetings and with the Board members is gradually diminishing. Board members nowadays want to know what the digital strategy for the business is. They want to know that IT is being used effectively and efficiently. They want to know whether the use of IT will be sufficient to withstand business disruptions. They want to hear from the CIO and in the CIO's own words.

CIO's that are able to make this jump into the shark tank need to be cautious and careful. As they say, the higher you climb, the further you fall. Some CEO's assert that the reason they keep the CIO away from the Board is to help preserve the CIO. All it takes is for the CIO to blurt out the wrong thing at the wrong time to a Board member, and the CEO might have no choice but to axe that CIO. In any case, let's take a look at what

CIO's should be doing to prepare for getting their time in the limelight and being closer to the flame.

––––––––––

CHAPTER 17: THE CIO AND THE BOARD OF DIRECTORS

Little discussed, and rarely considered, firms need to determine what role their Chief Information Officer (CIO) will have regarding their Board of Directors. I realize that some CEO's might react in horror that their CIO might do anything at all related to their Board of Directors. Sadly, there are many CIO's that rightfully should be kept away from the Board. I say this because those types of CIO's are the ones that are likely to say the wrong thing, or do the wrong thing, and doing so with the Board of Directors is about as high-up a goof-up that one can do.

There are though some CIO's that are well suited for interacting with the board. And, in those circumstances, even if perhaps rare, you ought to be thinking about how that interaction can best be structured and undertaken. Yes, you can just ignore the notion and figure, well, why even try to involve my CIO with any aspects of the Board. The basis for claiming that there is a right time and place for the use of the CIO with the Board is based on numerous instances where the CIO has helped the CEO and other topmost executives, by adroitly having done something regarding the Board that provided a big pay-off from the perspective of the executive team having their act together.

Some instances are relatively small, but are large in symbolic value and the creation of trust. Other instances are large of their own right. We'll take a look at both small and large instances, and then see how to establish the nature of CIO interaction with your particular Board.

SMALL BUT BIG

Allow me a moment to provide a story of a circumstance where as a CIO, I had a moment of involvement with a board, doing so after I had just joined the firm. You'll see that there are some instructive lessons to be learned. For an upcoming board meeting, I was working closely with the CEO to brief her about the latest status of several major Information Technology (I.T.) initiatives. I had prepared a top-level slide for the board book, depicting a summary level of the initiatives. Just one slide, which was in keeping with the normal style of the briefing book put forth for the board meetings.

I also had prepared back-up slides that showed underlying details, in case the CEO got quizzed.

When a board quizzes a senior executive, if they cannot respond adequately, they will seem potentially aloof of the business, and the board members might lose confidence in the executive. The CEO asked me to be on stand-by, in case something came up and she wanted me to come into the board meeting. This notion was somewhat commonly accepted at the firm, namely, occasionally bringing in a "guest expert" when needed, such as the time that the firm was facing a tough legal issue, and the chief counsel had a specialist legal expert waiting in the wings, in case the board wanted to get into some particular detail or had a question that was relatively obscure but perceived as important to answer right away.

I opted to sit in a waiting area just outside the official board room, figuring that if I was called to come in, I should be right there, ready to enter. I was doing other work on my laptop, and so using the time well, while also being essentially on-call. The board meeting got underway. Turns out that one of the board members was a few minutes late. As he came into the waiting area, heading to the board room, he saw me, and noticed that I was typing away on my laptop, and seemed to know what I was doing. He looked at me, and so I stood-up and introduced myself.

When he found out that I was the CIO of the firm (newly doing so), he told me that his laptop had a problem and he wondered if I knew why. I offered to take a look, doing so while he was in the board meeting, and mentioned that I might be able to at least diagnose the problem, and that subsequently then he might know what needed to be done to fix it. He handed his laptop to me, and into the board meeting he went. I figured that the clock was now ticking.

Now that I had his laptop, and since I wanted to show that I could earnestly be of help, I'd better make sure that I could deliver on being helpful. I rushed over to one of my PC techs, and we jointly looked at the laptop. We diagnosed that there was a Windows patch that had not been applied. I decided that it was safe to apply it, and so we did, and the error no longer occurred. You might say this was a bit chancy, since making any change to his laptop could have done harm, but, in this instance, it was relatively benign, and my PC tech agreed it was a low risk act.

I then rushed back to the waiting area, sat down, and resumed my own work on my laptop. Soon enough, the board meeting doors opened, and the board members decided to take a brief break. Out comes the board member, and he came directly to me – but he had an odd expression on his face. He blurted out that since I seemed to be still sitting there, he realized that maybe I had not had a chance to take a look at his laptop. Oh contraire, I told him that actually, not only had I looked into it, I had fixed it. He was pleasantly shocked.

And he even emitted disbelief – he told me that at the company that he was an executive, they would have never done something so quickly and that he normally would have waited at least to week to get his laptop back, and even then, it would probably be still untouched. We started up his laptop, and he saw that the error no longer existed. He was profusely thankful.

The board members went back into the room, and the doors closed. When the board meeting ended, the CEO came out, and upon seeing me, had a big smile, and waved for me to follow her back to her office. Arriving at her office, she explained that when she presented the one slide about I.T., that one particular board member spoke-up, and asked if I had been involved in the preparation of the slide. The CEO, not knowing why such a question had been asked, said, yes, I had been the one that prepared it.

The board member then spoke-up and said, well, in that case, he believes it to be true and that the projects are likely being well undertaken. Not wanting to look a gift horse in the mouth, the CEO happily accepted the compliment, and then went onto the next topic. I think you can see that the relatively "small" act of having solved the board member's laptop issue, translated into a "big" act of his expressing confidence in me and the I.T. group, which, otherwise, might well have not been the case. His speaking up probably also curtailed anyone else on the board that maybe have a beef with what was shown, and especially since he was one of the senior board members that carried a lot of weight on the board.

Furthermore, this single act had established an all-important first impression with the board member, which later on came to play many times. It also set the tone for the other board members too, in the sense that they now knew (or were led to believe) that I.T. was doing just fine, thank you.

LESSONS LEARNED

A few important lessons arise. First, a CIO can have an indirect relationship with a board by doing background work, such as preparing the CEO for a discussion involving I.T.

This preparation can also include preparing materials for the board. Most of the time, a board will have a prescribed board book and format for their meetings, so it is essential that whatever the CIO prepares is compliant with that approach. Departing from that approach can be confusing to the Board, and also make the CIO seem out-of-touch with what the board does. Notice too that it is important the CEO be briefed sufficiently, and have back-up materials, so they can look well informed.

This does not mean that the CIO should provide arcane and detailed techie stuff, which, unless the Board is somehow composed of techies, would be quite out of place. Instead, the material should be carefully crafted to be pitched in business terms, and also be technologically accurate, just in case someone does try to question it. That covers part of the indirect interaction of the CIO with the Board.

There can also be direct interaction. In this case, the accidental meeting with the board member that was late the meeting, turned out to become something significant. By providing assistance, and doing so promptly and professionally, it created a first impression that would have long lasting value. And, it even had immediate pay-off, due to the board meeting taking place and his willingness to show support for the I.T. slide presented by the CEO.

So, there are opportunities for the CIO to aid the board in indirect ways, by working with the CEO and other executives of the firm, and helping them regarding their preparations for their direct interaction with the Board. And, there are opportunities for the CIO to directly aid the board, such as this circumstance of helping the board member with his laptop problem.

MULTIPLE PATHS TO GLORY

There even more ways for the CIO to provide assistance regarding a Board. Shortly after I had spoken with my CEO and found out the results of the meeting, I also realized that there was another step I could potentially take. I happened to know the CIO of the firm that the board member was an executive at. I called up the CIO, and explained that I had helped patch the laptop. I then also mentioned, politely, carefully, the frustrations expressed by the executive about how poorly his own I.T. was functioning.

I tried to be sensitive to the aspect that I was telling a fellow colleague that one of his key stakeholders held little regard for his I.T. This probably also likely meant that the board member had little regard for him, the CIO, too. After some defensive comments, my colleague, the CIO of the firm that the board member was an executive in, said that he knew that things weren't going well, but had been so preoccupied with one of their major I.T. projects that he had let his I.T. infrastructure group fall to pieces.

He realized that this was a wake-up call, and vowed to overcome it. I later found out that he went to the board member, and with hat in hand, so to speak, he explained that he was making changes to how they handled their laptop issues, and was revamping their Help Desk and other elements. I got further "credit" from the board member since he was surprised at first that the CIO knew what had happened, but when he explained that I had called, it further reinforced to the board member the conscientious nature of how I do my job.

It was a win-win, in that I had helped my colleague, and at the same time had gotten further trust built-up with the board member. So, another lesson learned – CIO's can be contact with their fellow CIO's at the companies represented by the board members. This can be smart thing to do, for several reasons.

Besides the circumstance that I just described, it can also come to play if a board member were to during a board meeting bring up that their I.T. does such and such, and the CEO might wonder why they are doing so and we are not, by having a relationship with their CIO, I could readily follow-up to find out. Indeed, I often proactively contact the CIO's of the board members, doing so just before a board meeting of our firm, so that I can be aware of anything unusual or that might be top-of-mind by a board member.

This indeed has happened, for example, one time wherein I had talked to the CIO of one of the board members, and he mentioned that they had just rolled-out a new Data Warehouse that allowed their executives to retrieve on their smart phones the latest metrics of performance of their firm. I realized that it was possible that the board member might ask whether our firm is doing the same. Had I not realized the potential for such a question, I probably would not have thought to brief my CEO on the topic, especially since there were already a lot of other I.T. related topics that she needed to bring up during the board meeting.

Fortunately, on a chance that it might come up, I briefed my CEO beforehand. Sure enough, the topic was brought up by that board member, and my CEO looked quite sharp to have been on-top of a topic that wasn't even listed on the agenda.

BOARD MEETINGS GO TECH

Another example of interacting with the board as a CIO can involve the use of technology during a board meeting. Nowadays, board meetings often involve all sorts of high-tech stuff, whether doing teleconferencing, or bringing up real-time stats, or showcasing impressive presentations involving grand graphics, and so on. If the technology used during the board meeting is stilted or not working, it can be perceived that the I.T. group is likewise ineffective.

This might be completely unfair, in that sometimes the board meetings are not arranged by or involve the internal I.T. group, and might be done by some other third party, but, hey, the board members don't know that and so just assume all I.T. is all I.T. It is therefore useful for the I.T. group to be involved, and presumably make sure that things go smoothly with the technology during the board meeting.

Not doing so can lead to the false assertion that the company I.T. is fouled up, and, it not only smears the CIO, but it makes the CEO look bad too. Presumably, the CEO should be ensuring that their I.T. is well managed, and that they have a CIO in place that is doing the job needed for the firm. In that sense, the CEO has as much at stake about the technology used during the board meeting, since otherwise they might need to dig out of a hole with their board about why the technology is not working.

KNOW YOUR BOARD

I have met many CIO's that do not even know the members of their own Board of Directors. They do not know who they are, what they do, etc. This can be crucial to know. One board member that was with a company that I knew, I was aware that the company had been hacked and a lot of their private information had been leaked onto the Internet.

I had contacted the CIO there, and offered to have my security team and my Chief Information Security Officer (CISO) confer with his team, helping them to setup ways to stop further entry by hackers, and also how to approach dealing with the leakage. The CIO had been relatively close to the executive that was on our board, and told him about how I had helped out their firm. Once again, this came to play, during a board meeting, the board member was supportive when our Chief Compliance Officer (CCO) made a presentation and explained why our cybersecurity budget was so high, and he remembered that we had a top notch team that his own firm had tapped into.

BE READY FOR PRIME TIME

There are some circumstances wherein having the CIO directly participate in a board meeting is advantageous. As an example, I was briefing our CEO and COO on a proposed plan to roll-out tablets and mobile apps to our multi-thousand workforce, in anticipation of their presenting the topic at an upcoming board meeting. While preparing the CEO and COO, it became apparent to me, and to them, that they were not well versed in the nuances of the proposed plan, and they were concerned that two of the board members were at companies that were high-tech and might pepper them with various roll-out specific questions.

They decided to go ahead and have me attend the board meeting, and provide that portion of the briefing to the board. If the CIO does present to the board, the CIO should make sure they are well rehearsed and ready for intense action that can occur. Board members are sometimes very active in their role on the board, and want to exercise that fiduciary oversight responsibility that the carry on their backs.

And, in this example, sure enough, the two board members were quite vocal and challenging. I was ready for it, and had made sure that my ducks were all aligned. The CIO has to remain cool and calm, and systematically walk the board through whatever matter is at hand, including being able to expertly respond to questions.

PARTICIPATE ON BOARDS AS PRACTICE

CIO's that are interested in directly participating in their own firms' Board of Directors meetings ought to consider getting some time in as a board member of other boards. For example, take a look at possibly joining a board of a professional association in I.T. or in your industry. Or, look at joining a board of a non-profit in your community.

And, another popular way might be to consider getting on the board of say a start-up high-tech firm that might value your CIO related background and expertise. Naturally, it is important for you to avoid any conflicts of interest in serving on any of these boards, and you need to take any such board service as a serious and important matter.

Nonetheless, having such board experience will make the CIO more confident when interacting with the board of their own firm, and will potentially too impress their own firms' board by showcasing that the CIO is more than just the head-in-the-sand type of CIO. By the way, serving on such boards can also be a means to make sure that the CIO is up-to-speed on the latest practices of industry, and can also be inspirational to other members of their I.T. staff when they see that their CIO is sought after and doing things to aid industry or the community.

WRAP-UP ON BOARDS AND CIO

In recap, here are some ways that CIO's can help with Boards:

a) Prepare the CEO for any IT topics that the Board might bring up,

b) Provide materials for the Board Book that apply to IT related topics,

c) Aid directly Board members for aspects that might be of IT related,

d) Be in contact with CIO counterparts of the firms of the Board,

e) Aid those CIO counterparts when appropriate,

f) Find out from those CIO counterparts about those Board members,

g) Ensure that any tech needs at Board meetings are ready and working,

h) Know your Board members and be up-to-speed about them,

i) Consider serving on other Boards of say non-profits, associations, etc.,

j) Participate in Board meetings as needed and do so with aplomb.

Those are some of the ways that a CIO can be of value to a board. Not all CIO's are able and versed enough for those actions, and it is crucial to judge whether your CIO is ready for such interaction. The right interaction can make a big difference for the CEO, for the other executives, for the firm, and for the board. Make sure to make good use of your CIO with your board, when appropriate, and ensure that you leverage the benefits thereof.

CHAPTER 18

MERGERS & ACQUISITIONS (M&A) AND IT

PREFACE

In the past, companies would undertake a merger or acquisition and not particularly consider the IT aspects. Usually, as an afterthought, the CEO would announce after-the-fact that they are acquiring the Widget Company and then expect that whatever needed to be done on the IT side of things would just magically happen. Many CEO's got a rude awakening when they suddenly found out that the IT systems of the acquired company were a mess and would drive up the cost of the acquisition by a significant factor. Furthermore, the valuation of the acquired company had implicitly included a significant portion for the value of their systems and data, which upon closer scrutiny was mainly smoke and mirrors.

Today, companies that are astute at doing mergers and acquisitions involve the CIO at day one of the effort. There is a realization that needing to properly value the IT systems and data of the other firm is best done with the CIO involved. There is a realization that to be able to readily marry together the acquired company that there will be a substantive effort to interconnect the systems of both firms.

For the CIO, there are other factors to be considered when looking at a company merger and acquisition. They need to not only look at how the systems will mesh together, but also how the respective IT groups will mesh together. The systems of the acquired company are likely being run and maintained by the IT function there and if those people leave or are tossed by the wayside, the underlying systems might fall apart or otherwise not provide the value expected.

————

CHAPTER 18: MERGERS & ACQUISITIONS (M&A) AND IT

Last year, there was an estimated $4.86 trillion in worldwide M&A deals (according to Bloomberg figures). We seem to be once again on a rising slope of M&A activity. Those of you that lived through the horrors of the Dot.com bust will remember how M&A activity plummeted during that time period. And, maybe equally horrifying was the bust that hit the economy and M&A as the doldrums around 2010 hit.

Thankfully, M&A activity seems to be heading upward and the deal volume is generally sound. I want to share some insights about the role of IT as an element for consideration during the M&A process. I've worked in companies that got acquired, and I've worked in companies that were doing the acquiring, and helped firms involved in aiding the M&A process, and throughout I have seen what works and what doesn't work in terms of the valuing of IT as part of the overall deal calculus.

That being said, some of you might be scratching your heads and saying to yourself "what is Lance talking about?" since you maybe have not previously given much thought to the IT component of firms and how it relates to the M&A deal. I don't blame you for being somewhat perplexed. For most of the history of modern day M&A, the IT elements of an enterprise were not much on the radar for M&A transactions. I call this the "Don't Care" era with respect to IT. If you looked at most M&A transactions, you would nary see any particular mention about the IT assets and IT resources of a firm being acquired. Maybe a sentence or two.

We then seemed to enter into the next era that was what I call the "Risk Watch" era. Occurring around the Dot.Com boom of M&A activity, acquiring companies and entities wanted to know that the IT was not going to kill the deal. By this I mean that the view of IT was that it could harm the value of the acquired firm by having bad exposures. Typically, during due diligence, someone would be assigned to figure out whether the IT had any big risks that might undermine the M&A transaction.

In more recent times, I have seen the emergence of a third era, what I call the "Digital Value" era. As part of the M&A effort, there is emerging a realization that the company's IT products and services can be of a strategic nature and provide great value to a firm. Being able to grab hold of that IT value is something that savvy acquirers are looking closely at. The IT is no longer a footnote, but becoming sometimes even a driver for an M&A deal.

VALUING THE IT IN M&D DEALS

I see M&A efforts embodying the IT aspects in several ways, namely:

- IT is strategic and highly-valued (the "Golden Eggs")
- IT is useful to consider (the "Meat and Potatoes")
- IT is of little importance (the "Discard")

The IT in a firm might be so enticing that it is considered the Golden Eggs and adds distinctive value to the firm. This is happening more and more, and gradually will become a standard part of the M&A process. There is most of the time a view that IT is perhaps useful to consider, and as long as the meat and potatoes exists of the usual kind of IT keeping the lights on, it otherwise does not especially enter into the M&A picture.

Then there are the instances where nobody cares at all about the IT of the firm being acquired, and besides giving it little or no import, the view is that if needed too you could just discard all of the IT anyway and it would just not make any difference in the particular M&A deal. The status of IT in a being acquired firm can make a difference throughout the M&A stages.

Impact of IT Status During M&A Cycle of Stages

M&A Stage of Cycle	IT Helps	IT Hurts
Buyers Kick-the-tires	Attracted by IT capabilities	Repulsed by IT system problems
Preliminary Due Diligence	IT robust and ready for integration	IT costly mess and overhaul needed
Negotiations and Value Estimation	Higher worth due to prized IT	Perceived value lessened by IT shambles
Deal Establishment & LOI	Structure clear and IT Road Map laid out	Clogged IT disorder which muddies the deal
Closing the Deal	Able to close, speedy IT leveraging to occur	"Tail wagging the dog" of IT blockage quagmire

Figure 1: Eliot - How the IT Status impacts the M&A Stages

Usually, one of the first stages in M&A is the buyers that are kicking the tires of prospective firms to acquire. If the IT of a firm that is a candidate for acquisition is really topnotch and stands out, it can be an added attractor for a buyer. They might want to be reassured that the IT is providing the business with whatever it needs to be disruptive in its market niche. Not only might they like this due to it being a crucial element of the firm to be acquired, they might also have thoughts of leveraging those same IT systems and capabilities for themselves.

The buyer kicking the tires can go the other direction though if the IT is a shambles and the company being acquired can barely make use of IT. This could be a repulsing factor that causes a potential buyer to either walk away from considering the firm or that it might knock down the perceived value so much that the buyer decides it is not a worthy acquisition target.

The IT elements can help or hurt during each M&A stage, ranging from the preliminary due diligence, and during the negotiations and value estimation, and during the deal establishment and the Letter of Intent (LOI), and during even closing of the deal. Some involved in M&A don't put any thought to the IT side of things until toward the end of the M&A stages life cycle. This can be troublesome, bringing forth sudden adverse surprises that nearly spoil the deal, and can be both vexing and costly to the acquirer and the acquired firm since it can force the discussions to go backward and begin to unwind the deal.

WHAT MAKES IT VALUED

You might next be wondering as to why IT might be considered valued during an M&A effort. Suppose a firm has put together a mobile app that is widely adopted by consumers and has a tremendous loyal base of users. This is the kind of IT aspect that could be a big attractor to a prospective buyer of the firm.

The buyer might believe that the firm's mobile app has huge future potential as it furthers adoption among consumers. Or, maybe the buyer wants to use that same channel to push their own products and services, and will piggyback onto the mobile app that comes along with buying the firm.

The same can be said for web sites of an acquired firm. The firm being acquired might have an incredible e-commerce presence and have web traffic that can be further monetized. This is another example of an IT aspect that can add value. There is the social media penetration of a firm, perhaps having a strong base of followers on Facebook or Twitter, and for which that provides added value of the target firm.

IT Value Aspects	Why Value Add
Mobile apps	Specialized mobile app that is widely adopted and loyal base
Web sites (e-commerce)	Invested branding via web site with e-commerce presence
Social media	Strong social image and vested eyeballs for this sector
Big Data	Vast data sets on customers with insightful patterns and analytics
Cloud-based Integration	Agile cloud use able to shift systems to marketplace changes
AI/Machine Learning	Deep AI learning capabilities that leverage customer info insights
Other IT	Top IT talent that jells and can be leveraged; IT Intellectual Property (IP) stout resources; etc.

Figure 2: Eliot – IT Elements that can add deal value

Big Data is another hot area of potential added value. A buyer might want to grab hold of tons of rich data that can be used to aid not only the acquired firm but also be used by the buyer for other allied purposes. Cloud-based integration is another IT aspect that can be seen as allowing an acquired firm to have agility in being able to shift as marketplace changes occur. The acquiring firm might even decide to jump into the cloud by leveraging the capabilities established by the acquired firm.

AI/Machine Learning is another upcoming IT aspect of keen interest. A firm that has been toying with using Artificial Intelligence (AI) and deep learning could provide a future capability that has tremendous value down the road to the buyer. In the Other IT category, a buyer might want to have the IT talent that exists in an acquired firm. Nowadays, trying to find a topnotch team of programmers can be hard to do. So, one means to get that capability is to acquire a firm that has already honed such a team. The buyer might even not be especially interested in what else the acquired firm does, and just want to get that IT talent. Also in the Other IT category is the potential Intellectual Property (IP) that a target firm might have. The IP alone could be worth high value (maybe even for trolls).

REVIEWING IT DURING A DEAL

Assuming that there is some interest in considering the IT aspects during an M&A instance, I next provide insights about how to consider and review IT for valuation purposes. I show in Figure 3, the typical circumstances involving an M&A activity wherein two firms are involved in an M&A activity (side note: if the buyer is seeking to make the acquisition but is say a PE, these principles still apply and so please adjust accordingly as you read this – I will also be doing a future blog on PE's). Usually, the M&A will involve unequal's in the sense that one of them is being acquired and the other is doing the acquisition. Of course, there is the true "merger" situation too, which is also shown on the diagram.

M&A IT: Strategy During the Deal Process

M&A **Acquisition** (of Unequal's)	IT → *Takeover of* IT	**As Takeover Target** • Hostile or friendly? • Want your IT or not? • Readiness for IT inquiry • Systems stability during process • Your IT Team considerations
M&A **Acquisition** (of Unequal's)	IT → *Reverse Takeover of* IT	**As Taking Over Of** • Hostile or friendly? • Want their IT or not? • Conducting the IT inquiry • Systems stability during process • Acquired IT Team considerations
M&A **Merger** (of Equal's)	IT ↔ *Mutual "Takeover"* IT	**As Mutual Targets** • Hostile or friendly? • Which IT is "best" to prevail • Dual IT inquiries • Systems stability during process • Joint IT Team considerations

Figure 3: Eliot – M&A IT Strategies and Target aspects

If a firm of say a larger size is doing a takeover of a firm of a smaller size, I depict this by showing the larger sized blue box and taking over the small sized orange box. Let's further assume that both entities have some IT capabilities already. As a takeover target, the company being acquired should be considering whether or not the acquiring company will want their IT. In some cases, the acquiring company is like the Borg and will simply be stripping out the IT of the acquired company and be absorbing the acquired company into the IT of the acquiring company.

The acquired company should prepare for an IT inquiry from the buyer. During the M&A process, and even if done secretly, the odds are that one way or another word might spread amongst the IT team of the being-acquired company. This can create difficulty in that the IT team might start to get worried about their jobs. They might begin to defect to other firms. They might resist providing information about the IT systems of the company. They might even sabotage the systems and sneakily insert computer viruses or back-doors.

It is crucial that the acquiring company be thinking about these aspects, and likewise the target company. Planning for and anticipating these matters are key to seeking an M&A process for which the IT side won't get things stuck or go off-the-rails. There is a similar set of considerations for a reverse takeover of having a smaller firm essentially acquire a larger firm.

And when there is a merge of equals, the same kinds of considerations occur. Though, if the situation is truly a merger of equals, it can become more problematic trying to figure out which IT aspects are to stay and which IT aspects are to go. Indeed, trying to determine this in a piecemeal way such as by ranking as "best-in-class application" can be misleading since the odds are that the systems in a firm are intertwined and it is not so easy to untangle them for use in the other firm.

IT M&A SCAMS

I have witnessed many situations whereby the potential buyer was misled into believing that the IT aspects of the firm they were acquiring was much better than it really was. These subterfuges or disguises are hard for a non-IT executive or analyst to poke through, and it highlights the importance of getting someone well sophisticated in IT to participate in assessing the IT of the target firm.

There is the "Shiny Rotten Apple," wherein the target firm showcases some wonderful PowerPoints about how great their IT is. In reality, the IT is rotten to the core. This requires going past the pretty slides and actually digging deep into the systems in order to ferret out the truth.

The "Hidden Train Wreck" is another frequent scam. The system is wobbling, error prone, and ready to fall apart. But it is hidden from the buyer and/or the buyer does not even think to ask about IT, and so gets the train wreck which derails after the whole deal is done and closed.

The "One Man Band" involves a circumstance of a target firm having its key systems known by and only known by one person. This is the proverbial guy that whipped together systems in their garage syndrome. The buyer might think they are getting some really great IT systems, but then afterward realize it is all in the head of the one man band. This then can be a rough path since the person might try to get their own deal to stay with the acquired firm, or they might leave and so the value of the systems drops accordingly without the wizard to keep them going.

IT M&A Scam Aspects Under Disguise

IT M&A "Scams"	Description
Shiny Rotten Apple	Attempt to make systems look good by polished PowerPoints, but reality is rotten at the core
Hidden Train Wreck	System is wobbling and massive ticking time bomb
One Man Band	Knowledge about the systems is all in one person and collapse when the person exits
Legal Limbo	IT licensing for systems lacks ownership and will invite ugly lawsuit in ownership change
Duct Taped Systems	So-called integrated systems are kept together by thin duct tape and ready to fall apart
Techie Buzzword Bamboozle	Wild claims using hot buzzwords, mainly hot air and no substance

Figure 4: Eliot – How typical IT M&A "scams" occur

The "Legal Limbo" occurs when the various licenses for software and systems are lacking in the appropriate protections and limitations, and so the target firm really does not have ownership in the systems that the buyer thinks they are getting. This not only undermines the value, but can lead to ugly, costly, and distracting lawsuits later on.

The "Duct Taped Systems" are ones that are supposedly well integrated, but upon closer look you discover that the so-called integration is being done with very sloppy and thin pieces of code, and maybe a lot of manual intervention to make it work.

Finally, my favorite that sometimes gets me laughing on the inside are when I hear a target firm that touts its systems and IT, and does so by using every buzzword in the techie vocabulary. This kind of bamboozles often work pretty well with non-IT executives, and makes it seem like the target firm is up and running with the latest in everything. This is usually not the case. It is usually bamboozling.

TASKS ASSOCIATED WITH M&A AND IT

To make sure that IT is being properly considered during an M&A effort, it is advisable to use a methodology that guides the type of tasks to be performed. Here's a representative indication of such a methodology:

- Pre-Planning (Before M&A)
  - Examine IT Alignment with Corporate Strategy
  - Evaluate IT Culture and Capabilities
  - Identify Budget
  - Evaluate Legal and Compliance Risks
  - Evaluate IT Technology
  - Identify the Due Diligence Team

- Due Diligence (Day 0 to Close)
  - Assess Acquisition Target

- Planning (Day 0 to Close)
  - Create Integration Team and IT PMO
  - Develop Change Management Plan
  - Determine Schedule
  - Prioritize Projects
  - Create Risk Migration Plan
  - Evaluate Vendor Contracts'
  - Create Systems Integration Plan
  - Create Staff Retention Plan

- IT Integration (Day 1 Close to Cutover)
  - Implement Change Management
  - Integrate Systems
  - Integrate Functions
  - Implement Staff Retention Plan
  - Perform Data Migration

- Readiness & Adoption (Day 2 Separation to Integration)
  - Manage IT Changes
  - Conduct Employee Training

- Post-Integration Review (Day N Realize Value)
  - Assess M&A Value
  - Conduct Post-Mortem

You would need to tailor any such template like this to the particulars of a specific M&A IT effort. There are various such methodologies and I have used many of them, each having their own respective strengths and weaknesses, so carefully review any particular methodology to see if it is useful for your particular use. You might also do a head-to-head comparison between two or more, and either pick one that seems most suitable or do a pick-and-choose of the details to cobble together your own version.

There is a handy free IT M&A life cycle published for open use by Microsoft (the template does not have anything to do specifically with only Microsoft products per se, so no need to be thinking that you can only use this methodology if the IT is already using Microsoft products). The methodology conveniently shows the steps and then also indicates the tasks that are technology oriented, tasks that are process oriented, and tasks that are people oriented. The excerpted version shown on the previous page was based on that version and provide herein simply for illustrative purposes.

Overall, I hope this has provided you with some insights about the M&A IT trends and why it is becoming increasingly important to consider IT during M&A. If you don't consider IT during M&A, you might unpleasantly discover after-the-fact that what you thought was of no value was actually of strong value, or that what you assumed was of good value was actually worthless.

.

CHAPTER 19

IT STEERING COMMITTEES

PREFACE

Some CIO's find it especially helpful to put together a top-level executive committee that can help with the governing aspects of IT at the firm. This IT Steering Committee is used to help provide guidance regarding what kinds of projects and systems the firm should have. The committee often gets involved in aiding IT during budgeting and establishing the nature and size of the IT budget. The committee is at times an escalation point that provides "the buck stops here" when there are disputes lower in the organization about how IT should be used.

Not all CIO's are sold on the use of an IT Steering Committee approach. Such CIO's believe that having a committee is like wearing an albatross around their neck. They are constantly beholden to the committee. They feel stifled by having to go hat-in-hand to the committee for the littlest thing. Members of the committee might become overly inflated in their perceived importance to IT.

Part of whether you like the idea of having an IT Steering Committee is partially shaped by how well you manage it. For those CIO's that just let it happen, they are indeed likely to find that what they thought was helpful can become very obstructive. If you are embarking on having an IT Steering Committee, you need to plan for it, put it into being, and keep it well tuned.

CHAPTER 19: IT STEERING COMMITTEES

Some Chief Information Officers (CIO's) love having an Information Technology (IT) Steering Committee. Many hate having one. Why the big disparity? And, which of the two opposing viewpoints is right? Well, the answer can be found in the behavior of the desert shrub, Prosopis velutina, commonly known as the velvet mesquite, and found primarily in the Sonoran Desert of California and Arizona. I know this might seem a bit zen-like, but allow me a moment to explain.

This desert shrub manages to survive in the harshest of conditions, suffering amid summer temperatures easily toping one hundred degrees Fahrenheit. During the winter, temperatures drop well below freezing. There is little rain in this environment, and seemingly anything living in the desert appears to have achieved an incredible miracle. How does the Prsopis *veluntina* stay alive? Its seedlings are quick to send out roots the moment they hit the ground, and rapidly establish a shallow, but crucial, initial foundation.

Next, they extend out those roots, doing so over time, eventually stretching their reach to a distance equal to about the height of an 11-story building (about 160 feet). By doing so, the mesquite is able to survive, and thrive, as a result of having very deep roots (i.e., by tapping into sources of ground water that are deep underneath the dry and barren surface).

What does any of this have to do with CIO's and IT Steering Committees? By and large, savvy CIO's know that an IT Steering Committee is a means to establish a vital foundation in their organization, and then they utilize that foundation to extend their roots and gain traction throughout the rest of the organization. Usually, if a CIO changes jobs and enters into an organization that lacks an IT Steering Committee, it is one of the first – and most important – steps that they will take. But, you might ask, if that's the case, then why are there some CIO's, in fact a lot of CIO's, that don't like an IT Steering Committee. The answer to that seeming paradox will be described next herein.

IT STEERING COMMITTEE TRADE-OFF'S

Let's first make sure that we are all talking about the same thing. An IT Steering Committee is a high-level group of usually the topmost executives of a firm, and they meet on some kind of regular or semi-regular frequency to help provide guidance to the IT function of the organization. This sounds nice. In practical terms, this is very, very hard.

The reason it is hard involves the dynamics of the topmost executives of a firm. When you bring together the topmost executives, you are putting yourself into the limelight, all at once, among your peers, and you are either going to come out shining or come out torn to shreds. It is a dual-edged sword. You are enabling a group-like condition wherein the entire group can all at once denounce what you are doing, and do so in a circumstance where there is no place to hide. Imagine a pile on, with maybe the CIO at the bottom. Ugly.

Saw one circumstance where the CIO showed-up, and rather than the executives debating each other, they reamed out the CIO, with one starting the pile-on as a trigger, and the others gleefully joining in. Like sharks that smell blood and cannot help themselves but to go in for the kill. For some CIO's, it is just too risky, and they prefer to instead try to work with the topmost executives one-on-one, and avoid entirely the chance that they all might get together and want to collectively talk about IT.

Furthermore, the topmost executives usually have very strong personalities, and like they say, trying to get them to do anything of an aligned nature is like trying to herd cats. In that sense, there are certainly rational reasons to NOT have an IT Steering Committee. If trying to get together the topmost executives is going to mean that you, the CIO, are going to get bounced out of your job, well, naturally, job suicide is not something one seeks normally to voluntarily do. In addition, there are some CIO's that are just not suited to handle an IT Steering Committee. They are not the socio-political types that know how to appropriately establish and navigate the rough waters of an IT Steering Committee.

They would be wise to stay at least a hundred miles away from having an IT Steering Committee. OK, you might now be thinking, if it's that hard, then why even try? Usually, without an IT Steering Committee, the CIO is going to be between a rock and a hard place, over and over again. Here's a good example of the rock-and-a-hard-place, which I could see coming but the CIO refused to acknowledge that it could happen. There was a big budget IT project that the Chief Marketing Officer (CMO) really wanted to have done.

Meanwhile, there was a large IT project that the Chief Financial Officer (CFO) also wanted done. There was not enough IT budget to do both (and, by the way, this is pretty much the situation all of the time!). How does the CIO choose between the CFO and the CMO? Suppose the CIO chooses the CFO, and does so maybe because the CIO reports to the CFO. Seems sensible, you say. But, now, the CMO has their sights on the CIO, and hopes one day to knock the CIO out of the firm. That's not a good monkey to have on your back.

Well, you say, the CIO should have done the CMO's IT project, instead of the CFO's I.T. project. I think that not doing the IT project of your boss is probably not the best career move, if you know what I mean. So, the CIO ends-up in that terrible rock-and-a-hard place circumstance. This happens over and over again, across and among all things that the CIO is doing, whether choosing IT projects to work on, whether allocating laptops and tablets, or providing break/fix services to users, and so on. How to get out from this squeeze play?

Have an IT Steering Committee. The topmost executives meet, do some verbal arm wrestling, and make compromises among each other for the limited resources available from IT. The attention of who approved something shifts from somehow the CIO having to make that decision (and thus be the one squarely in the gun sights), and instead it is an outcome of the interactive negotiations among the topmost executives. Sure, the CFO might lose out to the CMO on that IT project, but it is not because the CIO was forced into making some Gordian knot like choice, but instead due to the CMO making a more compelling case and winning out over the CFO during the IT Steering Committee meeting.

Thus, the IT Steering Committee is tremendous vehicle to help provide governance for the IT function. Driving that vehicle takes some genuine smarts and hard work. The CIO has to know that they have the "Right Stuff" to do it. And, the CIO must know that the organization is ready for doing so – some firms have no other kind of similar top-level steering committees, and so it is especially hard to start-up an IT related one in that circumstance, and so it is worth reconsidering the situation if the organization has not done anything akin to it, and perhaps has a company culture antithetical to such a notion.

In recap, if the CIO is the Right Stuff, and if the organization already has a culture that accepts such a notion, the creation and ongoing use an IT Steering Committee can be a core aspect of ensuring that IT achieves its organizational mission, and that the CIO is able to succeed in the organization. Let's next get into some specifics about how to make this actually work.

CHOOSE THE RIGHT VERBIAGE

The word "committee" can be a death knell for the IT Steering Committee. In some companies, they detest committees, and think of a committee as overly bureaucratic, and something that is a waste of time and effort. You don't want to get stopped before you even get out the gate. So, if needed, give the thing a different and more palatable name.

Some call their IT Steering Committee an IT Steering Council, or an IT Steering Commission, etc. Figure out what fits for your organization. For example, one CIO tried to at first use "IT Steering Board" but the CEO didn't like the use of the word "board" since it sounded like the Board of Directors and so it was potentially misleading and confusing. Though you might think the name of the thing is relatively unimportant, it can be extremely important. If the name gives the wrong connotation, or if the name is seen as off-kilter (one firm tried "IT Steering Command"), it is not going to be attractive to the participants and will fail before it hits the ground.

Another one that I got a laugh about, and fortunately the CIO wisely changed, was "IT Steering Tribunal" – which I pointed out sounded like a witch hunt and maybe someone getting burned at the stake.

GET THE RIGHT STAKEHOLDERS

Let's assume that you have thought carefully about the name, and you have devised an appropriate naming for your IT Steering Committee (a name that fits for your firm). Now, who will serve on this august group? Usually, you aim for the highest executives that you can get on it. The reason to aim high is simple, if you have an IT Steering Committee that has say Vice Presidents, they are unlikely to be actual decision makers, and so whenever the IT Steering Committee meets, it won't make any decisions, and you'll have to wait to see what happens when those VP's all go back to ask what the true decision makers want to have done. I realize that you might say, well, suppose those VP's have been authorized to act on behalf of the topmost executives that they represent. Yes, that can be done, but, I assure you, in the end, when big decisions need to be made, they are probably not going to stick out their necks, and will want to play it safe by saying that they still need to check-in with their respective bosses.

In short, if feasible, get the highest executives on the IT Steering Committee, which might mean say the CFO, CMO, COO, etc. It might also mean the various Business Unit heads, since they are likely to have a stake in IT too, and if they don't believe they are getting their fair share, they ought to be in the IT Steering Committee too. Does this mean that only the topmost executives should be members? Not necessarily. Had one circumstance where the organization had a SVP of Strategy (reported to the COO, and so technically was not a topmost executive), and he was instrumental in shaping the overall direction of the firm. He was well liked by the topmost executives, and they tended not to make any big decisions without his input. Added him to the IT Steering Committee. He was pleased and became a big ally of the vehicle.

Had he been left by the sideline, the odds are that he would have taken potshots at it, doing so behind-the-scenes, and likely undermined its long-term viability. One thing though to keep in mind, if you start to open the door to members that are less than the top, it can open the floodgates, and all of sudden you have a one hundred person sized IT Steering Committee, which is unwieldy, diluted, and impractical. What you can do is establish a base set of members (hopefully the topmost executives), and then always allow for "guests" that are able to attend meetings from time-to-time, which are not actual members, but can attend as needed. It is like creating a secret club, for which the members feel honored and special, and others will want to be a part of.

This is contrast to having an IT Steering Committee where the members don't want to be there, and no one else wants to be there either. Best to be on the side of having something that is being sought and considered highly desirable. One other quick point, watch out for the classic "substitutions" ploy. Here's what happens.

For one IT Steering Committee, the COO said he could not attend a particular meeting and would send his right hand person – seem innocent enough. Upon attending the meeting, the CMO and the CFO both noticed that the COO was not there, and found out that the COO had sent a substitute. You can probably guess what happened next. At the next meeting, the CMO and CFO both sent substitutes. Soon, the IT Steering Committee consisted of the clerks that worked on the factory floor (well, not really, but the point is that it can be a slippery slope to allow substitutions so be on the wary).

ANGST IN GETTING UNDERWAY

One CIO decided that having an IT Steering Committee was great, and he had run one at the firm he used to be at. He had not started it at the predecessor firm, instead he had inherited it. Well, he opted at his new firm to send out an email to the topmost executives, invited them to be members, and set a date for the first meeting. He had a party to which few guests arrived.

He had failed to properly establish the basis for the IT Steering Committee, and he had relied on email to convey the value and importance of it. Bad move. This worked at his prior firm because it was already an ongoing mechanism and well accepted in the firm. Use of emails to setup meetings was fine. When you want to start something like this anew, you'll need to put together a campaign, just like running for office. You'll need to make sure that your boss is OK with the notion, and will be supportive.

You need to go see each of the members, individually, and explain what it is all about. You need to do your homework and figure out how the I.T. Steering Committee will be run and operated. All of that needs to be done prior to even having the initial meeting.

Remember the tale above of the CIO that had his first meeting and virtually no one showed-up,, he then found it much harder to try again, since he had already used up his initial goodwill, and digging out of the hole was now much worse than if he had started it well.

Also, one other handy tip. Try not to have the first meeting be especially meaty. If you start with some really tough topic, let's say the company is considering dumping its core ERP system, and you bring that up at the first meeting, the odds are that it is so contentious that the meeting will leave a foul taste in the mouths of your members. And they might not want to come back for further such meetings. Therefore, avoid anything overly ambitious for the first meeting.

There is another side of that coin, though. Do not do "nothing" at the first meeting. If the first meeting only consists of handshakes and hellos, it will leave the impression that nothing important will be done by the IT Steering Committee, and the members will view it as unworthy of their time. It is the Goldilocks phenomena. The porridge should not be too hot, not too cold, but just right. Pick a topic that has some meat, so that the members will get a chance to exercise their wings, but not so blazingly complicated or tremendous that it becomes a battle royal.

ONGOING CARE AND FEEDING

Running an IT Steering Committee is a commitment. If you start one, be ready to keep it going. Otherwise, you'll look incompetent and unable to get things done. Some CIO's take on the duties entirely by themselves. This is likely a mistake. There is a lot to be done, including for example taking minutes of the meetings, publishing the minutes, doing follow-up with the members and their staffs, preparing briefing materials, and so on.

A CIO that devotes their attention to all of this is likely to be missing doing other tasks for the IT group, and though the IT Steering Committee is pretty important, you cannot do it to the disservice of forsaking the other areas of IT. Generally, a CIO will involve some other trusted member of the IT group to help with the IT Steering Committee. Though some might turn to their secretary, and though such a person might be highly valued, it is usually better to use someone versed in IT per se, such as a top notch Business Analyst in your IT group.

Of course, do not pick some IT member of your group that is a heads-down techie, since this is an effort that requires the kind of business diplomacy not usually seen in the typical techie. You should also consider establishing a regular schedule for the meetings. At first, if there are lots of important items to be covered, and if time is an important factor, you might have the meetings say monthly. This is a lot of burden though; both on the members (busy topmost executives) and you, so only go monthly if the circumstances warrant doing so.

You normally would then drop down to bimonthly, and then quarterly. If you start-up on say a quarterly basis, the problem is that it takes so long for the next meeting to arrive that there is no momentum and no sense of connectedness by the members. A higher frequency at the start gets things underway, and then it can settle into the lesser frequency.

One firm was doing their IT Steering Committee only on an annual basis. This is bound to be less effective since it is so rare to occur. It would have to be an IT group where there was nothing especially happening, or where the outside effort by the CIO to confer with the members one-on-one was going so well that it did not warrant using up the time and attention by bringing the members together more frequently.

CALLING FOR A SPECIAL MEETING

In addition to having a regular schedule, make sure to be prepared for the need for a special meeting. One firm had been hit by a severe virus. The CIO decided that it made sense to bring together the IT Steering Committee so that at one time, in one place, he could brief all of the topmost executives, and also share with them what he was planning to do about the virus. There is likely going to be circumstances where a crisis or something unusual occurs that will make the potential for having an off-schedule I.T. Steering Committee meeting beneficial.

As always, only call for such a meeting if it makes sense, and if you are prepared for it. When I had talked to the CIO in the case above of the virus hit, he was merely going to inform the members about the virus, but he had not prepared any kind of solution. A wise CIO goes into such a meeting with solutions in-hand, otherwise, the members, all being strong egos and problem solvers that daily solve company problems, might take the matter into their own hands, and suddenly the CIO is on the defensive, trying to explain why some crazy plan they have devised won't work.

Go into such a meeting with a solution in-hand. But, be also ready to listen and adjust. I say this because if the CIO walks into such a meeting and appears inflexible, and even though the members might silently go along, they probably will afterward take shots at the plan, doing so in the cover of darkness. Plus, they will realize that coming to the meeting is like some kind of old Russian governmental committee trick, wherein all decisions have already been made, and they are merely the puppets expected to rubber stamp it. Most topmost executives want to have their say, and you've got to allow for room in your solutions for that kind of latitude.

LOT OF EFFORT INVOLVED

I mentioned earlier that there is a lot of work involved in a well-run IT Steering Committee. Indeed, one aspect involves preparing for the meeting. If you are going to be discussing say the IT budget, you'd better have a well prepared presentation about the IT budget. And, you should be prepared to be potentially attacked about how the budget is being spent. There are many CIO's that walk into their IT Steering Committee asking to increase their budget. Little do they realize that they might immediately get attacked that the budget they already have is not being used well.

Members are not going to pour more money into something that they think is not spending its money well to begin with. I remember one IT Steering Committee where the members not only complained about how badly the IT budget seemed to be spent, but they even started to discuss taking money away from IT, and the CMO even said that he would take the money that was spent toward marketing systems and start his own shadow IT group with the money (which he claimed would be better spent).

Preparation is key. Meeting with members beforehand is key, especially if there is something particularly being brought up for one of the members. There was a Data Warehouse that the COO wanted, but the CIO had not conferred beforehand with the COO, and the CIO assumed that whatever was proposed about the Data Warehouse would be quickly supported by the COO during the IT Steering Committee meeting. When the CIO revealed the price tag, which had not been shown to the COO beforehand, the COO spoke up and said he could not support such a cost.

As I say, meeting with members beforehand is a crucial part of preparations. Likewise, after the meeting, the odds are that you'll need to follow-up with the members. If someone feels they got blindsided during the meeting, you'd better get over to see them right away, and figure out how that happened, and find a way to placate the matter. The follow-up will often include making contact with subordinates of the members. Some CIO's go to the subordinates before having gotten the go ahead from the topmost executive, but this can be considered an intrusion onto someone else's turf, plus possibly lead to confusion as to what is going on.

During an IT Steering Committee meeting, it is handy to indicate that follow-up is needed, and get an indication from the members as to whom they would like the follow-up to occur. This opens the door to doing so, allows the designated subordinate to freely communicate with you and do so without concern that their boss will crush them for doing so, and serves as an indication that the CIO is thoughtful and does follow-up to what they say they will do.

By the way, it is best to have an agenda for the IT Steering Committee meetings, and run the meetings with proper facilitation. Some CIO's take on the facilitation role themselves. If the CIO has that kind of acumen, then it is probably OK to do so, but it also means that the CIO is no longer readily able to function as a fellow member of the tribunal. Usually, it is better for the CIO to use someone as the facilitator, and remain therefore able to act in other capacities, and it is also easier too that if the facilitation is failing that the CIO can do something about it (note: if the CIO is the facilitator, and if the facilitation is poorly done, it can be an awkward situation since no one wants to tell the CIO that they are doing a rotten job of it!).

I remember one IT Steering Committee where the CIO decided to have each member of the group became the facilitator, doing so on a round robin basis. Usually a bad idea. Topmost executives might be good at many things, but not usually being a facilitator. Though I get the notion that it is perhaps a means to have them have a stake in the meetings and get involved, it is probably not the ideal way to achieve that end. You can always have them give a presentation or do something during the meeting that creates that same kind of commitment, but avoids them having to act as a facilitator, which is a special skill.

Speaking of which, asking some lowly member of the IT group to be the facilitator might also be difficult, since they might be intimated by the members of the IT Steering Committee. Keeping in mind that they are the topmost executives, you need a facilitator that has the style and seniority to be able to sufficiently and adroitly handle such a group. You also need to establish rules about how the group will be run. There is the vaunted "Roberts Rules of Order" and it can be a guide. Do not though decide to make the IT Steering Committee meetings into a congress-like affair of looking up arcane rules of order, and trying to impose some lengthy laborious process onto the meetings.

Will there be voting on actions? If so, will the vote be done anonymously or explicitly? What carries the vote in terms of a majority rules or some other basis? These aspects need to be figured out beforehand, and also shared with the members so they know what to expect, but shared in a fashion that they appear to be logical and helpful, and not appear to be drudgery and mired in stuffiness.

MORE THE MERRIER, SOMETIMES

Should there be one IT Steering Committee, or more than one? I get asked this question all the time. Generally, there should be one IT Steering Committee that is the topmost, consisting of the topmost executives at the topmost position of the company. That being said, suppose you have a major business unit for one of your subsidiaries. Can it also have an IT Steering Committee? Sure, but I would normally say that it should be considered subordinated to the mighty one, the one that is at the topmost of the firm.

Likewise, suppose that you are starting a major IT project that will introduce a new ERP system across the whole company. Rather than the IT Steering Committee getting mired in that particular project, though it is an

800 pound gorilla of IT projects, I would suggest that you form an IT Project Committee that focuses on that particular project. It too would then ultimately report to the grand IT Steering Committee. In short, I am saying that there can be multiple IT related committees that have a steering-like purpose, but you should have a topmost one to which all others ultimately report.

If you don't do so, and if you allow lots of so-called "IT Steering Committees" then it will be quite confusing throughout the organization and no one will likely care or respect any of them. To distinguish them, you might call them sub-committees or use some other naming that fits to your firm.

For example, one company called their topmost committees as "Committee" while the subordinated ones were called a "Team" as a naming convention. They were in the midst of focusing on improving quality throughout the firm, so they for example started a high-level group called the "Strategic Quality Committee" and then had setup subordinated groups for quality initiatives in specific areas, such as the "Finance Quality Team" and the "Operations Quality Team" (this was within their accepted norms of organizational groups and groupings).

The downside of having lots of such committees and subcommittees can be that it eventually becomes an army of groups running around the company, and no one knows what one is doing versus another one, leading to mass confusion and personnel dreading the notion of yet another committee coming at them. Keep this in mind of you spawn a lot of subcommittees from your main IT Steering Committee.

ONE SHOE DOES NOT FIT ALL SIZES

An IT Steering Committee can be the savior for CIO's that otherwise will get sliced and diced by the executive team, doing so by shredding the CIO behind-the-scenes. By getting the executive team together, it allows for the dynamics among the executives to play out, and can take undue attention away from the CIO, and shift things toward the nature of the IT budget, IT resources, IT priorities, and lead to doing so in such a manner that the topmost executives understand how things came to be.

Notice that I am not saying that the executives will necessarily be happy about the outcomes, in the sense that if the CMO gets his project pushed down in priority by the IT Steering Committee, he or she is not going to be a happy camper simply because it was a group decision. But, at least the CMO cannot as readily attack solely the CIO, which, without an IT Steering Committee, could easily be the case, since the CIO is often perceived as the one that decides who gets what from the IT resources bucket.

And, the collective wisdom of the topmost executives must have been that the CMO's project was not as important, not as valued, not as beneficial, as some other efforts, and so in that sense the organization presumably is better off, because if the CMO project had gone forward, it would have perhaps denied or delayed other presumably more important and more valued efforts.

An IT Steering Committee can be an important way for the organization as a whole to understand how it is using its limited and precious IT resources, and hopefully more optimally allocate those resources. It can also be a means to spur innovation. In one IT Steering Committee, at a healthcare firm, the Chief Medical Officer identified some nifty new technology that she had been reviewing, and the other executives suddenly realized the value that it could provide for the products and services of the firm.

It is unlikely that the Chief Medical Officer would have brought up the topic to the executives in any other forum, and also would not have had the opportunity to share it with the entire group, and also that the group was able to quickly brainstorm, since they were there assembled as a group.

When it works, the IT Steering Committee is a wonderful mechanism. Research studies show that by-and-large, firms that have a working IT Steering Committee (one that is properly run), tend to have greater satisfaction with their IT and tend to put it to better use. If you firm is the right kind of firm to effectively make use of such a mechanism, and if the CIO and the CEO see eye-to-eye about the value, it is something you ought to get underway. Some circumstances do not warrant the IT Steering Committee, and can potentially make things even worse, and so as they say, one shoe does not fit all sizes. Make sure you have the right shoe, and the right size..

CHAPTER 20

MASLOW'S HIERACHY AND IT

PREFACE

Abraham Maslow has become famous for his now classic Hierarchy of Needs. It is a pyramid or triangular shape that has multiple layers, the lowest of which allegedly expresses our most basic needs of survival, while the topmost layer expresses the human need for the highest of our aspirations.

His theory is taught in most foundation courses of college that involve psychology or sociology. In most schools of business his theory is covered during discussions about managing of people. His approach is a handy framework. It is intuitive and easy to remember and use. IT managers and IT executives should become familiar with Maslow's Hierarchy of Needs and keep it in mind as a management tool. The popularity of Maslow's hierarchy has led to it being used for other allied purposes. One such allied purpose in IT consists of thinking of the services that IT does in a similar hierarchy of needs manner.

CHAPTER 20: MASLOW'S HIERARCHY AND IT

Nearly every introductory class in psychology, sociology, or management tends to introduce what has now become popularly known as Maslow's Hierarchy of Needs. It seems to be a de rigueur topic for any starter class or sometimes referred to as the "101" beginner class in many related disciplines. The Maslow hierarchy seeks to depict the various aspects of human needs, doing so in a series of layers, rising from a foundational layer at the base of the hierarchy and proceeding upward to higher levels of human needs.

At the base, survival kinds of needs are indicated such as breathing, eating, sleeping, and the like. At the very top of the hierarchy is the loftiest of human aspirations. We will take a closer look at this hierarchy later on in this piece. Abraham Maslow first introduced the concepts underlying his envisioned hierarchy of human needs in a paper published in 1943 for the journal Psychological Review (here's a link to the original article: http://psychclassics.yorku.ca/Maslow/motivation.htm).

Later on, Maslow expanded his notion of the hierarchy and its elements, doing so famously in his 1954 book entitled "Motivation and Personality (here's a link to the book: http://s-f-walker.org.uk/pubsebooks/pdfs/Motivation_and_Personality-Maslow.pdf). In today's column, we'll take a close look at Maslow's hierarchy of needs. His hierarchy can be useful as a tool for IT managers and leaders when considering how to guide the behavior of their IT teams, and is overall a recommended tool for managers in business, regardless of area of functional specialization. In other words, managers and leaders in finance, marketing, accounting, operations, and such are usually versed in and potentially make use of the Maslow hierarchy, and naturally IT managers and leaders should likewise consider doing so.

In addition to using the Maslow hierarchy directly, there have also been efforts to reuse the hierarchy toward other ways of viewing business aspects. Various researchers and practitioners have borrowed the Maslow hierarchical concept and tried to apply it to other domains. Indeed, his hierarchy has been also reapplied into the IT realm and we'll take a look at the nature of such re-applications.

MASLOW'S HIERARCHY DEFINED

Take a look at Figure 1 to see a typical depiction of Maslow's hierarchy. Notice that it is in the shape of a triangle or some call it a pyramid. Note that I'll refer to it as a pyramid, though some argue that it is not rightfully a pyramid since it lacks the proper three-dimensional shape. On the other hand, some depictions try to show it as a three-dimensional shape and add other augmented information to the other sides of the pyramid in order to make it more rightfully into an actual pyramid. I'm not going to get carried away about whether it is proper or not to refer to it as a pyramid, since most everyday mentioning of his hierarchy does tend to call it pyramid, and that it seems easy enough to describe it as such, and there is nothing particularly wrong or harmful in doing so.

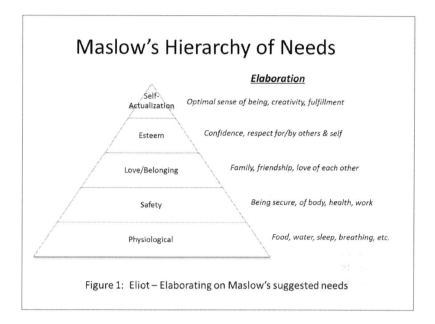

Figure 1: Eliot – Elaborating on Maslow's suggested needs

There are five layers in the pyramid. There have been some that have tried to reduce the five layers to say four or three, and others that have tried to expand the layers to six or seven in size. The five layers is pretty much the standard that most have come to accept, and other variants are certainly interested and allowable, but we'll stick with the five layers for now. Five is kind of a handy number anyway, given that we have five fingers and five toes, and find a certain familiarity in uses of the number five.

The word "Physiological" is at the base of the hierarchy and represents survival kinds of human needs. Just above that base, the next layer is labeled as "Safety" and refers to securing oneself and ensuring safeness in one's environment. The middle layer is labeled as "Love/Belonging" and refers to being able to have a sense of human belonging with others and an ability to embrace love. The layer just above it is the "Esteem" layer and suggests having a sense of respect for oneself and others. Finally, the topmost layer is labeled as "Self-Actualization" and refers to a higher order of human fulfillment.

Maslow had described essentially this same kind of hierarchical depiction, though he did not use a triangular shape or pyramid shape that has now become part-and-parcel synonymous with his hierarchy. His description was narrative in style and others helped out by concocting a visual hierarchy. This is actually significant in that it is hard to imagine that his hierarchy would have gained such tremendous popularity without the diagram. As they say, a picture is worth a thousand words, and more succinctly conveys the lengthy narrative of his original works.

It is also noteworthy to mention what Maslow was trying to accomplish in his work. Keep in mind that the time period was the early 1940s. At that time, there were lots of lists being developed about the nature of human needs. List after list was making the rounds. Maslow sought to put an end to these atomistic lists and provide a grouping or categorization which would embody the lists.

You can see this same devotion to the upgrading of lists in other areas of study. For example, in biology, rather than having simply longs lists of various organisms, there is an accepted taxonomy that you likely remember from your introductory biology classes. There are the levels or layers ranging from Domain, Kingdom, Phylum, Class, Order, Family, Genus, and to Species. A taxonomic structure is helpful in organizing biological organisms and being able to get a grasp of what they are and how they relate to each other, more so than just an exhaustive laundry list.

Maslow was trying to collect together these various human needs lists and put them together into a sensible framework. He thought that describing them into a hierarchical structure would be helpful in better understanding human needs.

CRITICISMS OF MASLOW'S HIERARCHY

Most people intuitively accept Maslow's hierarchy as a sensible framework. It is easy to understand, and the depiction makes it memorable. You can readily share it with others and use it as a guiding post. When you think about your own efforts, you likely find that it makes sense that you seek to appease your physiological needs, without which it is hard to do anything else. Once you appease the physiological needs, it makes sense that next you would be worried about safety. And so on, up the hierarchy, whereupon by satisfying each of the lower layers it allows you to make your way to a higher layer.

Not everyone is convinced that the Maslow hierarchy is appropriate. Take a look at Figure 2 for some of the criticisms of Maslow's hierarchy.

First, he admitted in his seminal paper that there was no scientific support per se for his approach. He stated that the approach was based on his observations and what he took from the reading of the literature on the topic. In that manner, those concerned about having a solid basis for theories about human nature were somewhat appalled that he ventured his approach but did not have a scientifically sound basis for it.

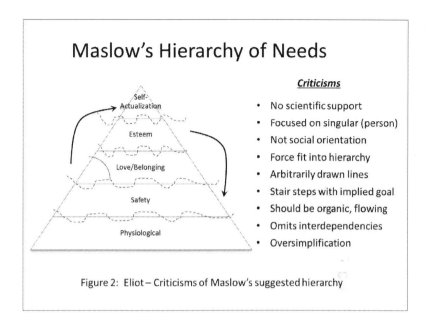

Figure 2: Eliot – Criticisms of Maslow's suggested hierarchy

Second, his approach is based on a single individual and their human needs. There are some that criticize this and claim that his approach lacks a social orientation. Humans are considered social animals and are driven by social customs and mores. Maslow's lack of seemingly putting human needs into a larger social context is considered by some critics to be needlessly narrow and potentially flawed thereof.

Third, the attempt to force fit the lists of human needs into a hierarchy is what rankles most critics the most. They would argue that the lines drawn between the layers are arbitrary. It also tends to overlook the interdependencies that exist between each of the many elements. A hierarchy implies a stair step kind of progression, making your way one step at a time, climbing upward. Critics say that this is a tremendous oversimplification and that the reality is that human needs are much more organic and flowing than can be accommodated in a hierarchy.

Critics point to the aspect that you might defer satisfying your hunger (an item in the Physiological layer) in order to say do something mundane like paint a picture (perhaps an item in the Self-Actualization layer) or help a friend (an item in the Love/Belonging layer). This immediately demonstrates that any kind of strict one-step-at-a-time hierarchy of human needs is misleading and in some ways incorrect.

COUNTER-ARGUMENT TO THE CRITICISMS

If you carefully read Maslow's work, you would become aware that he did not envision the hierarchy as a strictly one layer at a time kind of structure. In that sense, the pyramid depiction perhaps is both a positive in that it is easy to understand and communicate, but it is also easy to mislead. Maslow had indicated that each level when reaching a threshold of satisfaction would no longer become dominant as a human need.

In other words, if you were literally starving to death, the odds are that you would be putting Physiological pretty high up on your set of priorities and that painting a picture would be pretty low in your priorities (unless it led to getting fed). Any item in a particular level if it was missing to an extreme, he postulated it would preempt attention or a willingness to move to the next higher level. Until some semblance of physiological needs is met, it is very hard to move upward to safety, and likewise until some semblance of safety needs is met it is hard to move upward to love/belonging, etc.

He considered the hierarchy to be one of relative prepotency. He also acknowledged that this might not apply in all circumstances, such as say a martyr that has chosen to give up food to make a statement of a political or social nature. Maslow emphasized that our collective desire to try and make the world into a predictable and orderly structure is bound to be difficult and potentially lose some essence along the way, but that nonetheless seeking to discover and try to create a lens by which we can see the world as orderly is a proper goal.

Maslow also indicated that we can become complacent at a given level and not necessarily seek to rise higher. If you are satisfied at the first four layers, you might not necessarily seek to achieve the fifth and highest layer of self-actualization. There is also the chance that you will become somewhat habitual at a given layer, undertaking so-called automatic behavior. Think of how you satisfy your daily food cravings, perhaps falling into a daily routine of breakfast, lunch, and dinner, doing so without having to expend much thought toward what or how you are doing so.

Some have tried to put a percentage of relative satisfaction for each layer, demarking that once that level of satisfaction is reached that you are then able to move upward to the next layer. For example, once you have satisfied Physiological needs at 85%, you then can move into Safety, and once Safety is at 70% you then move into Love/Belonging, and then once it is 50% you move into Esteem, and once it is 40% you then move into Self-Actualization.

Moving into the next layer does not mean that you cannot move back down into the lower layer. Like a flight of stairs, you can move up and down each of the steps. Indeed, you can be on many steps at the same time, though this is where the image of a flight of stairs starts to weaken since we normally think of ourselves as standing on one stair at a time.

ALTERNATIVES TO A HIERARCHY

It is one thing to criticize; it is another to actually offer some kind of constructive alternative. There are some that favor Maslow's categories but are upset about the use of a pyramid and so have offered a non-hierarchical variant. Imagine that we had circles revolving around a core circle, similar to planets around a sun. We might put in the core the Self-Actualization, and then have orbiting around it the Esteem, Safety, Love/Belonging, and Physiological elements. In this manner, none of the elements are considered above or beneath any of the other elements. They are all equal. They are all interacting. Though this is an interesting way to consider Maslow's work, it has certainly not caught on. Generally, it is unlikely that this non-hierarchical depiction would resonate as well as does the famous pyramid. There are other variants too.

Another variant is to stack the elements side-by-side, like a series of parked cars in a parking lot. We would have Self-Actualization, Esteem, Love/Belonging, Safety, Physiological all side-by-side An arrow across all of them that was pointing in both the left and right direction could be used to suggest that we span all of the five categories and flow back-and-forth among them. Again, this kind of depiction is interesting but unlikely to dethrone the pyramid.

REUSE OF MASLOW'S HIERARCHY

Maslow's hierarchy has been reused in numerous other contexts. People like to parlay his hierarchy into other domains, which is handy because it leverages what someone already knows (the Maslow hierarchy) and can extend from that basis into some other area of endeavor.

In the IT realm, Robert Urwiler, CIO at Vail Resorts, and Mark Frolick, Xavier University, presented an IT maturity framework that leveraged Maslow's hierarchy. They opted to call this re-application the "IT Value Hierarchy" and offered that it be used by IT leaders to describe the value of progressively sophisticated IT use. Take a look at their interesting paper as published in the journal of Information Systems Management: http://site.xavier.edu/crable/it_value_maslow.pdf).

They propose that at the foundational layer are aspects involving the IT infrastructure and network connectivity, considered the Physiological needs. Then, they offer a Safety layer which consists of IT aspect involving system stability and computer security. The middle layer for Love/Belonging becomes what they coin "Integrated Information" and then above it is the Esteem layer which they depict as IT providing a strategic form of differentiation. Finally, the topmost layer of Self-Actualization is depicted as shifting the overall direction and approach of a firm by helping to change its paradigm via the use of IT.

Their framework resonates well with IT leaders and managers. It can be an eye opener that explains the daily grind of running IT, and brings together the lists of atomistic things that IT does, in the same manner that Maslow sought to bring together the various atomistic lists of what human nature consists of. Their efforts to reuse the Maslow hierarchy are laudable. Other IT researchers have also made use of their framework and tried to explore it further. In their paper, they offer suggestions of ways in which the framework can be validated and extended. There are other variants, as we'll see next.

IT MODEL AS A HIERARCHY

Another variant of reusing the Maslow hierarchy into an IT realm could be as follows:

- IT Transformative (at top)

- IT Specialized (below the top)

- IT Advances (in the middle, such as mobile, social media, etc.)

- IT Core Systems (such as ERP, etc.)

- IT System Fundamentals

At the bottom layer are the aspects that involve keeping the IT plumbing going, or as some say keeping the lights on or the trains running. Above this layer are the IT core systems such as ERP systems and the like. The middle layer involves advances in IT such a mobile technology, social media, and so on. Just below the top layer is specialized systems that are relevant to the particular business at hand, and then at the top of the pyramid is IT being transformative for the organization.

A CIO or CTO that wants to gain traction in an organization for transformative use of IT is likely to find themselves unable to get very far if say the lowest layer of the IT system fundamentals is not being met. Suppose that email is not getting delivered in the company. Suppose that the networks are constantly on the blink. Suppose that the companywide scheduling for calendars is prone to mistakes and is hard to use. If the business cannot reliably depend upon email and calendaring, for example, they are likely to be unwilling to listen to how great IT can be for transforming the enterprise.

In that sense, the lower layers need to be satisfied to make ones way up the pyramid to higher and more wide sweeping uses of IT. Similar to the earlier points about Maslow's hierarchy, one should be cautious in interpreting this Systems Hierarchy as being strictly a progression of one stair step to the next. For example, a percentage of relative satisfaction at any given layer is likely to be sufficient to make your way up further.

There are also interdependencies and the flow between the layers should be considered fluid. In some instances, having a solid ERP would allow the IT executive to then adopt mobile technology and even the higher specialized applications. That being said, there are instances where upon putting in place mobile technology and specialized systems will spur the organization to realize it needs to improve its ERP system. The pyramid should be seen as having a back-and-forth among the layers, rather than strictly proceeding from one layer to the next.

IT PARTNERSHIP MODEL AS HIERARCHY

Looking at the Maslow hierarchy on a systems perspective is one way to reuse the model. Another way to reuse the Maslow hierarchy is to consider the alignment of IT and the business. Alignment of IT and the business is an ongoing matter of significant difficulty and need. When IT and the business are misaligned, the odds are that the business will suffer in many ways, and likewise IT will tend to expend resources without meeting business needs.

Some argue that when IT is merely an order taker, it is not well aligned with the business. An order take is considered a negative posture for IT because it suggests that IT waits for the business to provide ideas of what needs to be done and then mindlessly tries to carry that out. This order take mindset is bound to produce systems that don't fit to the business, and can be duplicative or off-target of business needs. Take a look at Figure 3.

The most basic level of IT alignment on a partnership basis with the business is listed as being an order taker. Above this layer is IT as a service provider, and then at the middle layer is IT as a collaborator. Just below the top layer is IT as a business partner, and then at the top of the pyramid it is IT as a co-leader. These labels for each of the layers can be argumentative and have different meaning to different people within and outside of IT, so take it with a pinch of salt. The overarching point is that we can use the Maslow's hierarchy as a handy means to depict other aspects of IT.

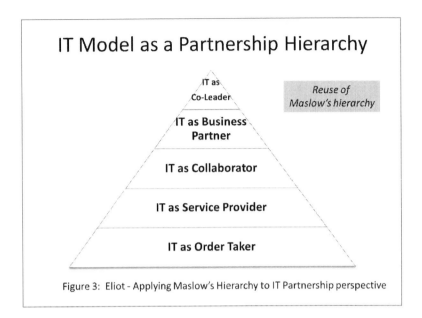

Figure 3: Eliot - Applying Maslow's Hierarchy to IT Partnership perspective

FURTHER ADAPTATION FOR IT USE

Any IT leader or executive can make use of the Maslow's hierarchy as-is for the day-to-day and overall management of their IT group. IT leaders and executives can also make use of Maslow's hierarchy as adapted specifically to an IT use. Maslow's hierarchy provides a helpful foundation to think about and communicate about IT, due to the great popularity that Maslow's hierarchy has. It is easy to understand and people find it quite intuitive. The adaptations to IT can be used when working with an IT Steering Committee and trying to convey the aspects of what IT does and what it wants to do next. Such an IT adaptation can be used as part of the IT Strategic Planning process. It is powerful, simple, and easy to communicate. And, it has that scientific glow to it that can provide a sense of robustness.

If you are considering making use of an IT adaptation of Maslow's hierarchy, make sure that it well applies to your circumstance, and also consider the earlier described advantages and disadvantages of the inherent Maslow's hierarchy. You don't want to get caught off-guard by someone in the firm attacking your IT adaptation without already being aware of the limitations and general criticisms of Maslow's hierarchy. Overall, the odds are that the cleverness and memorability of an IT adapted Maslow hierarchy would outweigh the negatives and it should be another tool in the toolkit.

CHAPTER 21

WHAT KEEPS CIO'S AWAKE AT NIGHT

PREFACE

One of the popular questions these days is "what keeps you awake at night?" and it is asked of executives, politicians, celebrities, and even during job interviews. The power of the question is that it presumably goes to the heart of what someone is most concerned about and thinking about. The answer to the question can be very revealing of what that person considers to be most important to them.

Vendors often use the question to find out what they can do to help a CIO. CIO's can use the question to find out from the CEO what is on the mind of the CEO, and then use this as a means of perhaps finding a way to have IT help get the CEO some sleep at night.

What does keep CIO's awake at night? I provide next some highlights of what is keeping CIO's awake. These are topics that indeed should be keeping the CIO awake. If you are a CIO, compare what's on your list to what is on this list here. Maybe you are losing sleep over the wrong things. Or, maybe your peers have different concerns than you do. Anyway, let's all try to find a means to not stay awake at night and ultimately get a good night's sleep, which might just solve those problems that seem to be keeping you awake.

CHAPTER 21:
WHAT KEEPS CIO'S AWAKE AT NIGHT

Things that go bump in the night. Scary sounds. Shivers up the spine. A nationwide poll of American's identified some of their biggest fears, but it turns out that a close analysis of those fears revealed that the things they feared most were ill founded fears. Experts assessed the risks associated with the identified fears, and produced an alternative list of what Americans should be afraid of. It is a kind of parlor game of fear this, not that.

Let's do the same for the sphere surrounding Chief Information Officers (CIO's). What do CIO's fear most? What should CIO's fear most? The answer to those two questions is surprisingly different. Based on a recent poll of selected CIO's, I have crafted a list of what they seemed to fear most (well, at least on the job), and then assessed whether there are other fears that have greater risk and would be a better use of their fear induced energies. Fear this, not that. Let the games begin.

FEAR C-SUITE LOSS OF FAITH IN YOU

CIO's tend to fear budget cuts that are frequently and seeming unceasingly aimed at Information Technology (IT). Many firms just don't get why IT costs so much (well, they think it costs so much, regardless of actually comprehending why and what the costs are). Will I be able to keep my IT staff, or do I have to do lay-offs? Can I keep the systems running or do I need to cut-back on maintenance and support? Are those IT projects next year going to survive or will they get dropped from the budget?

These are the fears of many CIO's, and rightfully so. But, a bigger fear, and one that some CIO's fail to perceive, involves a C-suite of executives that are not willing to step-up and say they believe in the IT group and its CIO. In other words, if a CIO can gain the support of his C-suite colleagues, they will help find a means to make the IT budget work out.

I've seen Chief Marketing Officers that handed over chunks of their own budget to the CIO, and heads of Operations that snuck part of their budget under-the-table to the CIO. Often, the wave to cut IT budgets arises because the CIO has not been able to secure the behind-the-scenes support of the C-suite. C-suite members might perceive that the CIO has not delivered on IT systems that support their needs.

Or, they might believe, rightly or wrongly, that they could do more with the monies going to their own budget than what IT can do with that same money. When I hear about IT budget cuts, rather than thinking about the symptom, akin to someone having a sore throat or a runny nose, I go for the underlying cause, which often is the faltering support of the C-suite toward IT and the CIO. That should be the CIO's bigger fear.

FEAR THE CYBER ATTACKERS

There are CIOs that lament the advent of Bring Your Own Device (BYOD). This is the notion that the employees of a firm come to the office armed with their own tablet or smart cell phone, and want to use it while doing work. Though this might seem innocent, it actually raises lots of thorny issues. Imagine that vital corporate data is being stored on someone's personal cell phone. What might they do with it? Suppose they let their kids play with the phone and they do something to that corporate data? Suppose the employee loses the phone and it gets into the hands of someone nefarious? Ownership and privacy issues abound.

At first, some companies put outright bans on employees using their own devices for work purposes. This created some confusion and consternation, and led to some employees having to carry around at least two phones, one that is the company provided phone, and one that is their own personal phone. Same might be true for a tablet, a laptop, etc.

Fortunately, technology offers a solution to this problem. There are ways to do containerization on such devices, effectively separating the work stuff from the personal stuff on a personal phone. Virtualization is another such technology solution. And, the creation of Mobile Device Management (MDM) systems has made it much easier to be able to monitor and control such devices. In that sense, the fear of BYOD is sometimes overblown today.

A bigger fear should be of cyber attackers or sometimes called hackers. We have increasingly seen that there are hackers of all different flavors that are aiming squarely at company data. There are hackers that do it for fun, hackers that do it for profit, hackers that are country sponsored that want to attack other countries, insider hackers, outsider hackers, and so on. The number and flavor of those kinds of hackers just keeps growing and expanding. By the way, I am reluctant to use the word "hacker" because it is a word that has multiple meanings and at one time was considered a badge of honor, but, now, in today's headlines, it seems that the hacker notion has become synonymous with cyber crooks, so I am adopting it herein, though I don't like doing so. CIOs should be fearing the hackers, more so than BYOD.

FEAR SOCIAL MEDIA OSTRICH EFFECT

Chief Digital Officers (CDO's) were momentarily the new darling of the C-suite. As the mania over firms going digital has gained ground, there has been a call by some that we need to have a new top-level C-suite role to focus on that aspect. Thus was borne the CDO role. A few firms jumped right away onto that bandwagon. Others opted to rename a CIO or CTO as their CDO. Or, sometimes anointed them with a dual title. Meanwhile, some said that a CIO or CTO is just not the right stuff to be a CDO, and it needs to be a completely different person and role.

I am not going to settle that debate here, especially since it has the markings of a classic "religious wars" kind of heated discussion. Take a look at the chapter in this book that covers the details on this topic But, I think it safe to say that CIO's should not be fearing CDOs as much as they should be fearing something more dangerous.

Namely, they should fear the social media ostrich effect. This might be also described as the head-in-the-sand of not putting due attention to social media at the firm. Sadly, there have been some CIO's that have essentially ignored the social media wave for business, and have kept out of it, thus, creating a huge vacuum in their firm, and which has thus led to the call for someone to plug that hole, namely, the CDO. In that sense, the CDO is once again a type of symptom solving a more vexing problem that really is at the root of the matter.

I realize that some readers are going to have heartburn over the notion that the phrase "social media" is being used herein as though it refers to all things digital within and for a firm, which, admittedly though somewhat implied, does not fully convey that notion. Likewise, some clever readers will say that an ostrich really doesn't stick its head in the sand to avoid danger and that it is a false myth.

Anyway, let's not lose sight of the main point, namely, the importance of CIO's to embrace the value and significance of social media in their firms, and do something substantive about it. Of course, there are CIOs that want to do something about it, but their firms view their interest as over extending the reach of what they consider a proper role for a CIO. Bottom-line: Fear the danger of not being on top of social media, rather than the oft chance of a CDO stepping into your turf.

FEAR YOURSELF, NOT THE FUTURE OF CIO'S

Finally, the last fear is that the future of the CIO might be doomed. Some people have been saying that there will no longer be a need for

CIO's. Indeed, the catchy phrase is that CIO stands for Career Is Over. I doubt this. I seriously doubt this. I would say that CIO's should be more fearful of themselves.

They should be fearful of themselves in the sense that if they aren't business savvy enough, if they don't have the right kind of business acumen, it will doom them. It is once again the root of the problem. Firms are tempted to do away with CIO's because they don't comprehend what a CIO brings to the table. And CIOs that don't bring much to the table are regrettably the "bad" apples that spoil the entire barrel for all CIO's. CIOs need to fear themselves, more so than the future of CIO's. If they can properly tackle that fear and overcome it, there will always be a future for CIO's.

I think that's enough fears to cover for now. Ralph Waldo Emerson said it best when he said, "Always do what you are afraid to do." Whatever fears a CIO has, they need to confront those fears, and crush them. It is hard to do, and it has to be done in the right way. No fear in saying that.

CHAPTER 22

CEO'S REFLECT ON THEIR CIO

PREFACE

What do CEO's say when they are asked to describe CIO's? The answers are similar to being asked about your legislative representative. Most people tend to have a relatively positive view of their own legislative representative, but have a dim view of politicians overall. Unfortunately for CIO's, most CEO's seem to have a dim view of CIO's overall, though when asked about the CIO they now have they are usually a little more satisfied.

One could argue that the reason that CEO's are generally dissatisfied with CIO's is because they historically have not liked the ones they've experienced. It could also be a branding issue, namely that CIO's aren't working hard enough to create a strong enough brand image for CIO's.

I was invited to write a column piece on the topic of CEO's reflecting upon their CIO's, doing so for the popular blog of one of the IT industry's top executive recruiters. I include here an edited version of my blog piece, providing some added material into it.

————

CHAPTER 22: CEO'S REFLECT ON THEIR CIO

The Oxford Dictionary declared that the word-of-the-year winner was "selfie," the social media self-portrait phenomena that even ensnared President Obama in some controversy when Denmark's Prime Minister

Helle Thorning-Schmidt and British Prime Minister David Cameron snapped a selfie shot with the President.

A selfie, though, can be more than just a narcissistic exercise. Now, as the New Year gets underway, undertaking a CIO Selfie can be illuminating and instructive. Take a moment to look at yourself via your smart phone's camera, and reflect upon how you are perceived in your CIO capacity. I recently had an opportunity to chat with several CEOs about their perceptions of CIOs, and you might find it useful to augment your own internal reflections by the external views that CEOs hold of our vaunted CIO role.

I've boiled down the CEO feedback into three key areas. The numbering of the areas is intended for ease of reference, rather than a priority ranking.

1) Be more politically adroit

Several CEOs complained of CIOs who lack political savvy. One CEO told the story of a CIO who convened an IT Steering Committee meeting and seemingly got blindsided by the CFO about IT budget issues and a major ERP implementation that was underway. The CIO complained afterward to the CEO that the CFO had been unfair. But, it turned out that the CIO had not done his homework and had failed to prep with the CFO before the meeting.

Thus, from the CEO's perspective, the CIO had not exercised good political judgment. He called an important meeting and did not work out critical issues with his peers before the meeting took place. Even though the notion of "politics" is currently eschewed, being politically savvy is part and parcel of success in the executive suite.

In short, CIOs need to improve their politicking skills, which includes having the motions that exhibit political acumen, but that do not overtly trigger the stench of political maneuvering that can then undermine their actions.

2) Observe the doctrine of absurdity

For those of you with a passing familiarity with the American legal system, you might be aware of the so-called absurdity doctrine. It states that adhering to the strict interpretation of something is potentially absurd, especially when it violates common sense reasoning. One CEO shook his head in disgust as he told me about a recent circumstance involving the doctrine of absurdity and his CIO.

The CIO had reworked her IT Service Desk and decided that henceforth, all callers to the IT Service Desk would be treated equally. This was a reaction to some callers that had tried to elevate their priority by either trickery or subtle bribes to get on the top of the Service Desk response heap.

Though an "every person is equal" policy may seem fair, in a business environment there are top executives making crucial business decisions and others who should be treated as high priority. A caller from the sales team who is about to land a big account, and requesting help with their tablet to close the sale, is far more important than the R&D junior staffer requesting a memory upgrade in her PC.

This new "equality" policy put in place by the CIO seemed to defy common sense reasoning, and the CEO was aghast that the CIO could have purposely instituted such an approach.

In short, CIOs need to look at their operations and activities, and make sure that common sense prevails and that the doctrine of absurdity does not overtake their heroic efforts.

3) Be a heads-up team player

On a day-to-day basis, it is easy to fall into the trap of narrow mindedness, failing to see what is going on around us, or opting to ignore aspects that do pertain to us. One CEO described his CIO as having the proverbial head-in-the-sand on a recent rollout that was promulgated by the Chief Marketing Officer (CMO).

The CMO had pushed hard for a saturation social media campaign (perhaps something akin to actor Will Ferrell's recent nonstop scorched-earth marketing for "Anchorman 2"). In the case of the CEO's tale of woe, he lamented that his CIO had stepped away from the CMO, and blindly let the CMO work on his own using powerful technology to execute a social media campaign. Unfortunately, the CMO was not especially technically gifted, and the customer file that had been used to do various email blasts got posted onto a web site that was easily lifted by nefarious hackers.

The black eye on the company, along with potential lawsuits and legal ramifications, though perhaps not as striking as the recent 40 million swiped credit cards at Target, nonetheless presented a large financial and PR nightmare for the company. Had the CIO and CMO worked together, it seems likely that the CIO would have been able to foresee the potential technical hazards and help to secure the valued data.

Only recently have there been any major CIO/CMO Conferences. At these events, it is readily apparent that gaps still exist between CIOs and CMOs. One way or another, the gap needs to get closed, especially since the rise of social media has increased the ways in which technology can help, or potentially harm, an organization as it pursues new and exciting marketing techniques.

CONCLUSION

There are various studies that purport to describe how CIO's spend their time. Generally, those studies suggest that something like 65% of their time is used toward running IT, 20% toward growing the business by adopting new efficiencies or capabilities via IT, and about 15% towards transforming the business and taking a long-term strategic view. If that's the case, it means that only 15% of their time or roughly 6 hours a week is time focused on the bigger picture and transforming the business (assuming working 40 hours a week, though most CIO's are working a lot more hours than that!).

Given the swirl of activity surrounding a CIO, I'd suggest that even those few hours of less than a day per week are splintered into an hour here and a few minutes there. In the end, it really is insufficient to provide the kind of thoughtful consideration needed to help ensure the future of the firm and the ongoing role of IT. When possible, it can be handy for the CIO to have a #2, perhaps you might think of this person as their COO for IT, taking care of at least the 65% of the time being used toward running the business. This #2 also then gets aligned for succession planning, which I am a big believer in too, and frees up a chunk of time for the CIO to become more strategically focused (it's the same reason that hectic CEO's often put in place a COO, allowing the CEO to focus less on the operations of the firm and more so on the strategic overarching direction of the firm).

Some say that IT is there to support the business. I see that as a somewhat reactive kind of statement rather than proactive. Saying that you "support" something implies that once the business figures out what it wants to do, then and only then does IT step into the picture. I often say that IT has the potential to "drive" the business, opening new doors to products and services and being an enabler of business opportunities.

This use of the word "drive" though at times is misinterpreted to suggest that IT should do so alone, acting as a maverick, and not involve the business until IT has magically figured out what the business should do next. We seem to have a conundrum here. Use of the word "drive" gets us in hot water as being a loner, while using the word "support" seems to get us into the leftover bin.

Let's combine it and offer that the CIO is there to both support and drive the business, seeking to ensure the sustainable competitive edge via the use of IT. I am intending to indicate that IT and especially the CIO can work collaboratively with the C-suite and find ways via joint brainstorming to reboot the business or recast the business. The rest of the C-suite might not have had any chance of seeing ways that this could be done, were it not for the CIO being in the midst and offering ideas and approaches of how to do so. I also use the word "sustainable" because you want to find ways to keep the competitive edge viable over time, and not settle for something that is a one-time short-lived competitive edge (which would be great too, but just not as good as one that has sustainability).

LESSON OF THE CARGO CULT

One final quick story before wrapping up. Allow me to use a metaphor or analogy to describe what it takes to be a successful and Smart CIO. It is said that during World War II, there were natives on an isolated island that carefully observed the Allied military when they setup a base on the island. The natives were not familiar with the practices and customs of the Allied troops, and were quite behind in terms of Allied deployed technology and modern conveniences of the times.

The natives had seen how the Allied troops created a tower, used headsets to communicate, and would witness planes landing over and over onto the runways created by the soldiers. They watched as the planes were unloaded. With amazement, they saw that crates of supplies were brought to the island. Fresh food was aplenty. Clothing and other items appeared from those boxes and crates.

When WWII ended, the Allied troops left the island. The natives wondered how the flow of supplies could be somehow resumed. Reportedly, the natives built mock-ups of headsets, airfields, airplanes, and towers, and then sat in the towers and spoke into the headsets. They tried to make the supplies come again to the island, doing so by mimicking what they had seen before. It didn't work, of course.

This is part of what is known as "cargo cult" and has been used to describe circumstances whereby there is a hollow but sincere effort to undertake a task but do so without an inherent and deep understanding of what it actually takes to do it. In my view, a Smart CIO is one that does not rely (solely) on magic, but also has the depth of understanding to know what works and what does not work.

I hope that the material in this book provides an indication of that underlying body of knowledge. I faithfully continue to try and help enhance the capabilities and the branding of the CIO's that we have and those that are someday to be CIO's, and if you want to keep in-touch then please do catch my blog from time-to-time (**www.lance-blog**).

There are some doom-and-gloom pundits saying that the CIO will soon be an occupation that belongs only in the history books, but I firmly believe that CIO's are destined to *be making history* and will increasingly be appreciated for the value that they provide to business.

APPENDIX

TEACHING WITH THIS MATERIAL

The material in this book can be readily used either as a supplemental to other content for a class, or it can also be used as a core set of textbook material for a specialized class. Classes where this material is most likely used include any business classes at the college or university level that want to augment the class by offering thought provoking and educational essays cover IT and CIO's. Specialized classes in IT at the undergraduate and graduate level can also make use of this material. An MBA seminar class at the graduate level on trends and the future of IT is one such example of how this material has been used.

For each chapter, consider whether you think the chapter provides material relevant to your course topic. There is plenty of opportunity to get the students thinking about the topic and force them to decide whether they agree or disagree with the points offered and positions taken. I would also encourage you to have the students do additional research beyond the chapter material presented.

HANDY SOURCES ON IT

They can readily find most of these topics in the usual business publications such as the Harvard Business Review, Forbes, Fortune, WSJ, and the like. For IT publications, I'd suggest they look at CIO.com, along with exploring the research publications put out by IDC, Forrester, Gartner Group, Computer Economics, and other accepted think tanks. MIS Quarterly is one of the most established and strongest of the IT academic journals and would be well worth having your students use as a research source (see http://www.misq.org/).

At the Society for Information Management (SIM) web site, www.simnet.org, there are materials that can be accessed and provide an IT practitioner leader and management perspective. Consider joining too, since it is a great professional association for IT leaders and managers. The Association for Information Systems (AIS) is kind of the equivalent for academics in terms of richness of materials in the IT and IS field, and its journals, including the JAIS, would be fruitful material to consider too (http://aisnet.org/).

The Association for Computing Machinery has been a crucial element of my career, which I joined while a freshman in college, I competed in their annual programming contest (won in the Western Region), I volunteered at their conferences, I later published in their publications and served on editorial boards when I became a professor, and eventually helped even establish a SoCal OC professional chapter and served as the Vice Chair while as a CIO. The ACM is well worth joining. The repository or library of materials is also tremendous and available online (see https://www.acm.org/).

In terms of the ranking of IT-related publications, this is done by various academic groups from time-to-time, and over time some publications move up and some move down. On a relative ranking basis, without being overly concerned about who is first per se, here's a list from one of the more typical rankings (starting in order with the most highly ranked:

Ranked starting at highest in IT or IS research publications, here are the Top 10 (subject to change over time):

1) MIS Quarterly,
2) Information Systems Research,
3) Comm. of the ACM,
4) Management Science,
5) Journal of Management Information Systems,
6) Artificial Intelligence,
7) Decision Sciences,
8) Harvard Business Review,
9) AI Magazine,
10) European Journal of IS

Here are the next publications after the Top 10: Decision Support Systems, IEEE Software, Information and Management, ACM Transactions on Database Systems, IEEE Transactions on Software Engineering, Journal of Computers and System Sciences, Sloan Management Review, Communications of the AIS, IEEE Transactions on Systems, Man and Cybernetics, ACM Computing Surveys, Journal on Computing, Academy of Management Journal.

GUIDE TO USING THE CHAPTERS

For each of the chapters, I provide next some overall ways to use the chapter material. You can assign the tasks as individual homework assignments, or the tasks can be used with team projects for the class.

a) What is the main point of the chapter and describe in your own words the significance of the topic,

b) Identify at least two aspects in the chapter that you agree with, and support your concurrence by providing at least one other outside researched item as support; make sure to explain your basis for disagreeing with the aspects,

c) Identify at least two aspects in the chapter that you disagree with, and support your disagreement by providing at least one other outside researched item as support; make sure to explain your basis for disagreeing with the aspects,

d) Find an aspect that was not covered in the chapter, doing so by conducting outside research, and then explain how that aspect ties into the chapter and what significance it brings to the topic,

e) Interview an IT practitioner in industry about the topic of the chapter, collect from them their thoughts and opinions, and readdress the chapter by citing your source and how they compared and contrasted to the material,

f) Interview an IT academic in a college or university about the topic of the chapter, collect from them their thoughts and opinions, and readdress the chapter by citing your source and how they compared and contrasted to the material,

g) Try to update a chapter by finding out the latest on the topic, and ascertain whether the issue or topic has now been solved or whether it is still being addressed, explain what you come up with,

h) Have the students role play as CIO's and ask them to consider the chapter material in light of being a CIO, and explain what they would say or comment in a CIO capacity,

i) Have the students role play as non-IT executives of the C-suite and ask them to consider the chapter material in light of being a CIO, and explain what they would say or comment in a CIO capacity,

j) For students that work in a business, have the student describe how IT takes place in their business and whether the issue or topic of the chapter is relevant to their firm or not, and say why,

k) Make use of case studies, such as a relevant case study from the Harvard Business Review library, and analyze the case from an IT and CIO perspective and make use of the chapter material as a means to do so.

The above are all ways in which you can get the students of your class involved in considering the material of a given chapter. You could mix things up by having one of those above assignments per each week, covering the chapters over the course of the semester or quarter.

As a reminder, here are the chapters of the book and you can cherry pick whichever chapters you find most valued for your particular class:

Chapter 1: Role of the CIO, CTO, CDO
Chapter 2: On Being a Smart CIO
Chapter 3: SMAC: Social, Mobile, Analytics, Cloud
Chapter 4: CIO's Top 10 Lists
Chapter 5: Tech Trends and Business Value
Chapter 6: The CIO 100 Notables
Chapter 7: DevOps: Development and IT Operations
Chapter 8: Human-Computer Interaction (HCI)
Chapter 9: Ransomware and Digital Extortion
Chapter 10: Hybrid IT
Chapter 11: Consumerization of IT
Chapter 12: Bimodal IT
Chapter 13: Shadow IT
Chapter 14: To Whom Should the CIO Report
Chapter 15: Interim Temp CIO
Chapter 16: Social Intelligence and the CIO
Chapter 17: CIO and the Board of Directors
Chapter 18: Mergers &Acquisitions (M&A) and IT
Chapter 19: The CIO and the IT Steering Committee
Chapter 20: Maslow's Hierarchy of Needs and IT
Chapter 21: What Keeps CIO's Awake at Night
Chapter 22: CEO's Reflect on Their CIO

ABOUT THE AUTHOR

Dr. Lance B. Eliot, MBA, PhD is known as a Thought Leader in high-tech and business, and has over 20 years of industry experience, including serving as a corporate officer, Chief Information Officer (CIO), and was a Partner in a major executive services firm. He is a serial entrepreneur having founded, ran, and sold several high-tech related businesses. He previously hosted the popular radio show *Technotrends* that was also available on American Airlines flights via their in-flight audio program. Author or co-author of four books and over 300 articles, he has made appearances on CNN, and has been a frequent speaker at industry conferences.

A former professor at the University of Southern California (USC), he founded and led an innovative research lab on Artificial Intelligence in Business. He also previously served on the faculty of the University of California Los Angeles (UCLA), and was a visiting professor at other major universities. He was elected to the International Board of the Society for Information Management (SIM), a prestigious association of over 3,000 CIO's/CTO's worldwide.

He has performed extensive community service, including serving as Senior Science Adviser to the Vice Chair of the Congressional Committee on Science & Technology. He has served on the Board of the OC Science & Engineering Fair (OCSEF), where he is also has been a Grand Sweepstakes judge, and likewise served as a judge for the Intel International SEF (ISEF). He served as the Vice Chair of the Association for Computing Machinery (ACM) Chapter, a prestigious association of computer scientists. Dr. Eliot has been a shark tank judge for the USC Mark Stevens Center for Innovation on start-up pitch competitions, and served as a mentor for several incubators and accelerators in Silicon Valley and Silicon Beach. He serves on several Boards and Committees at USC, including the Marshall Alumni Association (MAA) Board for Los Angeles and Orange County in Southern California.

Dr. Eliot holds a PhD from USC, MBA, and Bachelor's in Computer Science, and earned the CDP, CCP, CSP, CDE, and CISA certifications. Born and raised in Southern California, and having traveled and lived internationally, he enjoys scuba diving, surfing, and sailing.

ADDENDUM

On Being a Smart CIO:

Lessons I've Learned
as a Chief Information Officer (CIO)
and Trusted C-Suite Adviser

By

Dr. Lance B. Eliot, MBA, PhD

———

For supplemental materials of this book, visit:

www.lance-blog.com

For special orders of this book, contact:

LBE Press Publishing

28987479R00144

Printed in Great Britain
by Amazon